The Marble Wilderness

The Marble Wilderness
Ruins and Representation in
Italian Romanticism, 1775–1850

CAROLYN SPRINGER
Stanford University

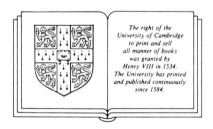

*The right of the
University of Cambridge
to print and sell
all manner of books
was granted by
Henry VIII in 1534.
The University has printed
and published continuously
since 1584.*

CAMBRIDGE UNIVERSITY PRESS

Cambridge
New York   New Rochelle
Melbourne   Sydney

Published by the Press Syndicate of the University of Cambridge
The Pitt Building, Trumpington Street, Cambridge CB2 1RP
32 East 57th Street, New York, NY 10022, USA
10 Stamford Road, Oakleigh, Melbourne 3166, Australia

First published 1987

Printed in the United States of America

Library of Congress Cataloging-in-Publication Data
Springer, Carolyn.
The marble wilderness.
Based on the author's thesis (doctoral) – Yale
University.
Bibliography: p.
Includes index.
1. Italian literature – 19th century – History and
criticism. 2. Romanticism. 3. Archaeology in
literature. 4. Excavations (Archaeology) – Italy –
History – 19th century. 5. Italy – Civilization – 1789–
1900. 6. Italy – Politics and government – 1789–1900.
7. Papal States – Civilization – 19th century.
8. Papal States – Politics and government – 1815–1870.
9. Papal States – Antiquities. 10. Italy – Antiquities.
I. Title.
PQ4086.S638   1987   850'.9'006   86-32682

British Library Cataloguing in Publication Data
Springer, Carolyn
The marble wilderness : ruins and representation in Italian romanticism, 1775–1850.
1. Italian literature – 18th century –
History and criticism 2. Italian literature
– 19th century – History and criticism
3. Archaeology and literature
4. Romanticism
I. Title
850'.9145   PQ4084

ISBN 0 521 33472 1

CONTENTS

ILLUSTRATIONS

GCS: Gabinetto Comunale delle Stampe.

ACKNOWLEDGMENTS

MUCH OF THIS BOOK was written on the Janiculum hill, across from the Villa Savorelli (Fig. 18). The villa, which served as Garibaldi's headquarters in the legendary 1849 defense of the Roman Republic, has since been rebuilt and rebaptized as the Villa Aurelia, and now serves both as residence of the Director of the American Academy and as public lecture hall where many of the ideas in this book were first tested.

It is a pleasure to thank the many friends and colleagues who have contributed to my project of reading Rome: not only at the Academy but at Stanford, Rutgers, and Yale University, where this book began as a doctoral dissertation under the expert guidance of Paolo Valesio. I am especially grateful to A. W. Allen, who patiently read every draft of the manuscript, and to others who helped me along the way with their advice and suggestions: Shirley Allen, William Arrowsmith, Gian-Paolo Biasin, Peter Brooks, Jane Crawford, Dante Della Terza, Umberto Eco, Alban Forcione, John Freccero, Bernard Frischer, Donna Mancusi-Ungaro Hart, Aden Hayes, Charles Henderson, Fred and Meg Licht, Giuseppe Mazzotta, John O'Malley, Cathy Popkin, Alfonso Procaccini, Brook Thomas, Marc Treib, Gianluca Trivero, and Alice and Helmut Wohl. Silvio Pasquarelli opened his library to me and freely shared his knowledge and love of Rome. Don Engelman and Eileen Reeves were a source of unfailing friendship and support. I am also grateful to have found in Elizabeth Maguire a resourceful and wholly sympathetic editor.

The research and writing of this book have been generously supported by an Andrew W. Mellon Fellowship in the Humanities at Stanford University, a National Endowment for the Humanities/Rome Prize Fellowship at the American Academy in Rome, and a Rutgers University Faculty Research Council Fellowship.

Parts of several chapters have appeared in earlier versions in the *Stanford Italian Review*, *GRADIVA*, and *Quaderni d'italianistica*. I thank the editors for permission to reprint the revised versions here.

Carlo Pietrangeli, General Director of the Vatican Museums, provided

Acknowledgments

a photograph of a painting recently acquired by the Vatican Pinacoteca (Fig. 5). Fernando Mazzocca kindly contributed a copy of a lithograph in his personal collection (Fig. 17). The provenance of the other plates is given in the preceding list. Special thanks are due to Edith Cicerchia, of the Archivio Fotografico Vaticano, and Elisa Tittoni, of the Museo Napoleonico, for their warm interest in this project and their help in assembling the illustrations.

This book is dedicated, with love, to my parents.

INTRODUCTION:
MODES OF ARCHAEOLOGICAL
REPRESENTATION, 1775–1850

> The Niobe of nations! there she stands,
> Childless and crownless, in her voiceless woe;
> An empty urn within her withered hands,
> Whose holy dust was scatter'd long ago;
> The Scipios' tomb contains no ashes now;
> The very sepulchres lie tenantless
> Of their heroic dwellers: dost thou flow,
> Old Tiber! through a marble wilderness?
> Rise, with thy yellow waves, and mantle her distress!
>
> Byron, *Childe Harold's Pilgrimage,* IV (703–11)

N O ONE COULD DISPUTE the importance of archaeology to the romantic imagination. The revival of interest in the ruins of classical antiquity that characterized neoclassicism remained a primary component of the romantic experience. Italy, which for generations of eighteenth-century travelers had been a paradigm of picturesque decay, in turn became a privileged ground for the emerging romantic sensibility and the preferred setting for a "poetry of ruins" that reached its climax in the early decades of the nineteenth century in poets like Byron and Shelley. Byron's image of Rome as a "marble wilderness" recalls, then, a rich literary and figurative tradition that portrayed the classical landscape as a locus of decay; as in Piranesi's engravings we see the forest of fallen columns choked with marble and masonry, watch nature gather in the broken monuments of man, and we see it all, inevitably, with a slight thrill of *Schadenfreude:* as Henry James would later admit in his own reflections on Italy, "To delight in the aspects of sentient ruin might appear a heartless pastime, and the pleasure, I confess, shows a note of perversity."[1]

The "perversity" of such romantic pleasure in ruins contrasts sharply with the prevailing mood of Italian literature of the early nineteenth century. This book attempts to show how the metaphor of archaeology was used in Italian literature of the period, by examining the connections between archaeology and politics in a range of texts from the formative years of the Risorgimento. These texts represent a broad ideological spectrum, from the papal classicism of Monti's early poetry to the democratic and anticlerical tradition of Foscolo and Mazzini.

It is my contention that religious and political pressures specific to Italy between 1775 and 1850 generated a distinctly political iconography of ruins in Italian literature. If this has not previously been noticed or discussed, it is because the critical vocabulary we use to describe romanticism was largely elaborated in reference to other national literatures. Not surprisingly, the Italian nineteenth century has been almost entirely neglected by critics of European romanticism; in fact, its failure to conform to their categories of explanation has led some scholars to conclude that Italian literature knew no romantic period at all.[2]

But I am less interested in proposing a new definition of romanticism (or of neoclassicism, with which it is inextricably intertwined) than in suggesting a set of critical categories that may enable us to chart some of its transformations with greater precision than has yet been possible. These categories are essentially rhetorical, and reflect the political crisis catalyzed in Italy by the French Revolution and Napoleonic conquest. I have chosen to focus on the archaeological metaphor because of its rich and ambivalent political connotations; during the period that I will discuss (roughly, the years between Winckelmann and Schliemann), despite its struggle to constitute itself as a science, archaeology was widely exploited for ideological ends. Napoleon's raid of the art works from Rome, his Egyptian campaign, the archaeological patronage of the restored papacy, and Garibaldi's march on Rome are a few of the more spectacular examples that are elaborated in Italian literature of the period.

In contrast to the elegiac mode of archaeological representation that we have come to regard as "romantic" (the poetry of the "marble wilderness"), this book proposes two typologies of archaeological representation of more direct relevance to Italian literature: the encomiastic mode of the Church and the exhortatory mode of the democratic opposition.

These categories correspond to two of the three types of classical rhetoric, the epideictic or *genus demonstrativum* and the deliberative or *genus deliberativum*. Like its classical model, the first distributes praise and blame (praise, as we will see, of the *pax cristiana* and blame of democratic revolution), while the second tries to persuade its audience to a definite course of action (the overthrow of the papacy and unification of Italy). The revival of these classical genres in reference to the imagery of ruins is a doubly archaeological move; it is certainly not new to the Church, which had revived the epideictic genre in sacred rhetoric as early as the fifteenth century, but it proves formative in the evolution of democratic imagery and thought in the Risorgimento.[3]

How does each of these strategies work in the literature of the nineteenth century? The elegiac mode is the most familiar: In Canto IV of *Childe Harold's Pilgrimage,* for example, Byron ranges among the principal sites and antiquities of the Italian peninsula ("Visto ho Toscana, Lombardia, Romagna, / Quel Monte che divide, e quel che serra / Italia, e un mare e l'altro, che la bagna,")[4] weaving an impressionistic reverie on the decay of Italian civilization and the irreversible erosion of its heroic past.

If Byron reads the ruins of Italy as the sign of an absence, both the Church and its democratic opposition celebrate antiquity as a palpable presence, daily restored through the agency of archaeology. Thus they concur, despite dramatic ideological differences, in invoking archaeology as a figure of political rehabilitation.

By recovering Italy's monuments, the shards and scattered fragments of its history, as emblems of survival rather than decay, both factions implicitly reverse the valence of romantic *Ruinenstimmung.* To the nostalgic evocation of an irretrievable past they substitute, respectively, the pious idealization of the present and the apocalyptic projection of a democratic future.

While the Church, opposed to unification and reform, consistently exploits archaeological occasions in the apology of power as proof of the providential continuity between classical and Christian Rome (only briefly interrupted by the Napoleonic occupation), the democrats demand a search for Italy's authentic republican traditions beneath the rubble of throne and altar and the excavation of civic and national ideals long suppressed by the Church (ironically, the short-lived Roman Republic of 1849 would prepare a vast plan of excavations in the Forum, to be carried out in part by the restored Pius IX).[5]

It is clear that the ideological duplicity of archaeological imagery is that of neoclassicism in general, which has been shown to range from a highly conservative cult of academic authority (and of the political and cultural institutions that embody it) to the self-styled "revolutionary classicism" of David and other artists of late eighteenth-century France.[6] Thus the metaphor of archaeology informs contrasting modes of discourse and proves equally adaptable to the reinforcement and subversion of prevailing symbols of political authority in nineteenth-century Italy.

The essential difference, then, between the elegiac mode of European romanticism and its Italian counterparts is a difference between opposing rhetorical strategies. The elegiac strategy is one of *metonymic reduction* of the whole into its component parts. The encomiastic and exhortatory modes, instead, both operate on the principle of *synecdochic assimilation* – the reintegration of the whole into a unified object. We might say that the figure of synecdoche is the single rhetorical principle which governs and motivates archaeological practice in the nineteenth century.[7]

It will be the purpose of this book to assemble a wide range of examples from contemporary sources to illustrate the encomiastic and exhortatory modes of archaeological representation. Before examining each model individually, however, I will return to the text of Byron to trace in greater detail some strategies of the elegiac mode, and to suggest some preliminary terms of comparison from the rival Italian traditions, to be developed in the following chapters.

The section of Canto IV of *Childe Harold's Pilgrimage* devoted to Rome (lines 694–1467) provides an excellent illustration of the elegiac representation of Roman ruins. In the tradition of eighteenth-century topographical poetry, Byron explores the remains of the ancient city and comments in turn upon each of its monuments. But the iconographical vocabulary of the canto is already distinctly romantic:

> Come and see
> The cypress, hear the owl, and plod your way
> O'er steps of broken thrones and temples, Ye!
> Whose agonies are evils of a day –
> A world is at our feet as fragile as our clay.[8]

The poet begins by comparing Rome to the figure of Niobe (recalling to us a statue which enjoyed unparalleled popularity in the nineteenth century and which Byron had certainly seen in the Uffizi).[9] The choice is significant: Niobe is a personification of loss, and Byron in fact defines her through figures of negation (childless, crownless, voiceless). Like an allegorical mourner carved in a Canova stele she stands, "an empty urn within her wither'd hands," lamenting the death of her children and the dispersal of their ashes. Not only have her children died: their tomb has been violated and their "holy dust scattered long ago."

The Niobe passage is significant because it leads, by association, to a description of the Scipios's tomb ("the Scipios's tomb contains no ashes now; / The very sepulchres lie tenantless / Of their heroic dwellers"). Byron reads this ruin, like the sculptural figure of Niobe herself, as the sign of an absence. Just as Niobe, through the very fact of her survival, paradoxically signifies death (she survives only to mourn the death of her children and by extension, the end of her line), Rome's ruins testify to the death of a civilization. Byron focuses on the void created by the excavation of the Scipios's tomb, not on the spoils that it yielded.

Consider the difference between Byron's representation of the tomb and an encomiastic representation of the same archaeological site. To the poets of the papal court, the discovery and excavation of the tomb of the Scipios in the spring of 1780 was a spectacular rhetorical occasion. It dramatized the continuity between classical and Christian Rome – indeed, the triumph of the Cross over the artifacts of antiquity, now restored to the Church's possession. The sarcophagus of Cornelius Scipio Barbatus, consul in 298 B.C. and ancestor of the great Scipio Africanus, was in fact expropriated by Pius VI and prominently placed in the atrium of the Pio-Clementine Museum at the Vatican; and it was this occasion that such an unlikely candidate as the Milanese Enlightenment intellectual Alessandro Verri celebrated in his prose fantasy *Le notti romane* (begun as a parody of papal antiquarians, this work evolved into a genuine panegyric of Pius VI).[10]

To the democrats, on the other hand, such republican spoils as the sarcophagus of the Scipios were the legitimate property of the people, and belonged with the Capitoline bronzes (the Roman wolf, the bust of Lucius Junius Brutus) in a secular and public collection consecrated to the resurrection of Rome's republican traditions.

Throughout the Fourth Canto Byron emphasizes the pathos of Rome's ruined landscape. Rome's ruins are inscrutable, opaque; they resist formal reconstruction and historical explanation. "Chaos of ruins!" he writes, surveying the seven hills, "who shall trace the void, / O'er the dim fragments cast a lunar light, / And say, 'here was, or is,' where all is doubly night?" (718–20).

Wrapped in the "double night" of time and ignorance, in exploring Rome we can not steer a rational course: "The ocean hath his chart, the stars their map, / And Knowledge spreads them on her ample lap; / But Rome is as the desart, where we steer / Stumbling o'er recollections . . ." (724–7).

Again, on the Palatine, Byron prizes the disorder of the scene and denies that it can be reduced to a rational plan:

> Cypress and ivy, weed and wallflower grown
> Matted and mass'd together, hillocks heap'd
> On what were chambers, arch crush'd, column strown
> In fragments, chok'd up vaults, and frescos steep'd
> In subterranean damps, where the owl peep'd,
> Deeming it midnight: – Temples, baths, or halls?
> Pronounce who can; for all that Learning reap'd
> From her research hath been, that these are walls –
> Behold the Imperial Mount! 'tis thus the mighty falls.
>
> (955–63)

Byron's bias is anti-archaeological; like Keats interrogating the Grecian urn, he implies that what is gained for erudition is lost to the imagination.[11] Byron's fiction is that Rome is "still unravish'd" by archaeological or historical scholarship, and that she still withholds all explanation of her origins. The poet protects this fiction at the expense of the most blatant anachronisms, as in his invocation of the Column of Phocas: "Tully was not so eloquent as thou, / Thou nameless column with the buried base!" he declares. Yet the Column of Phocas was not "nameless" in Byron's time; its base had in fact been cleared in 1813 during the widely publicized excavations ordered by Napoleon. John Cam Hobhouse, in his explanatory notes to the Fourth Canto, includes the entire text of the Phocas inscription and adds in an ironic note that the identification of the monument, long disputed by papal antiquarians, was well overdue: "It must appear strange that the simple expedient of digging to the base to look for an inscription, was delayed until 1813, on purpose, as it were, to give scope to further conjecture."[12]

Byron's own strategy in the poem is consistently designed to "give scope to further conjecture," at whatever cost to the archaeological care of his commentator. "Whose arch or pillar meets me in the face, / Titus or Trajan's? No – 'tis that of Time: / Triumph, arch, pillar, all he doth displace / Scoffing . . ." (986–9).

By inscribing the names of Titus and Trajan – among the most familiar points of reference in Roman topography – only to erase them, Byron subverts the very notion of archaeological attribution. In the same way he consistently subverted the efforts of his collaborator, by suppressing and obscuring the very dimension of archaeological detail which it was Hobhouse's responsibility to elucidate. Byron's interest is not in the "labyrinth of external objects" represented by Rome, but in the processes of his own imagination. Therefore it is not surprising that having ordered the *Historical Illustrations* as a companion volume to *Childe Harold,* he "took cruel pleasure later in informing others that he had never read them."[13]

Byron's Rome is above all a gallery of private images and hallucinatory reflections, a landscape overgrown and "fantastically tangled" where the soul may freely "meditate amongst decay . . . a ruin amidst ruins." Ruins are indeed central to Byron's work; but far less in a historical and political sense than as generic metaphors of the human condition.[14] Just as Rome fell from the height of her creative powers, crippled by the passage of time, man himself falls away, inevitably, from his felt potential for activity and experience. Byron embraces the entire classical landscape as a figure for the ruin of his own imagination; and in lamenting the limit, even the loss of his own powers, he writes one of the great romantic poems. Perhaps no better visual analogue for this posture could be found than in the work of the Swiss artist Johann Heinrich Fussli (1741–1825), whose drawing, "The

1. Johann Heinrich Fussli, "The Artist's Despair before the Grandeur of Ancient Ruins,"
1778–9 (Zurich, Kunsthaus).

Artist's Despair before the Grandeur of Ancient Ruins" (Fig. 1), conveys all
the drama and pathos of Byron's own encounter with the ruins of Rome.

Like pictures in a gallery, Byron's views of Rome are aligned throughout
the canto, linked by his freely modulating remarks, fantasies, and reflections. The structure of his meditation on the tomb of Cecilia Metella (883–
954) again illustrates his resistance to all archaeological elucidation that
might cripple the movements of the poetic imagination. The first three
stanzas present a series of questions, increasingly insistent, regarding the

identity of Cecilia Metella: "But who was she . . . Was she chaste and fair? / . . . What race of chiefs and heroes did she bear? / What daughter of her beauties was the heir? / How lived – how loved – how died she? . . ."

In the following two stanzas he imagines (just as Keats imagines the "little town . . . emptied of its folk" on the morning of the sacrifice portrayed on the urn) all the possible circumstances of her life and death. Yet, abruptly, he concludes: "But whither would Conjecture stray? / Thus much alone we know – Metella died, / The wealthiest Roman's wife; Behold his love or pride!" (925–7).

The poet preempts his own series of conjectures and concludes with relief that the scholars can tell us nothing about this Roman site.[15] There is no need here to blur the contours of the object: this tomb is in fact still inviolate, "unravish'd," and it is its very reticence that gives voice to the poet, as he continues:

> I know not why – but standing thus by thee
> It seems as if I had thine inmate known,
> Thou tomb! and other days come back on me
> With recollected music, though the tone
> Is changed and solemn, like the cloudy groan
> Of dying thunder on the distant wind;
> Yet could I seat me by this ivied stone
> Till I had bodied forth the heated mind
> Forms from the floating wreck which Ruin leaves behind.
>
> (928–36)

For Byron the ruin is primarily a vehicle to meditation, an otherwise irrelevant object in the foreground of his poetic consciousness that is left behind by the imagination as it turns inward again upon itself. From the "floating wreck" of the primary visual image, the poet fashions his own private forms (here, the "little bark of hope" that might return him to the "solitary shore / Where all lies foundered that was ever dear," 941–2). Byron's movement then is to interiorize the classical landscape, to read it as a figure of his own spiritual condition and field of his private struggle to build a poem more lasting than marble or bronze.

━━ ━━

If Byron's tendency is to interiorize the classical landscape, Italian political poetry and rhetoric of the early nineteenth century project the same monuments into a shared public dimension, where they serve alternately as signs of the restored power of the papacy and of the emerging force of the nationalist movement. The most prominent monument of ancient Rome, the Colosseum, enjoys pride of place for both factions and is central to the

2. Domenico De Angelis (?), "The Restoration of the Colosseum" (episode from the
biography of Pius VII), 1818 (Vatican Library, Galleria Clementina).

political iconography of both the Church and the Risorgimento. Raffaele
Stern's restoration of the Colosseum under Pius VII was one of the most
widely celebrated acts of the Chiaramonti papacy; the Pope's name is
inscribed on the southwest spur built to buttress the crumbling arcade,
and the restoration is celebrated both in the lunettes of the Chiaramonti
Museum and the frescoes of the Galleria Clementina in the Vatican library
(Fig. 2).

In the papal tradition of "converting" classical monuments into Christian
symbols (as in Sixtus V's placement of the statues of Peter and Paul on the

3. Domenico Russo, "Garibaldi and Rome," 1862 (Naples, Museo Nazionale
di San Martino).

columns of Trajan and Marcus Aurelius), the popes consecrated the Colosseum to the Christian martyrs, reclaiming the site as a point of pilgrimage
for the Christian world; and one of Pius VII's first acts after the Napoleonic
occupation was to fill in the steps, vomitoria, and corridors cleared by the
French Prefect Camille de Tournon and restore the stations of the Cross
first placed in the Colosseum by Benedict XIV in the mid-eighteenth
century.[16]

Despite papal attempts to reclaim the Colosseum as a religious symbol, in
the democratic imagination it had long served as a sign of the survival of
pre-Christian Rome (despite centuries of papal violation and pillage), and a
promise that the ancient republic would one day be restored. Garibaldi is
conventionally portrayed in contemporary painting against a landscape of
Roman ruins; one famous portrait by Domenico Russo (Fig. 3) shows him
standing outside of Rome against a crumbling wall overgrown with thorns
and acanthus, while the Colosseum and dome of St. Peter's rise in the
distance – the Colosseum that he had pledged to reclaim from the papal
usurper. Garibaldi himself wrote a novel in which the Colosseum serves as a
locus for the democratic opposition; in a fictionalized account of the actual
uprising at the Villa Glori in 1867, his conspirators gather in the Colosseum,

like ghosts of the ancient Romans, to plot the overthrow of the temporal power.[17]

In his novel Garibaldi derides the sentimental tradition that had stripped the Colosseum of its political significance; the public arena had become a private pleasure garden, picturesquely overgrown, where the foreign visitor might wander in melancholy reflection. Travelers to Rome had always marveled at the Colosseum; but the romantic vision of the monument owes more to Byron than to any other author. By comparing his passage on the Colosseum in *Childe Harold's Pilgrimage* to a typical papal panegyric view, we can again gauge the distance between the elegiac and encomiastic representations of Rome.

> the moonbeams shine
> As 'twere its natural torches, for divine
> Should be the light which streams here, to illume
> this long-explored but still exhaustless mine
> Of contemplation; and the azure gloom
> Of an Italian night . . .   (1147–52)

It would become a romantic *topos* that the Colosseum is best viewed at night, when the scars of human history are obscured and the moon lends a ghostly and shimmering light:

> It will not bear the brightness of the day,
> Which streams too much on all years, man, have reft away.
>
> But when the rising moon begins to climb
> Its topmost arch, and gently pauses there;
> When the stars twinkle through the loops of time,
> And the low night-breeze waves along the air
> The garland-forest, which the grey walls wear,
> Like laurels on the bald first Caesar's head;
> When the light shines serene but doth not glare,
> Then in this magic circle raise the dead:
> Heroes have trod this spot – 'tis on their dust ye tread.   (1286–96)

It is in this scene, "divinely desolate," that the poet raises a prayer to Time, "the Beautifier of the dead, / Adorner of the ruin" (1162–3). He offers up his own "ruins of years – though few, yet full of fate" (1174–5). Again the figure of the poet stands "a ruin amidst ruins"; and the most disturbing phantoms he conjures up are neither ancient (nor modern!) Romans, but the shapes from his own troubled past.

How different then the sanguine rhetoric of the papal court, and its official reading of the "ruin'd battlement" that for Byron had such uneasy imaginative power! One such poem predates Byron by thirty years, but is typical of a genre that survived unchanged well into the era of Pius IX. Recited at the awarding of prizes in architecture, sculpture, and painting by the Accademia di San Luca at a ceremony on the Capitoline in 1786, this sonnet, "La Mole di Flavio, o sia il Colosseo," was written by Niccolò Ardizzoni, a minor poet of the Arcadian Academy, and accompanied as an extra archaeological flourish by a Latin translation:

> Questa mole, che sorse al ciel vicina,
> È chiara immago del poter romano.
> La strugge il tempo, e nella sua rovina
> Stanca la falce, ma la stanca invano.
>
> Giove, mentre sù lei lo sguardo inchina,
> Quasi al riparo suo stende la mano,
> Che ama tuttor la maestà latina,
> E Venere rammenta, e il pio Trojano.
>
> L'arte col guardo la misura, e gira,
> E mentre scorge i sparsi avanzi a terra
> La gloria sua ne' danni suoi rimira.
>
> O Roma, o Roma! fosti grande allora,
> Quando sorgesti a dominar la terra,
> Grande sei tu nelle rovine ancora.[18]

(This mass, which rose close to the sky, is a clear image of Roman power. Time consumes it, and in laying it waste he wearies his scythe, but in vain. Jupiter, as he lowers his glance, extends his hand as if in protection, for he still loves the majesty of the Latin race, and remembers Venus and the pious Trojan. Art measures and encircles it with her gaze, and as she sees its remains scattered on the ground she admires its glory in its destruction. Oh Rome, oh Rome! You were once great, when you rose to rule the earth; you are great in your ruin even now.)

The polemical message of the poem is clear: "quanta fuit Roma ruina ipsa docet." It is the ruins themselves that prove the magnificence of ancient Rome, and by extension, the might of the papacy. The ruins are not an emblem of loss but proof of a legacy that is indestructible. The vocabulary of the poem is strictly pagan, and there is no reference either to the Pope or to a Christian God; for it is the privilege of the Church to absorb and appropriate classical language and imagery for its own use, just as it gathers the spoils of its excavations in the halls of the Vatican museums.

The personification of Time with his scythe is of course an ancient *topos*, but it had been widely revived in both the poetry and painting of the papal court in the 1770s and 1780s. This revival was due at least in part to the influence of Raphael Mengs's ceiling fresco in the Sala dei Papiri of the Vatican Library, commissioned by Clement XIV and completed in 1772 (Fig. 6). Ardizzoni's sonnet represents a variant on the basic iconographical scheme of Mengs's painting, the triumph of History over Time: Time, with his scythe, is an impotent adversary, powerless to destroy the relics of Rome that survive as proof of her privileged destiny.[19]

The papal iconography is explicitly political. Byron's concern instead is aesthetic and philosophical. Time is not the adversary of empire but the ally of the poet. "Beautifier of the dead" and "adorner of the ruin," he creates a consoling refuge from the poverty of the present:

> There is given
> Unto the things of earth, which time hath bent,
> A spirit's feeling, and where he hath leant
> His hand, but broke his scythe, there is a power
> And magic in the ruined battlement,
> For which the palace of the present hour
> Must yield its pomp, and wait till ages are its dower.
>
> (1155–61)

This was in fact the era of fabricated ruins; throughout northern Europe, the new propertied classes were planting columns and arches on their vast estates to lend an aura of legitimacy to their newly acquired wealth. But the Church, long heir to the classical landscape, had no need of plaster temples and towers; by incorporating the ancient landscape into its liturgy (as in the papal *possesso,* a triumphal procession through the Forum itself), the Church had long exploited the Roman ruins in a shrewd and complex choreography of power.

Those who praise Byron as a prophet and catalyst of the Italian Risorgimento rarely seem to notice how often his poetry subverts his own revolutionary sympathies. For despite the elegiac mood of *Childe Harold's Pilgrimage,* it is true that Byron was a passionate supporter of the Italian revolutionary cause and even briefly took part in the *carbonaro* movement in central Italy before leaving to fight for the independence of Greece.[20] It is the manner of his life – and death – rather than the mood of his poetry, that explains his impact on revolutionary movements throughout Europe in the nineteenth century.

If most English romantic poets of the second generation showed an ambiguous sympathy for the Italian cause when the continent was opened up to them after the Napoleonic Wars, French romantics like Lamartine showed a clear contempt for the Risorgimento movement. Returning to Naples in 1820 as secretary to the French embassy, Lamartine was indignant to discover this classic ground infested by *carbonari:* "Naples n'est plus Naples. Entendez-vous faire des motions au pied du sacré tombeau de Virgile! Et voyez-vous des clubs de carbonari dans les temples de Baia et de Pouzzoles!"[21]

Lamartine's return to Naples in the midst of the revolution shattered an adolescent myth of Italy as an enchanted ground, a picturesque refuge from politics. "La politique m'ennuie," he announced, after describing to a friend the political turmoil in Naples: "pour [se] désennuyer" he would write, several years later, a sequel to Byron's *Childe Harold* which flatly dismissed the "myth" of an Italian Risorgimento. For Lamartine, Italy could not be resurrected: it was a "terre des morts":[22]

> O terre du passé, que faire en tes collines?
> Quand on a mesuré tes arcs et tes ruines,
> Et fouillé quelques noms dans l'urne de la mort,
> On se retourne en vain vers les vivants; tout dort . . .
>
> Monument écroulé, que l'écho seul habite!
> Poussière du passé, qu'un vent stérile agite!
> Terre, où les fils n'ont plus le sang de leurs aieux,
> Où sur le sol vieilli les hommes naissent vieux, . . .
>
> Je vais chercher ailleurs (pardonne, ombre romaine!)
> Des hommes, et non pas de la poussière humaine!

The Italian response to such an attack can well be imagined. The exiled general Gabriele Pepe did his best to avenge the insult in a duel on February 19, 1826; but the debate continued for nearly two decades, culminating in the publication of Giusti's satirical poem, "La terra dei morti," in 1842.[23]

Giusti ridicules Lamartine's claim that Italy is an irreparable field of ruin: "O mura cittadine, / Sepolcri maestosi, / Fin le vostre ruine / Sono un'apoteosi" (O city walls, majestic sepulchres, your very ruins are an apotheosis). Italy's ruins themselves are a promise of her political regeneration; and if her inhabitants are to Lamartine nothing but "poussière humaine," Giusti reminds him that even the dead will be avenged at the Last Judgment:

Ah d'una gente morta
Non si giova la Storia!
Di Libertà, di Gloria,
Scheletri, che v'importa? . . .

Tra i salmi dell'Uffizio
C'è anco il *Dies Irae:*
O che non ha a venire
Il giorno del giudizio?   (17–20, 97–100)

(Ah there is no use in writing the history of a dead people! Liberty, glory, what are they to you skeletons? . . . Among the psalms of the Office there is also the *Dies Irae:* Can you doubt that the judgment day will come?)

The iconography of Giusti's poem is almost literally transcribed in a contemporary engraving by Gonsalvo Carelli, "Vendetta di Dio" (Rome, Museo Centrale del Risorgimento). Against the background of an angrily smoking Vesuvius, an angel addresses a group of skeletons who emerge from their tomb, pushing aside a stone inscribed "Italiani." The angel points to a sword in the sky, marked "Vendetta di Dio." The image is yet another example of the politicization of the Italian landscape in poetry and painting, as one by one its landmarks are reclaimed from the tyranny of the picturesque. Carelli's Vesuvius is no longer the placid backdrop of the traditional Neapolitan *veduta* but a startling image of apocalypse. Carelli's own career as an artist allows us to trace this transformation; having begun as a painter of Neapolitan genre scenes and views of Vesuvius for the tourist trade, he became a fervent patriot and fought both at the Cinque Giornate of Milan (1848) and with Garibaldi at the Battle of Volturno (1860).

The chapters that follow will trace the separate strategies of archaeological representation by the Church and its democratic opposition from 1775 to 1850. I have chosen to begin with the year 1775 because it marks the beginning of the papacy of Pius VI (1775–99), a period of extraordinary importance in Italian political history, encompassing the French Revolution and first Napoleonic invasions, the forced removal of the Pope to France, and his death in exile in 1799. The reign of Pius VII (1800–23) spans the Napoleonic occupation of Rome (1809–14) and the restoration of the legitimate monarchies throughout Europe, along with the first stirrings of the Italian Risorgimento movement. The 1840s mark the emergence of the neoguelph movement, with Gioberti's publication of *Il primato morale e civile degli italiani* in 1843 and the accession to the papacy of Pius IX in 1846.

The book ends in 1850, with the fall of the Roman Republic. To continue beyond this point, when the political valences of the ruins had been virtually established at both ends of the political spectrum, would have been valuable but beyond the scope of this study.

The essential novelty of my approach, in the context of previous studies of Italian romanticism, is its use of the techniques of rhetorical and semiotic analysis to explore the ideological conflicts articulated in the Risorgimento. My scheme violates certain assumptions of traditional literary history; first, because it refuses to privilege the established canon of Ottocento literature, and second, because it is grounded in a renewed understanding of rhetoric not as a specialized taxonomy of figures and tropes but as the fundamental structuring principle of human discourse.

Many critics have urged such a reappraisal of the ontological status of rhetoric and called for the revival of rhetoric as a contemporary instrument of cultural analysis.[24] Perhaps the most forceful theoretical defense of this position has been provided by Paolo Valesio, to whose work and example this study is deeply indebted. In his *Novantiqua: Rhetorics as a Contemporary Theory* (Bloomington: Indiana University Press, 1980), Valesio defines rhetoric as a phenomenon coextensive with discourse itself, "the functional organization of discourse, both in its internal aspect of syntactico-semantic structuring and in its external aspect of dialectic relationship with the surrounding semiotic frame" (p. 16). The implications for practical criticism are immediate; if no text is innocent of rhetoric, all texts at once invite analysis (including that of the critic himself), and we may choose to privilege "literature" only because its rhetorical structures are programmatically foregrounded. Valesio's theory calls for a radical reorientation of literary criticism; and this study takes that challenge seriously. Within a historically delimited discursive field, it maps the pervasive presence and manipulation of a single theme – the role of archaeology in the rheotrical practice of the nineteenth century.

It will be clear that "archaeology" functions both as a metaphor and theme in texts considered here. This ambiguity is not only unavoidable but an integral part of my project; for to eliminate either the metaphorical or referential sense of the term, in the interests of an arbitrary methodological "coherence," would be willfully to ignore half the evidence. Archaeology acquires new force as a metaphor in the literature of the nineteenth century precisely because of its enhanced "objective" status in the world; the urns and statues that populate its museums find their way into its poetry and finally cast their shadow on all the forms of its discourse.

My apparently eclectic choice of texts in the chapters that follow is motivated, then, by a deep methodological concern: to assemble a broad range of disparate materials from varying genres, registers, and disciplines, in order to enable certain broad rhetorical patterns to emerge. I offer only one extended analysis of a "major" work of literature, Foscolo's poem *Dei Sepolcri,* and devote considerable time and attention to "minor" genres both para- and extra-literary. From dialect poetry to legal discourse to academic orations and encomiastic verse I try to move as freely as possible, without erecting hierarchies or hazarding judgments on any text's poetic or political merit. My aim throughout is to be both thorough and systematic in my description of rhetorical strategies, and to align these unfamiliar texts in a perspective that renders them mutually illuminating.

As the title indicates, my primary orientation is in literature; but my method has drawn me inevitably to consider related visual materials. Because I understand rhetoric to be the structuring principle of all cultural activity, I have become increasingly concerned with those forms and genres of visual representation that make up the semiotic context of Italian literary romanticism. By alternating the discussion of literary texts with the analysis of architectural plans, fresco cycles, political festivals, museums, and other visual programs, I have tried to give a sense of the variety, mobility, and complexity of this period and its rich and largely unexamined cultural production.

In addressing questions traditionally belonging to political history (nineteenth-century struggles against the papacy), along with those reserved for literary history (the conflict between neoclassicism and romanticism), I have bridged two sets of categories as a critic; but this book is not, strictly speaking, a study of the relationship *between* literature and politics. From a rhetorical perspective, politics is always present in literature; as Valesio argues, "rhetoric *is* the political dimension of discourse" (p. 99, emphasis in original). Rhetorical analysis, then, gives access to the political dimension implicit in every act of representation, whether literary or nonliterary, verbal or visual, temporal or spatial in its primary coordinates (the recitation of a poem, for example, as opposed to the display of an artifact, festival apparatus, or theatrical tableau). The challenge is to engage the full rhetorical (and hence, political) complexity of each semiotic structure. The following chapters represent one such attempt. Whatever their limitations, I hope that they illustrate the advantages of a flexible interdisciplinary approach in a contemporary reappraisal of Italian romanticism.

My use of the term "archaeology" inevitably implies a debt to Foucault. In fact his influence is pervasive in my work; for it is Foucault above all who has catalyzed a return to history in literary studies. His concrete analyses of cultural artifacts and institutions alert us to the broad range of signifying practices at work in society as a whole, and remind us that literary texts are themselves "forms of power and performance,"[25] inseparable from the historical context in which they were designed to function.

Introduction

Most notably in *The Archaeology of Knowledge* (New York: Harper and Row, 1972), Foucault has used "archaeology" as a metaphor for his critical project. But it should be clear that my own use of the term is inevitably charged (and contaminated) by the meanings attributed to it in the nineteenth century, when archaeology was not a "neutral" science but an ideologically loaded enterprise. As Foucault himself notes, romantic archaeology "aspired to the condition of history" by restoring a voice to the silent monuments and traces of the past.[26] Foucault's "new history" in turn aspires to the condition of archaeology; but his relevance to my work lies not in his deployment of this metaphor but in his fundamental insights into the nature of discursive practices and larger account of the crisis of historical consciousness in early nineteenth-century Europe.[27] The texts that I examine are situated precisely at that rift between "classical" and "modern" that Foucault has identified and examined at length; and though he does not discuss the Italian situation, surely that "nostalgia for origins" that he attributes to Europe at large finds dramatic expression in the archaeological rhetoric of the Risorgimento.

One final note regarding the geographical focus and frame of this study: The impact of archaeology on the romantic imagination was a wide-ranging phenomenon, spurred by the rediscovery of Greek and Etruscan as well as Roman civilization. The practice of excavation at any site was inevitably politicized. Another book, accordingly, might have dealt with the ruins of Pompeii, Herculaneum, Paestum, Agrigento, or the Etruscan towns of central Italy. Instead I have focused, both in practice and principle, on representations of Rome: for it is here that the political iconography of ruins is most sharply polarized and it is here that the stakes are highest. This survey does not pretend to be complete (*Roma non basta una vita!*), but I hope that it will raise new questions in Italian literary and cultural history, and encourage other scholars to give their attention to a period that has not received the creative scrutiny it deserves.

PART I

PAPAL ARCHAEOLOGY:
THE ENCOMIASTIC MODE

1

MONTI'S "PROSOPOPEA" AND THE IDEOLOGY OF THE PIO-CLEMENTINE MUSEUM

OF THE VAST LITERATURE of archaeological encomium promoted by the eighteenth-century papacy, only the "Prosopopea di Pericle" is still read today. Even the "Prosopopea" is seldom taken seriously; written by Vincenzo Monti at the age of twenty-one, it finds its way into anthologies among his juvenilia as an amusing experiment with an archaeological conceit, an example of that "papal classicism" which Monti would soon abandon in the predictable metamorphoses of his career as a court poet.

In the context of Monti's individual development the "Prosopopea" is indeed of passing importance; it represents a position that he quickly dismissed as the political fortunes of the papacy changed. In the larger context of Italian literary history its importance might seem more limited still, for no one would claim that it is a great poem; in many ways it is a standard papal panegyric and lacks even the formal polish of Monti's later work.

My purpose in this chapter is not to defend the poem's literary merit, but to restore it to the sophisticated and complex ideological context in which it was designed to function. As the single literary text that was framed and incorporated into the program of the Pio-Clementine Museum (Fig. 4),[1] it is the best example we have of the ideology of papal collections in the eighteenth century; and as the most familiar example of a tradition of archaeological encomium now largely forgotten, it illustrates a series of *topoi* and rhetorical strategies long used by the Church to celebrate its repossession of Rome and renew its title to the temporal power.

This chapter will explore the synchronic dimension of papal classicism by restoring Monti's text to the context of the Pio-Clementine Museum in which it is literally framed. The following chapter will trace the diachronic dimension of archaeological encomium: its development as a poetic genre from the accession of Clement XIV to the death of Pius VI. It is hoped that these complementary perspectives will restore a sense of the political importance that the Church attributed to archaeology in the eighteenth century – a tendency which would increase dramatically in the early years of the Risorgimento.

The Pio-Clementine Museum, one of the first great museum complexes of Europe, was an international showpiece of the temporal power. Begun in 1770 by Clement XIV at the initiative of his treasurer Gianangelo Braschi (the future Pius VI), the museum initially consisted of a set of small rooms grouped around the Belvedere courtyard. But under the Braschi pope himself (1775–99), the museum grew by dazzling proportions. In the first few years of his papacy, Pius VI supervised one hundred thirty excavations in Rome, and by the end of his reign he had added nearly six hundred marbles to the Vatican.[2]

What explains the rapid growth of the Vatican museums? It would be cynical to attribute it entirely to Pius's personal vanity; though his zeal as a collector was certainly motivated in part by dynastic ambition. After a period of reform in the Settecento papacy, Pius VI was widely criticized by his contemporaries for the corruption of his finances; he amassed a private fortune from the papal treasury and installed his nephew, Luigi Braschi, in a palace which even a sympathetic biographer would call a "monument of nepotism."[3] Pius's family pride was universally suspect; his original choice of a papal shield (a grandiose device comprised of four fleurs de lis, two eagles, several rows of stars, and Boreas, the north wind, blowing against a lily) was a clear sign of his exaggerated ambition and the subject of countless pasquinades.[4] This version of the Braschi shield, though soon abandoned for a simpler design, can still be seen sculpted on some statue bases in the Pio-Clementine, along with the ubiquitous inscription, "EX MUNIFI-CENTIA PII VI."

Yet important as any individual psychological motives may have been in the growth of the collection, the political and economic context of the late Settecento papacy alone provides sufficient grounds for the creation and expansion of the museum. In the climate of archaeological enthusiasm that followed the discovery of Pompeii and Herculaneum, the artistic patrimony of Rome was endangered as never before. Although foreign collectors had steadily removed artworks from Rome since the Renaissance – despite formal prohibitions on export – the number of excavations and sheer quality of objects now available to the private market was unprecedented; and as the century progressed it had become increasingly clear that legislation alone would not be sufficient to curb the antiquarian trade.

It was to protect the archaeological patrimony of Rome, then, and to reassert the power of the Church against the economic pressures of the private sector, that Gianangelo Braschi as papal treasurer to Clement XIV urged the creation of the Clementine Museum. If the century had begun with the loss of several priceless family collections to the north of Europe (the thirteen hundred Giustiniani marbles, sold to the Earl of Pembroke in

4. Herm of Pericles flanked by Monti's "Prosopopea" (Vatican, Pio-Clementine Museum).

1720; the Odescalchi collection of Queen Christina's sculptures, sold to Philip V of Spain four years later; the Chigi and Albani marbles, both lost to Dresden), Clement XIV's own papacy was inaugurated by the purchase of the Fusconi and Mattei collections in 1770 to form the core of the new museum.[5]

For the next thirty years, through a shrewd program of excavations, preemptions, purchases, and gifts (directed first by Giambattista Visconti as Commissioner of Antiquities and then by his sons Ennio Quirino and Filippo Aurelio), the museum grew as a symbol of the renewed vigor and wealth of the papacy. With the mounting threat of revolution in France, the collection continued to grow, crowding even its new Vatican quarters: and the bankrupt monarchy in France could look with envy at the seemingly inexhaustible resources of Rome. In the words of one French historian, "Les fouilles semblaient remplacer au centuple les statues émigrées; le sol de Rome était inépuisable."[6]

The myth of Rome's inexhaustible wealth, coupled with the fiction of the political invulnerability of the papacy, was promoted by the vast publicity given to the ongoing excavations in Rome. Long before Ennio Quirino Visconti completed his monumental seven-volume catalogue to the Pio-Clementine Museum, archaeological inventories by Bartolomeo Cavaceppi, Francesco Piranesi, and Filippo Antonio Guattani circulated news of the recent papal discoveries and acquisitions.[7] The antiquarian and literary gazettes of Rome published lyrical accounts of the excavations; poets composed verses in praise of Pius's archaeological patronage; and news of the discoveries spread throughout Europe in the reports of travelers and artists invited to view the new Vatican collections.

To celebrate the visit of the Swedish king Gustavus III to the new gallery in 1784, Pius VI commissioned two paintings from Bénigne Gagneraux (Stockholm, Royal Palace). To commemorate the official opening of the museum several months later, in the tenth year of his papacy, he ordered from Bernardino Nocchi an "Allegory of the Creation of the Museo Pio" of which a preparatory study still exists in the Museo di Roma. The same Bernardino Nocchi may be the author of a painting recently acquired by the Vatican Pinacoteca (Fig. 5), which records the Pope's own visit to the new museum; he is escorted by classicists, artists, and antiquarians of his court, including the elder Visconti (who presents a small model of classical sculpture) and the architect Michelangelo Simonetti (who presents a map of the museum itself).[8] Countless texts such as these, both verbal and visual, conspired to publicize the museum and promote the prestige of the papal collections.

Papal propaganda created a demand for images of antiquity at the popular level as well. Reproductions circulated not only in scholarly publications but also in the less exalted forms familiar to us today as inevitably accessory

5. Bernardino Nocchi (?), "Pius VI visits the Pio-Clementine Museum," 1781 (Vatican, Pinacoteca).

to the tourist industry. The studio founded by the Fratelli Pisani at Florence in 1780 catered to such demands; it employed over a hundred workers and was, according to Hautecoeur, a "véritable usine de réproductions."[9] In an advertising brochure it offers along with the standard "bustes d'empereurs, des philosophes, des femmes illustres" and "statues en marbre copiés de l'antique de toute sorte de grandeur . . . ," a variety of paperweights, ink-wells, vases, lamps, and other ornamental objects ingeniously fashioned to "réprésenter les ruines," and all available by mail order.

But this plethora of reproductions only reinforced the appetite for the images whose originals still resided in Rome; so that in 1785 Visconti could remark with satisfaction, "les antiquités découvertes demeurent encore pour la majeure partie à Rome . . . Ces admirables restes des arts de la Grèce sont devenus l'école des arts modernes et font de Rome l'unique emporium du beau et le temple du bon goût . . . les nations se pressent autour de la mère commune des doctrines saines et des beaux arts."[10]

The Pio-Clementine Museum soon outstripped all other collections of classical sculpture in Europe, including its own rival and direct predecessor in Rome, the Villa Albani. The difference between the two institutions is clear. Unlike the Villa Albani – conceived and programmed (in part by Winckelmann) as the precinct of a scholarly elite, the projection of a private antiquarian dream[11] – the Pio-Clementine had a primarily public and cele-bratory function. This function was articulated in an intricate program, through the disposition of space, the ordering of objects, and the rich decorative schemes in fresco, marble, mosaic, and bronze. Before mapping out this program and its political implications in greater detail, we should consider some precedents in the fresco programs of earlier, related rooms in the Vatican.

Before the creation of the Pio-Clementine only one collection of pre-Christian artifacts existed in the Vatican, apart from Julius II's sculpture garden in the Belvedere: the Museo Profano, founded by Clement XIII in 1767. This was a small collection, confined to a single room, and consisted mainly of gems, cameos, ivories, and coins. The ceiling fresco by Stefano Pozzi (1768) is a straightforward allegory of papal patronage.

Against a turbulent landscape littered with the relics of ancient Rome (a broken torso and bas-relief, shattered friezes and severed capitals, with a pyramid and column rising in the distance), Minerva (goddess of wisdom but also patron of the arts) commands the winged spirit of Rome to rescue a marble statue from the spirit of Time: presumably to convey it from the disordered field of the picture to the orderly, "rational" frame provided by the new museum.

A similar ceiling fresco by Anton Raphael Mengs in the Sala dei Papiri of the Vatican Library, commissioned by Clement XIV to celebrate the creation of the Clementine Museum, develops the allegory of patronage in a more sophisticated way (Fig. 6). The same winged genie, here crowned by an oak wreath, rushes toward the seated figure of History to entrust to her the scrolls that he has rescued from the ravages of Time (who slouches against his scythe in the foreground). Resting her book on the shoulders of Time, History watches the Janus figure on the right (his youthful face turned to the light), who points toward the entrance of the newly inaugurated museum. Above the scene the figure of Fame with her trumpet announces the opening of the new museum, toward which she, like the Janus figure, is pointing. The painting represents, then, the Victory of History (which records and preserves) over Time (which destroys and disperses).[12]

But the painter introduces a number of references to the papacy's privileged relationship with History that stress the specific political function of the museum. Significantly, all these references are related to the theme of writing. In the first instance, History records in her book the inscription over the entrance to the museum (MUSEO CLEMENTINO). A second inscription, barely legible, on the ancient gravestone in the foreground, concludes with the acronym: H[OC] M[ONUMENTUM] H[EREDEM] N[ON] S[EQUITUR]. This legend, inscribed on an artifact destined itself to be incorporated into the museum,[13] implies that it is the Church's duty as legitimate heir to Rome to protect its monuments from desecration and alienation. As in ancient precedent, the acronym signifies that the heir may neither sell the ancestral plot nor allow it to fall into disrepair, but is re-

6. Anton Raphael Mengs, "Allegory of the Clementine Museum," 1772 (Vatican Library, Sala dei Papiri).

quired to maintain and honor the site, preserving it for transmission intact to all later descendants.

This message is reinforced by a second set of inscriptions in the figural frame of the *quadro riportato*. The first, on a tablet held by two angels hovering over the seated figure of Peter, consists of the words that Christ spoke to Peter: SUPER/HANC PETRAM / A [E] DIFICABO/ ECCLESIAM/MEAM (Matthew 16:18). The second, on a partially opened scroll at the feet of Moses, on the opposite wall, contains the opening words in Hebrew of the third Book of Moses, also a formula of vocation: "And the Lord called Moses and spoke to him."

By a trick of perspective the New Testament tablet reads visually as a base for the central picture, just as the seated figure of Peter seems a column supporting History as she records the moment of the museum's inauguration. Thus the central space of the *quadro riportato* (clearly recognizable as the space of the museum itself) creates a bridge between the figures representing the New and Old Testament, just as the museum provides a bridge between pre-Christian and Christian history. The museum is itself conceived as a discourse, an encomiastic narrative of papal piety toward antiquity; and through the formal syntax of its spatial organization and the rich vocabulary of its decorative forms, it conveys a political message of central importance to the Church.

These ceiling frescoes anticipate the program of Pius's museum, and help us to appreciate its nature as discourse. It is time now to take a closer look at the museum itself and some of the ways in which it expresses its ideological program.

The most striking example is in the articulation of space. Where Clement XIV, like all his eighteenth-century predecessors, had used only preexisting rooms to house his collection, taking great care to preserve their integrity and in some cases even to restore their original decoration, Pius VI built a series of vast rooms *ex novo,* which he wrapped around the Belvedere Courtyard. The Renaissance cortile (now Cortile Ottagono, updated in neoclassical dress) was not the focus or forecourt of his museum, as it had been for Clement XIV; it was just one of many rooms realigned on a new and ambitious plan.

Upon his accession to the papacy in 1775, one of Pius's first orders to the architect Michelangelo Simonetti (who had succeeded Alessandro Dori upon his death in 1772) was the extension of Clement's Gallery of Statues, in the north loggia of Innocent VIII's Palazzetto, and the construction of an entirely new wing that would more than double the size of the original museum. This necessitated the destruction of Innocent's chapel, completely frescoed by Mantegna, which Clement himself had carefully preserved. This act of vandalism seemed to give the lie to the new pope's professed archaeological "piety"; but it was a move implicitly sanctioned by a long papal tradition. To cite just one example, an earlier Pius (Aeneas Sylvius Piccolomini, the Latin humanist who became Pope Pius II in 1458) had seen no contradiction between his own edicts and Latin elegies deploring the destruction of ancient monuments and his subsequent destruction of the eastern colonnade of the Portico of Octavia, along with other important monuments, to provide building materials for the Vatican.[14]

In any case, it was with an act of destruction that Pius VI emancipated himself from his predecessor's scheme, opening up new possibilities for the Pio-Clementine both as a scholarly project and political statement. The sheer size of the new museum was of course significant, but equally important was the organization of space. By realigning Clement's collection along two new axes which converged in his spectacular Sala Rotonda, Pius gave a new unity and discursive force to the museum itself.

As we can see in an eighteenth-century plan of the museum (Fig. 7), the first axis led from the Sala Rotonda (a great round hall with coffered ceiling in imitation of the Pantheon) through the octagonal, domed Hall of the Muses and the Sala degli Animali, then bisected the Belvedere courtyard to end in Clement's tiny Vestibolo Rotondo. By closing the entrance to the Gallery of Statues from the Belvedere courtyard, Pius subjected the courtyard to an axial orientation; henceforth Julius's cortile could be "read" and traversed only in reference to the Braschi plan (poets paid analogous homage to Pius's "anxiety of influence" in their encomiastic verse; Pius's superiority to both Julius II and Leo X was a standard claim).

The second axis from the Sala Rotonda aimed straight down the library corridor toward the Sistine Chapel itself. The sequence of forms arranged along this axis (grand staircase / Greek-cross atrium / circular domed gallery) repeats the pattern of Clement's eastern wing (staircase / Atrio del Torso / Vestibolo Rotondo). Pius's joke on his predecessor seems quite deliberate; by imitating the syntax of the original entry in his own monumental wing, he dramatized the growth of the museum from its modest beginnings to a truly imperial scale.

At the same time this succession of forms established an important precedent in museum architecture. The combination of a formal staircase, square vestibule, and imposing domed gallery became a prototype for later art museums. Pius stressed the importance of this arrangement in the painting commissioned to Bernardino Nocchi on the opening of the museum; unlike Mengs's "Allegory of the Clementine" (Fig. 6), which situated the viewer in the Belvedere courtyard, this placed him at the foot of the Scala Simonetti, looking up past the figures of Painting, Sculpture, and Architecture toward the Atrio a Croce Greca and a high glimpse of the Sala Rotonda. A later painting attributed to Domenico De Angelis in the Sala Alessandrina of the Biblioteca paid homage to this same perspective in its portrayal of the pope's inaugural visit to his museum.

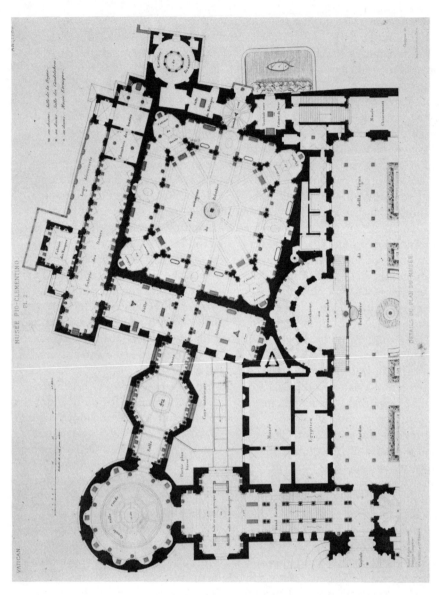

7. Plan of the Pio-Clementine Museum, 1780 (Vatican).

In addition to its primary rhetorical function as monumental entry to the Pio-Clementine Museum, the Scala Simonetti had a calculated visual impact on the adjoining library corridor. The imposing marble staircase subordinated the entire corridor to a new perspective function; and Pius enhanced this by widening the doorways in the gallery as far as the Museo Sacro, creating an uninterrupted perspective 318 meters long. Thus the visual and ideological thrust of the new museum extended beyond its formal spatial boundaries. From Benedict XIV's Museo Sacro through Clement XIII's Museo Profano to his own collection of classical antiquities, Pius VI traced a single axis of power – an axis which can itself be read as an iconic representation both of the continuity of the Settecento papacy and of the larger continuity between classical and Christian Rome that is the museum's main argument.

The relevance of the architectural plan to the ideological program is implied by the inclusion, at the beginning of the first volume of Visconti's folio catalogue, of a map of the museum drawn by Simonetti. Whereas earlier catalogues of antiquarian collections had commonly provided a different sort of illustration for the frontispiece, frequently an interior view of one of the rooms in the collection (Caylus's *Recueil d'antiquités* shows a bank of shelves cluttered with disparate objects), here the organization of space is considered fundamental to an understanding of the museum (the two axes converging in the Sala Rotonda are drawn into the plan, as an aid to the reader). The calculated articulation of space and arrangement of objects within the Pio-Clementine contrast with the essentially paratactic construction of earlier collections such as Caylus's *Recueil* and Kircher's museum at the Collegio Romano.[15] Despite the variety of its inventory, the Pio-Clementine is never an arbitrary arrangement, and when one object is privileged we can expect to find an excellent reason.

The frontispiece of Visconti's first volume displays the traditional figurative apparatus of papal encomium: below the title the Braschi arms, surmounted by a papal tiara and keys, rest on a pair of cornucopia, one spilling coins and the other ripe fruit. At the left are a painter's palette and brushes and a broken bas-relief; at the right a pair of books, a compass and quadrant, a set of floor plans clearly legible as those of the museum itself, and the marble bust of Pericles whose discovery at Tivoli prompted the composition of Monti's "Prosopopea."[16]

The privileged position of the Pericles statue within the program of the museum is not accidental. Visconti himself, who includes the bust so prominently here among the trophies of his patron, was the one to suggest to Monti the theme of his poem.[17]

Recited at the Accademia dell'Arcadia in celebration of the *voti quinquennali* of Pius VI, the "Prosopopea di Pericle" celebrates both the recovery of the Pope from a recent illness and the recovery of the Pericles statue from the ruins of Tivoli. The zeugma is deliberately precious and in keeping with the spirit of the Arcadia. Monti's poem was only one of a dozen compositions presented for the occasion; but it alone was singled out to be framed and permanently incorporated into the collection.

What does the "Prosopopea" tell us about the ideology of the museum? Its argument is simple: Monti claims (and here any question of his "sincerity" is irrelevant) that Pius VI surpasses Pericles himself as a patron of the arts, and that his reign has brought a new golden age to Rome – to all of Europe, if she will only acknowledge it.

> Io de' forti Cecropidi
> nell'inclita famiglia
> d'Atene un dì non ultimo
> splendor e maraviglia,
>   a riveder io Pericle
> ritorno il ciel latino,
> trionfator de' barbari,
> del tempo e del destino.[18]

(I of the great race of Cecrops in the noble family of Athens, once not the least source of splendor and amazement, I Pericles return to see the Latin sky, triumphant over barbarians, time, and destiny.)

It is "Pericles" who is speaking: the voice, that is, of the sculpted herm that is the historical Pericles's last incarnation. The syntactical inversions and archaizing diction serve to establish the authority of the speaker. In this prosopopea, which could be considered a dramatic version of traditional *ecphrasis,* the poet represents the artifact not by external description but by attributing to it a fictionalized voice. The mask of Pericles assumes the first person, as if to literalize the archaeologists' claim to make the "mute stones speak."

The stiff genealogical periphrasis by which the speaker introduces himself also introduces a theme that will be central to the poem – that of the idealized genealogy which will claim a direct link between Pericles and Pius himself.

Pericles is not only the heroic precursor of the Braschi papacy, according to the poem, but its humble beneficiary. In his last incarnation as sculptural mask, Pericles the former protagonist of political events is reduced to his representation in stone, and dependent upon the piety of the present age for his retrieval, restoration, and honorary appointment at the Vatican. Hence the fiction of his poetic homage to this golden age, far greater than his own:

Tardi nepoti e secoli,
che dopo Pio verrete,
quando lo sguardo attonito
indietro volgerete,
  oh come fia che ignobile
allor vi sembri e mesta
la bella età di Pericle
al paragon di questa!   (89–96)

(Future descendants and ages that will come after Pius, when you look back with astonished eyes, oh how ignoble and wretched will seem the glorious age of Pericles in comparison with this!)

The public recitation of the "Prosopopea" celebrates the consecration of a pagan idol and its incorporation into a formalized Christian space. The conceit does not originate with Monti; it recalls a long tradition of Christian ambivalence toward the relics of antiquity. Like the obelisks resurrected throughout Rome since the sixteenth century, all classical artifacts converted to Christian service had to be exorcised of their political and religious ambiguity before they could be accepted as univocal signs of the supremacy of the Church.

In the era of Sixtus V, who erected four obelisks in only five years as Pope (1585–90), explicit rites of purification were actually performed, in the presence of the multitudes kneeling in prayer, before the Cross was raised above each of the obelisks. "Esorcizzo te, creatura di pietra, nel nome del Dio onnipotente," pronounced the bishop at the inauguration of the obelisk erected in the Piazza San Pietro in 1586, "perchè tu divenga pietra esorcizzata per sostenere la Sacra Croce e resti priva da ogni immodezza di paganesimo e da ogni assalto di spirituale nequizia . . ."[19]

The same ritualistic, quasi-magical formulas of exorcism were permanently inscribed on the base of the obelisks. On two faces of the base of the same obelisk we read: "Ecce Crux Domini / Fugite Partes Adversae / Vicit Leo / De tribu Iuda" and "Christus vincit / Christus regnat / Christus imperat / Christus ab omni malo / plebem suam defendat."

In the Settecento liturgy of papal classicism, the recitation and inscription of Monti's poem on the Greek statue performed an analogous ceremonial function. Like the prayers and litanies chanted upon the consecration of the obelisks, this poem performed the double rites of exorcism and benediction of the pagan image. Pericles's disclaimer of his own godless age, coupled with his pledge of a new allegiance to Pius, frees the Church to take triumphant possession of his image.

The analogy I make here may seem misleading. Pius VI's age is no longer that of the Counter-Reformation; this had "officially" ended with Clement XIV's dissolution of the Jesuit Order in 1773. But the political pressures on the Church in the late eighteenth century were comparable to those faced by the first popes of the Counter-Reformation, though the enemy now was not Luther but Voltaire. In its precarious position on the eve of the French Revolution, the Church could not countenance secular readings of antiquity. (Voltaire's *La mort de César* would be performed on the Capitoline during the 1799 Roman Republic, with the bronze She-Wolf itself as a prop!) The only possible political justification for the Church's archaeological enterprise was to reclaim the classical tradition from its potentially subversive uses. Pericles must be made to bow to the Cross – and to Gianangelo Braschi.

Given the strict nexus between politics and archaeology, we can see that Pius VI's own interest in obelisks was not accidental. For of all the popes to succeed Sixtus V he erected the greatest number of obelisks in Rome (including one, facing the French church at Trinità dei Monti, only months before the fall of the Bastille). Pius's interest in the subject, like his passion for antiquities in general, was not innocent of political motives. Nor was the protection he provided to the Danish scholar Georg Zoega, author of a monumental study, *De origine et usu obeliscorum,* published in 1797 with a lengthy dedication to his patron.[20]

The "Prosopopea di Pericle" illustrates many of the basic themes and strategies of the literature of archaeological encomium at the court of Pius VI. But in some ways it is unique. This may help to explain its inclusion in the museum and its importance as an index to the ideology of papal classicism.

Unlike previous papal "poetry of ruins" such as that of Alessandro Guidi almost a century earlier, this text foregrounds not a Roman but a Greek artifact. The ideological range and resonance of the Greek icon is obviously greater than that of its Roman counterpart: for it enables the poet to celebrate the political continuity not only between pagan and Christian Rome, but between modern Rome and fifth-century Athens.

Monti's poem capitalizes on the Hellenizing enthusiasms of the papal court since Winckelmann, and provides an exemplary strategy of reading the icons of ancient Greece as signs of the future greatness of Rome. It admits no *querelle* between Greece and Rome; eliding the entire Piranesi/Winckelmann debate, the text simply incorporates Greece into a heroic genealogy of papal Rome. Of course, fifth-century Greece and its icons would not long remain in exclusive custody of the Vatican. Just as the Elgin marbles migrated to London, Greece would become a symbol of the anti-Napoleonic opposition.[21] But for the moment, Monti's text appropriated the prestige of ancient Greece for the benefit of the Pope, enrolling

Pericles himself, among "mille volti argolici," in the front lines of the papal court and Pio-Clementine Museum.

The poem is also original in its reinterpretation of the *topos* of the "progress of civilizations" common to neoclassicism and didactic poetry. Pericles's account of the decline of Greece and subsequent rise of Rome is at first formulaic:

> Dimentici
> della mia patria i Numi,
> di Roma alfin prescelsero
> gli altari ed i costumi.
>   Grecia fu vinta, e videsi
> di Grecia la ruina
> render superba e splendida
> la povertà latina.
>   Pianser deserte e squallide
> allor le spiagge achive,
> e le bell'Arti corsero
> del Tebro su le rive.
>   Qui poser franche e libere
> il fuggitivo piede,
> e accolte si compiacquero
> della cangiata sede.   (125–40)

(Forgetful of my homeland, the Gods finally chose the altars and customs of Rome. Greece was conquered, and the ruin of Greece rendered the Latin poverty proud and splendid. Then the Greek shores wept, deserted and dismal, and the fine Arts rushed to the banks of the Tiber. Here free and unmolested they rested their weary foot, and thus welcomed they rejoiced in their changed home.)

The passage of political and cultural hegemony from Greece to Rome is predestined by the gods. Athens is despoiled, its temples dismantled and its icons carried off as trophies of war: but Rome revives the arts and they continue to flourish in their new home until the first Gothic invasions (third stanza). They are fully restored and redeemed only through the efforts of Pius VI:

> Ed or fastose obbliano
> l'onta del goto orrore,
> or che il gran Pio le vendica
> del vilipeso onore.   (141–4)

(And now in their splendor they forget the disgrace of the Gothic
terror, now that the great Pius is avenging the affront to their honor.)

What is unusual in this synopsis is its omission of the Italian Renaissance,
grudgingly credited with the revival of antiquity even in the progress
poems of Augustan England (for example, in James Thomson's "Liberty").[22] The Braschi pope displaces all his precursors; Julius II (della Rovere)
may have discovered the Laocoön and Paul III (Farnese) the Hercules, but to
Pius VI is reserved the prize talisman of antiquity.

To anyone familiar with the heroic personification of Renaissance Sculpture in Thomson's "Liberty," triumphantly excavating her masterpieces
from the "tyrant's garden" of Renaissance Rome (and Thomson lists all the
favorites: the Farnese Hercules, Vatican Meleager, two Gladiators, Apollo
Belvedere, Flora, Medici Venus and Laocoön),[23] Monti's irony is clear
when in the "Prosopopea" he transforms her into a Magdalene figure,
despairing of the resurrection of the Pericles image:

> Carca d'alto rammarico
> sen dolse l'infelice
> del marmo freddo e ruvido
> bell'arte animatrice;
>   e d'Adriano e Cassio,
> sparsa le belle chiome,
> fra gl'insepolti ruderi
> m'andò chiamando a nome. (21–8)

(Burdened with great regret lamented the beautiful Art which gives
life to cold, rough marble; and with her beautiful hair disheveled she
wandered through the unburied ruins of Hadrian and Cassius, calling
me by name.)

By deferring the allegorical triumph of Sculpture to the Settecento Monti
not only indulges his patron's fantasy of surpassing his Renaissance precursors, but subverts the panoramic premise of the Augustan progress poems –
the theory of Albion's "manifest destiny" to displace a decadent Rome as
Rome had once displaced Greece. His thematic focus on an artifact admired
and sought after by the Renaissance but not discovered until the Settecento
dramatizes the claim that the Roman Renaissance is only beginning. Papal
Rome is not the "tomb of Empire" deplored by Thomson ("Need I the
contrast mark? Unjoyous view! / A land in all, in government and arts, / In
virtue, genius, earth and heaven, reversed," I, 107–9), but a thriving capital, secure in its custody of the icons of Greece already coveted by England.
The "Prosopopea" opposes then to the political moralizing of the Au-

gustan "poetry of ruins" a triumphal celebration of a specific archaeological occasion. Within the larger program of the museum it provides an exemplary reading of an individual artifact to guide the visitor in his understanding of the Church's privileged relationship with antiquity. Inscribed beside the statue of Pericles, it illuminates the legend of the pope who was creator and patron of the museum.

The "Prosopopea" is one of many auxiliary texts that enable the museum to comment on itself and clarify its function to the public. Some of these texts are verbal, like the inscriptions which document the history of the museum's construction; the proud notice that Pius's museum was a "wholly new building" ("A Fundamentis Extruxit") appears at three critical junctures in the plan (over the entrance to the Biblioteca from the Scala Simonetti, over the entrance to the Sala degli Animali from the Cortile Ottagono, and in a slightly altered form on the floor of the Galleria delle Statue).

Other such auxiliary texts are visual. Domenico De Angelis's hagiographic narrative of Pius's life in the Sala Alessandrina (1818), which stresses the theme of his archaeological patronage, is a posthumous tribute that cannot be considered here.[24] But one elaborate program completed during Pius's lifetime illustrates strategies of encomium similar to those which I have analyzed in Monti's poem, and deserves at least brief mention in any discussion of the Pio-Clementine.[25]

Commissioned by Pius VI and probably programmed by Ennio Quirino Visconti himself, this pictorial cycle is located in a hall on the second floor of the Vatican (now Galleria degli Arazzi), where Pius VI installed the first Vatican Pinacoteca. Though his collection of 118 paintings was dispersed after the Treaty of Tolentino, the decoration on the vaulted ceiling remains.

The cycle is a complex allegorical program that is explicitly archaeological in both form and content. Conceived as a trompe-l'oeil "stucco" ensemble of grisaille medallions on a pastel ground, the program makes several layers of archaeological allusions. The ornamental grotesques painted by Antonio Marini recall both the famous decorations by Raphael and Giovanni da Udine in the Vatican Loggie and the originals in the Domus Aurea that inspired them. The framed figural episodes by Bernardino Nocchi, distributed in geometrical compartments on the decorative ground, in turn are trompe-l'oeil imitations of antique sculpture – particularly of imperial Roman prototypes from the Forum of Nerva and the Columns of Trajan and Antoninus Pius.

Briefly, the program consists of two series of episodes from the lives of Roman emperors that converge on a central image of the Braschi arms. Each scene is an "exemplum virtutis" comparing the virtues of a chosen emperor to those of Pius VI. The individually framed moral paradigms, deployed in sequence, set up an illusionistic political narrative in apology of the temporal power. Like Monti's poem, this cycle of images argues that the pope is sole legitimate heir to the legacy of imperial Rome.

Thus the trompe-l'oeil "archaeology" of this decorative program reinforces the central message of the museum itself. This is clarified in the central section, which is devoted to the theme of artistic patronage. Both Augustus and Hadrian are represented examining architectural plans: Augustus studies the plan and elevation of his temple to Mars Ultor, while Hadrian holds the plan of his villa – which as one of the most extensive collections of sculpture in ancient times was both the prototype of Pius's own museum and the source of some of its greatest treasures.

Pius's literal resurrection of classical artifacts marks his resurrection of an imperial myth. Like Monti's poem, and like the Pio-Clementine Museum in general, the program of the Pinacoteca is an allegory of power. It represents a genealogical romance, a projection of idealized origins and a claim to political legitimacy that would soon be directly challenged.

The cycle was completed in 1789. As a political statement (if not for its artistic merit) it invites comparison with another group of images in the Vatican: Giulio Romano's Hall of Constantine, completed just a few years before the 1527 Sack of Rome.[26] In a climate of growing hostility toward the papacy, each of these visual narratives reasserted the legitimacy of the temporal power and the pope's uncontestable title to Rome.

Rome was sacked in 1797 as it had been in 1527. The Pio-Clementine Museum was dismantled and its sculptures carried off to Paris as trophies of war. Not all of the art works were returned from the Louvre in 1815, and new acquisitions somewhat altered the face of the museum; but Pius's program survives largely intact, as testimony of the importance of archaeology to the politics of the eighteenth-century papacy.

2

THE POETRY OF PAPAL ENCOMIUM:
ARCHAEOLOGICAL TEXTS
AND PRETEXTS

O N THE SIXTH NIGHT of his prose fantasy, *Le notti romane,* Alessandro Verri stages a visit of the shades of ancient Romans to the newly opened Vatican museums. It is the highlight of their tour of the monuments of papal Rome. Accustomed to their own colossal palaces on the Palatine, the visitors are at first unimpressed by the size and scale of the Vatican palace:

> But when they entered, and saw the marvelous artifice of the paintings on every wall . . . when arrayed in its spacious halls they admired the images of their gods, and heroes, and celebrated men, together with the urns, and inscriptions from their tombs, the altars and implements of their sacred rites, the domestic Penates, their furnishings, arms, feminine ornaments, and coins; when they recognized every emblem and accessory of their habits and customs preserved not out of simple curiosity, but with pious veneration, then I saw that all the shades were moved by inexplicable amazement and tender joy.[1]

It is a moment of deep satisfaction, both sentimental and rhetorical, for Verri's narrator. Impressed by the variety of objects assembled here to document their own culture, and grateful for Christian piety toward pagan artifacts, the shades range through the museum "like bees swarming through flowers," examining the relics of a world they had thought buried with them forever.

> I saw many whose eyes streamed with tears of joy; others with shining faces wandered anxiously, contemplating their own images or those of their relatives; others stood before the portrait of some famous man, silently and thoughtfully enjoying the prospect . . . What ineffable delight was mine, as great as any in heaven!

Not accidentally, as they wander through the palace, many of the shades stop with care to examine a painting, on the wall of a great chamber, representing a king bowing at the foot of the Highest Priest; and on another wall they observed scenes of battle, and bloody events, and enemies overcome by swift destruction. And they judged these triumphs no less perilous or proud than the ones which they themselves had celebrated.

This can only be a description of the Hall of Constantine. Although the shades themselves, new to the language of the imperial papacy, are unable to decipher its iconography here, Verri assumes that his own readers will recognize the cycle and remember the episodes that it illustrates: the baptism of Constantine by Pope Sylvester, the Battle of Ponte Milvio, allocution to the soldiers and vision of the Cross, along with the Donation of Constantine (here polemically reasserted over Valla's Quattrocento critique). It is a fitting conclusion to a tour of the Pio-Clementine, and another significant lesson in the glory of papal Rome.

Verri's ancient Romans are model pupils. At the end of their indoctrination it is Cicero himself who concludes, as their spokesman, that the empire of the Church surpasses all pagan precedent. Cicero's "Ragionamento sul Pontificato Romano" is an idealized recital of the political history of the papacy, which alone has ensured the survival of Rome and perfected the ancient ideal of empire. Founded on a principle higher than that of military conquest, it has based its authority on the shared faith and spontaneous consent of its subjects. Instead of despoiling its provinces, Rome has enriched them by serving as a peaceful and cosmopolitan capital, opening up its vast riches to the civilized world.

Cicero explicitly rejects any attempt to unify Italy under a secular power. All the nations should be grateful for the guidance of the Church, he argues:

> but certainly if any part of the world should appreciate the authority of the Papacy, it is Italy; which owes to Her its defense in calamitous times, its preservation in extreme vicissitudes, and its splendor; for as the seat of the Papacy Italy is still honored and esteemed throughout Europe and the world. Whereas without the Pope, even if Italy were the domain of a single monarch, she would still be less extensive and powerful than Iberia, Germany, Gaul, and many other kingdoms more vast and formidable. And yet now due to that magnificent power she rises again, revered by the nations, and extends her empire of peace to the remotest ends of the earth . . . therefore I rejoice to see my homeland raised again incorruptible, a perpetual instrument of that heavenly providence which prepares and accomplishes the principal revolutions of the earth.[2]

Cicero's conversion to the praise of the papacy parallels Verri's own ideological development during his long residence in Rome. Begun in the

Milanese enlightenment spirit of his earlier writings as a satire on Settecento archaeology, *Le notti romane* evolved in a direction unforeseen by Verri himself, who finally suppressed its introductory chapter, "L'antiquario fanatico," with the warning that Rome was not a fit subject for satire.

For both political and literary reasons *Le notti romane* was an unprecedented success throughout the early Ottocento, and not in Italy alone; thirty-two editions and eight translations appeared during Verri's lifetime and more than one hundred editions and sixteen translations in less than a century. The eventual appeal of its argument to the neoguelph movement can easily be imagined; its apology of the papacy as sole ordering principle of Italian unity later seemed a presage of Gioberti's *Primato*. At the same time Verri's representation of ruins, alternately sinister and sentimental, declamatory and macabre, appealed to evolving strains of European romanticism.

For the range of its appeal, the complexity of its treatment of an archaeological theme, and its ambiguous status as a literary genre, Verri's Roman romance was unique in the literature of the Italian Settecento. Less unusual, but arguably even more important to an understanding of the politics of papal archaeology, is the body of literature directly sponsored by the Settecento papacy to celebrate its vast archaeological patronage. Composed largely for recitation at ecclesiastical and academic ceremonies, this literature was a local product, not widely exported and (in most cases) quickly forgotten; Monti's "Prosopopea," preserved in the Pio-Clementine Museum, was only one example of a once thriving genre that deserves to be unearthed and reconsidered today.

The purpose of this chapter is not to provide a complete history of the poetry of archaeological encomium, but to present a significant range of examples to illustrate its primary themes and strategies. I have assembled these texts from three kinds of sources: the literary and antiquarian journals of the period, the proceedings of the Accademia dell'Arcadia, and the reports of the *concorsi capitolini* (competitions in painting, sculpture, and architecture sponsored at three-year intervals by the Accademia di San Luca, under the auspices of the Pope). The material, so far largely neglected by literary historians, is vast and needs to be studied in depth; but this discussion will serve as a preliminary sounding. Both as an illustration of the ideology of papal collections and as an informal chronicle of the Church's archaeological patronage, these texts are of extraordinary interest to the study of Settecento classicism.

Monti is remembered today for his single experiment with an archaeological theme – proposed, as I have said, by Ennio Quirino Visconti, the child prodigy turned papal antiquary and programmer of much of the Pio-

Clementine Museum. If Monti was at first reluctant to follow Visconti's advice, Francesco Preziado showed a firm and consistent preference for the genre. First as secretary and later Prince of the Accademia di San Luca, he was a tireless contributor of archaeological verse to the *concorsi capitolini* and designed the frontispiece long used for its published volumes of the ceremony's proceedings.

This engraving presents several of the major themes of Preziado's poetry: the parallel glorification of ancient and modern Rome, the need to mobilize all the arts (including poetry itself) to celebrate the return of a golden age, the call to preserve and emulate the classical tradition. The iconographical scheme is simple and recalls on a small scale more ambitious allegories in the Vatican. In the center of the picture Minerva, patron of the arts, extends three laurel crowns to the figures of Painting (identified by her brushes and palette), Sculpture (hammer and chisel), and Architecture (compass and quadrant). A mask and pen on the right allude to the shared responsibility of literature in promoting a renewal of the arts. In the background are the generic signs of a classical landscape – a round temple reminiscent of the Pantheon, framed by a pair of obelisks. In the foreground reclines the figure of the Tiber, beside the Wolf who suckles the twins Romulus and Remus.

The rhetorical occasion favored by the 1771 *concorsi* was the founding of the Clementine Museum. Preziado's sonnet, which inaugurated the collection of poems recited at this competition, is a canonical example:

> O diroccate al suol moli latine
> > Archi e colonne de l'antico impero;
> > O sassi che mostrate al passeggero
> > I segni de le gotiche rovine:
> Su le sette del Tebro alme colline
> > Ritornarete a lo splendor primiero,
> > Or che l'augusto Successor di Piero
> > Tante impiega per voi cure divine.
> Così dicean le tre bell'Arti industri
> > Nel mirar fatto asilo il Vaticano
> > De' già dispersi monumenti illustri;
> E quindi a gara affaticar la mano
> > A scolpir generose in fronte ai lustri
> > Il nome e l'opra del Pastor Sovrano.[3]

(Oh Latin palaces razed to the ground, arches and columns of the ancient empire; Oh stones that show to the passerby the signs of Gothic ruin: upon the sublime seven hills of the Tiber you will return to your original splendor, now that the august Successor of Peter ministers to you with his divine care. Thus spoke the three industrious fine arts, when they saw the Vatican become a refuge for the illustrious monuments once dispersed; and therefore they vied with each other, each wearying his hand to sculpt before the coming ages the name and the works of the Sovereign Pastor.)

Like the medal coined in the same year to commemorate Clement's founding of the museum (which represents the Pope, in the guise of Ripa's "Liberality," overturning a cornucopia of gold coins against the background of Innocent's Palazzetto with the Barberini candelabra and Fusconi Meleager – both fresh acquisitions – displayed in the foreground),[4] Preziado's poem employs the standard iconography of papal encomium to celebrate Clement's archaeological patronage. To the three figures of Painting, Sculpture, and Architecture (commonly personified in both poetry and painting as appreciative witnesses to the disinterment of Rome), the poet attributes the apostrophe of the first eight lines. Together they invoke the ruined Roman landscape not, as in the elegiac tradition, to deplore the destruction of the classical past, but to celebrate its reconstruction and assimilation into a Christian present. The Vatican museum, conceived as a refuge and sanctuary (*asilo*) for the relics of antiquity, represents the successful integration of the classical and Christian traditions and is the symbol of a new golden age and revival of the arts.

The disorder of the ancient landscape, reflected in the essentially paratactic structure of the opening lines ("O . . . moli . . . archi e colonne . . . sassi") is only provisional, the poem implies; for the Church, by its "cure divine," will restore the monuments and integrate them into its own complex representational structure. (Thus Mengs's painting in the Sala dei Papiri would illustrate the continuity between Old and New Testament civilizations: Pius VI, with his own passion for Egyptian antiquities, would flank the entrance to his expanded collection of Greek and Roman sculpture with two "Egyptian" telamones, probably Hadrianic, excavated at Tivoli.)

The Pope's gesture of assembling the scattered fragments of pre-Christian civilization and "re-membering" Rome's dismembered past is seen as a guarantee of stability and continuity in modern society. By offering examples of ancient monuments for young artists to study, the museum encourages the emulation of the classical tradition by young artists drawn to Rome from all parts of Europe; it reinforces Rome's position as a cosmopolitan capital and repository of traditions presumed immune to political change.

The very periphrasis used to designate Clement ("l'augusto Successor di Piero") implies a genealogy of power. By an inevitable paronomasia, the adjective "augusto" recalls Augustus and the entire Julio-Claudian dynasty as authentic ancestors of the Settecento papacy.

If Rome's ruins testify to the violence of human history (the palaces "razed to the ground," the stones bearing "signs of Gothic ruin"), the

Church's successful reconstruction of classical monuments implies its transcendence of history, the arrival of a new golden age beyond disorder and change. In a landscape which had been read as a representation of absence and loss, the Vatican museum is a new symbol of presence and plenitude. It is the responsibility of the arts then, the poet argues, to praise the institution that has finally prevailed over the vicissitudes of history, by inscribing the name and deeds of Clement in its own works of painting, sculpture, architecture, and poetry.

A sonnet by Giuseppe Aluigi recited at the 1773 competition, "Sonetto per la nuova Fabbrica del Museo Clementino ordinata da Nostro Signore," makes a similar exhortation to the artists currently at work on the construction and decoration of the new museum:

> Industri Fabbri, che ampia mole ergete
> Al cenno di CLEMENTE in Vaticano,
> E alle prische memorie altere e liete
> Novo aprir meditate asil sovrano:
> Voi, che su i bronzi, e i marmi ognor solete
> Alle bell'opre affaticar la mano,
> Pronti a gara le invitte arti volgete
> All'alto onor del gran Pastor Romano.
> Là degli eroi più eccelsi in mezzo ai busti,
> Di lui pur sorga il Simulacro altero
> A far argine, e fronte agli anni ingiusti:
> E mostri il grato vostro almo pensiero,
> Che col favor de' suoi bei geni augusti
> Dell'Arti egregie Ei ristorò l'Impero.[5]

(Industrious Builders, who raise a huge palace in the Vatican at the command of Clement, and plan to create a supreme new sanctuary for the proud and glad memories of ancient times: You, who are accustomed to wearying your hand in fashioning beautiful works from bronze and marble, turn your unrivaled skills to the contest, to honor the great Roman Pastor. There, amidst the busts of the noblest heroes, let his proud Image rise to block the advance of the unjust years: and let it show forth your affection and gratitude, for with the favor of his great and august genius he has restored the Empire of the distinguished Arts.)

Again the museum is referred to as an "asilo" or sanctuary, a structured refuge for memories long held hostage by time; and the poet urges his contemporaries to mobilize all their talents to fashion the "Simulacro altero" of a pope who has restored the empire of the arts and reestablished the supremacy of Rome.

As patron of the arts, in both poetry and painting the Pope is frequently figured as Minerva. A 1773 sonnet by Alessio Falconieri recalls the iconography of Stefano Pozzi's "Allegory of the Museo Profano" (1768; see Chapter 1) in its personification of "l'arte, che superba stassi / In atto di vietar, che appresso [alle sculture antiche] / Non osi il Tempo avvicinare i passi" (Art, who stands proudly in the act of forbidding that Time draw near to the antique sculptures).[6] Like Pozzi's allegory, this poem represents the function of patronage as that of protecting ancient icons (and the sovereignty they represent) from destruction. Grasping Time, with his scythe, is the enemy; while the patron, providing sanctuary for the art works, is the embattled hero. The function of patronage, then, is purely conservative; art does not instigate social and political change, but protects the community from it.

After Clement's death, the praise of his archaeological program was transferred to the newly elected Pius VI, who in fact, as we have seen, had been largely responsible for encouraging Clement's interest in collecting during his term as papal treasurer. Ennio Quirino Visconti, who himself would become Commissioner of Antiquities, director of the Capitoline Museum, and programmer of much of the Pio-Clementine, at the age of twenty-four wrote a poem for the accession of Pius VI that attributed Rome's return to peace and prosperity to the new "piety" shown toward classical monuments. In the poem, Rome's "genio guerriero" reawakens to find the fierce ancient city subdued and transformed:

> Vide il gran foro, i colli ameni, e tutte
> Nuovo aspetto di pace avean le cose.
> Su i Teatri, e le Terme arsi, a distrutte
> Cento la fronte ergean moli famose.
> Non più ai fieri spettacoli ridutte
> Vide esaltar le genti bellicose,
> Ma sugl'Idoli infranti, e i marmi sparti
> Sorgere la pietà; rinascer l'Arti.[7]

(He saw the great forum, and the gentle hills, and all things wore a new aspect of peace. Over the Theaters, and the burned and leveled Baths, a hundred famous buildings raised their head. He no longer saw the warlike peoples exult in fierce spectacles, but saw piety rise up over the broken Idols, and the scattered marbles, and the Arts reborn.)

Work on the Pio-Clementine continued throughout the Braschi reign; and his court poets persisted, with only slight variations, in their formulaic praise of the project. At the Capitoline competitions of 1783, Preziado contributed another sonnet, which began:

> No, non temer gran Figlia di Quirino,
>   Che cerchin le Belle Arti altro emisfero,
>   Or che con esse il Successor di Piero
>   Cotanto accresce lo splendor latino.
> Dal Celio, dal Tarpeo, dal Palatino
>   Pio le richiama al sommo onor primiero,
>   E vuol che in Vaticano abbian l'impero,
>   Il loro ad eternar nobil destino.[8]

(No, do not fear, great daughter of Quirinus, that the Fine Arts will seek out another hemisphere, now that through them the Successor of Peter so increases the Latin splendor. From the Celian, from the Tarpeian, from the Palatine Pius recalls the arts to their former honor; and he wishes them to have an empire in the Vatican, to immortalize their noble destiny.)

Again the poet conflates the notions of political and artistic empire. By assembling the scattered icons of Rome in the Vatican, he claims, the Pope has protected an inalienable inheritance. The Church's privileged access to the arts in turn grants it political immunity, a perennial centrality which can never be contested. "No, non temer gran Figlia di Quirino / Che cerchin le Belle Arti altro emisfero . . ." There can be no migration of the arts, Preziado boasts; no city in the world will ever displace Rome. The poet here may be whistling in the dark; in any case his words prove prophetic, for precisely the danger he denies becomes real within the decade. When Napoleon in 1798 finally raids the art works from Rome, his express intent is to transfer the capital of the civilized world to Paris, reducing Rome to a provincial outpost of the French empire.

The growing political threat to the papacy is repeatedly denied in encomiastic verse of the 1780s and '90s. "Roma . . . siegui pure ad alzar la fronte altera," Gaspare Rondanini insists, in a sonnet of 1783; for Time, the adversary, is impotent and Rome is inviolate, past all change and desecration:

> Vedrai, che or ruota la sua falce invano,
>   Invido di tue glorie il Tempo rio
>   Sù i prischi avanzi del valor Romano:

46

> E oh! quanti ancor preda sarian d'obblio,
> Se nel loro bujo non stendea la mano
> L'emulo degli Eroi Genio di PIO.[9]

(Rome, continue to hold your head high . . . You will see that now in
vain evil Time, envious of your glories, swings his scythe over the
ancient remains of Roman valor: and oh! how many of these would
still be prey to oblivion, if into their darkness the Genius of PIUS,
emulator of the Heroes, did not extend his hand.)

The figure of Time the evil reaper, swinging his blunted scythe among
the relics of Roman virtue, is by now familiar in the iconography of the
period. Yet the image of the Pope, reaching into the darkness to extract the
statues, gives us some small sense of the dangers inherent in the archaeological gesture; particularly for the Church, with its residual fear of resurrecting pagan idols that had long lain buried. But the poems I am presenting
do not dwell on the dark side; and no poet was ever paid to question the
motives of his patron.

Papal rhetoric, then, remains optimistic and continues to elaborate a limited repertory of themes. Even in 1789 Angelo Guiduzzi has little to add to
the scheme of Monti's "Prosopopea," written ten years earlier in a different
Europe:

> Il genio animator, che ai Re presiede,
> E ad Essi eterne opre di gloria inspira,
> Lieto intorno al Roman soglio s'aggira,
> Anzi in fronte al gran PIO contento siede.
> Ecco divien delle bell'Arti sede
> Il Vaticano, e Grecia invan s'adira,
> Che il Genio quì propizia aura respira,
> E di sua sorte pago altro non chiede.
> In van Pericle dunque or vanti Atene
> Nè il Tebro sol d'Augusto i dì rammenti,
> L'eccelse Moli e le vetuste Arene.
> Maggior monarca d'ogni età raccoglie
> Rari tesori, e nobili portenti,
> E altrui la speme d'ugguagliarlo ei toglie.[10]

(The animating genius that rules over kings and inspires them to
everlasting works of glory, moves joyfully around the Roman throne,
indeed sits gladly on the brow of the great PIUS. See the Vatican
become seat of the arts, and Greece becomes angry in vain, for here

the Genius breathes favorable air, and satisfied with its destiny desires nothing more. In vain then let Pericles boast of Athens, nor let the Tiber remember only the days of Augustus, the lofty buildings and ancient arenas. A greater monarch is gathering up the rare treasures and noble portents of every age, and denies others all hope of rivaling him.)

Despite the threat of revolution in France the Vatican collections continue to grow, Rome's own proud monument to the ancien régime. Surrounded by his "rare treasures and noble portents," Europe's "maggior monarca" seems braced for a siege. It is not long in coming; but papal rhetoric remains reassuring. As late as 1795, only two years before Tolentino, a poet with the appropriate name of Giuntotardi will declare to an audience assembled for the bicentennial celebration of the Capitoline *concorsi:*

> Nè vi turbi il fragor bellico e fiero
> Ch'Europa infausta orribilmente assorda!
> Veglia sul Tebbro il Successor di Piero.[11]

(Neither be disturbed by the fierce and warlike tumult which deafens unfortunate Europe! The Successor of Peter keeps watch over the Tiber.)

Not all of the poetry of archaeological encomium commissioned during this period addresses the Vatican museum as an institution. Many poems instead focus on individual sculptures, whether recently excavated (like the herm of Pericles) or old favorites from the Capitoline and Belvedere collections. Along with formulaic *ecphrases* of works such as the Dying Gladiator,[12] the bust of Lucius Junius Brutus,[13] and the much admired marble relief of "Curtius flinging himself into the Gulf," recently installed by Marcantonio Borghese in his newly decorated villa on the Pincio,[14] appear descriptions of less familiar pieces freshly acquired by the Vatican. One such poem, by Gioacchino Pizzi, celebrates the donation to Clement XIV of an Etruscan bronze recently excavated near Tarquinia:

> O Pargoletto, che nel bronzo annoso
> Serbi l'arte, e il valor d'etrusca mano,
> Non ti lagnar se lunga etate ascoso
> Nel Tarquinio giacesti altero piano:
> Dono d'un Cuor gentile or vai fastoso
> Di Roma augusta al REGNATOR SOVRANO,
> E fra i recessi del Museo famoso
> Ergi il volto ridente in Vaticano.

Forse già fu col ciglio alto indovino
Da gli Aruspici tuoi vaticinato
Il luminoso tuo nuovo destino;
E il lavoro immortal voller celato
A l'antica Terrena onda vicino
Per maturar di tua grandezza il fato.[15]

(Oh youth, who in ancient bronze preserve the art and valor of an
Etruscan hand, do not complain if for a long age you lay hidden in the
proud Tarquinian plain: The splendid gift of a gentle heart, you go
now to the Sovereign Ruler of august Rome, and in the shelter of the
famous Museum you lift your smiling face in the Vatican. Perhaps
long ago the soothsayers already envisioned your luminous new destiny; and they wished the immortal work concealed from the ancient
Tyrrhenian wave nearby, to allow the fate of your greatness to ripen.)

The poet appears innocent of the potentially subversive implications of
Etruscan archaeology. During the early decades of the nineteenth century,
in fact, such works as Micali's *L'Italia avanti il dominio dei Romani* (1810)
would promote a polemical revival of interest in the pre-Roman civilizations that the city had assimilated and destroyed during its conquest of the
peninsula. "Provincial" archaeology, both Etruscan and medieval, would
have a profound impact on Italian politics throughout the Risorgimento, as
opponents of a centralized Italian state with its capital at Rome used the
historical examples of Etruria and the medieval communes to dramatize the
dangers of Roman imperialism and argue the advantages of a federalist
system.[16]
    These considerations, however, remain alien to the papal court. Like the
columnist in the *Effemeridi letterarie di Roma* who enthusiastically reported
Clement's acquisition of this piece (No. 7, 15 Feb. 1772), and like the ranks
of poets later enlisted to celebrate Gregory XVI's founding of the Etruscan
museum at the Vatican (1837), Gioacchino Pizzi admits no ambivalence
regarding Rome's suppression of the Etruscans. Like the conquest of
Greece, he implies, this was providentially ordained and historically necessary to consolidate Rome's superior civilization and prepare the way of the
Church. The peaceful recovery of the spoils is itself providential, the sign of
the arrival of a new golden age and fulfillment of a perpetual *pax romana*.
The Pope, in his charity, grants amnesty to all the buried hostages of the
past and permanent asylum in his new museum.
    By delivering the Etruscan statue to the Vatican, the poet claims, Clem-
ent has fulfilled its privileged destiny to transcend the pagan culture by
which it was produced. He has both released and appropriated the power of

which it is the repository: the "arte" and "valor" preserved in the aged bronze.

The imagery of light and darkness that recurs in these poems (here the statue's "luminous new destiny," redeeming centuries of oblivion) is inevitably associated with archaeology; but it is itself politically ambivalent and undergoes a radical shift in the eighteenth century. Papal use of the metaphor resembles that of the "illuminated" monarchs throughout Europe, beginning with Louis XIV, the Sun King, himself. Like Louis XlV, Pius VI surrounds himself with the imagery of Apollo; most notably, by the resurrection of Augustus's "sundial" obelisk of the Camp Marzio, which Alessandro De Sanctis celebrates in a sonnet of 1795:

> Questa, ch'ergesi al cielo, eccelsa mole
>   Per lunga eternità da PIO fu posta
>   L'immense ruote a misurar del sole,
>   E a ricordar la lunga età riposta.
> Mill'anni stette al dì, mille nascosta,
>   E seppellìa con sé l'Egizio sole;
>   Or del gran PIO col nome al ver s'accosta
>   D'alta gloria immortal novella prole.
> Barbaro scempio la minaccia invano,
>   Come invan freme, ove or l'aratro fiede
>   La gran palude, il turbine montano.
> Rome in eterno dell'invitta Fede
>   La maestra sarà nel Vaticano,
>   E dell'arte sarà l'augusta Sede.[17]

(This lofty mass, which rises toward the heavens, for long eternity was placed by PIUS to measure the immense rotations of the sun, and to remember the long age when it lay buried. A thousand years it stood in the light of day, a thousand hidden, and buried with it the Egyptian sun; now it joins together with the truth through the name of the great PIUS, the new heir to high immortal glory. Barbarian ruin threatens it in vain, as the mountain gale rages in vain where the plow now tills the great swamp.[18] Rome for eternity will be in the Vatican the mistress of the unconquered Faith, and the venerable seat of the arts.)

With the new light of his golden age Pius claims to dispel the darkness of previous regimes. More specifically, as a patron of archaeology he reenacts the central Christian drama of resurrection, lifting pagan idols into the light of the true faith. Remembering, however, the rapid inversion of the imagery of light and darkness in eighteenth-century France (as light came to be identified not with royal or ecclesiastical authority but with the secular reason of the *philosophes*), we can see on the horizon of papal Rome the blaze of Blake's apocalypse and the incandescent rhetoric of the French Revolution.[19]

The objects singled out for poetic *ecphrasis* at papal ceremonies were not necessarily the ones of greatest artistic value. Monti's Pericles, believed to be the work of Phidias, was of course much admired, and the obelisk of Montecitorio was of colossal physical and rhetorical dimensions; but other objects, like the Etruscan miniature above, and the Roman sarcophagus celebrated in the following sonnet of 1773, may have been privileged simply because they suggested to the poet the genealogical theme that was crucial to the mechanics of papal encomium:

> O Nobil'Ara, che nel marmo altero
>   Mostri a noi per virtù d'industre mano
>   I tristi fati dell'Iliaco Impero,
>   E i bei principi del Valor Romano:
> Te scorge generoso alto pensiero
>   Ai lieti auspici del Pastor Sovrano,
>   Per cui scosso l'orror tacito e nero
>   Splendi chiara e famosa in Vaticano.
> Ben altro loco a te non si dovea,
>   O monumento luminoso e degno
>   Della stirpe di Romolo, e di Enea;
> Ch'or su quel colle da immortal disegno
>   Fu stabilito con eterna idea
>   Non men del mondo, che dell'Arti il regno.[20]

(Oh Noble Altar, which in proud marble shows to us through the skill of an industrious hand the sad fate of the Trojan Empire and the noble origins of Roman valor: a generous and lofty thought brings you to the happy protection of the Sovereign Pastor, thanks to whom, having shaken off the black and silent horror, you now shine forth bright and famous in the Vatican. No other place was worthy of you, oh luminous monument worthy of the race of Romulus, and of Aeneas; for now on that hill by an immortal plan has been established for eternity the kingdom no less of the world, than of the Arts.)

Implicit even in the isolated Etruscan artifact was a history of Roman conquest; but here the poet's task is considerably simplified, for unlike the free-standing figure the sarcophagus is itself a form of visual narrative. Beginning then with an allusion to the events portrayed on the relief (the Trojan War and origins of Rome), the poet completes its idealized narrative by adding his own encomiastic inscription. He applauds the donation of the altar to the museum as an act of restitution to the Church of a work that portrays its own distant origins. The pagan altar is part of the Pope's legitimate inheritance and rightly belongs to his collection of antiquities. Just as the medieval Church had appropriated the figure of Virgil as a prophet of the Christian empire, the Settecento papacy appropriates individual artifacts inspired by Virgilian texts.

The poetry of papal encomium is vast, and one could almost chronicle the growth of the Vatican collections by assembling the poems commissioned to celebrate new acquisitions. But any review of this literature would be incomplete without a description of the context for which it was created. All of these poems were composed for performance; they are ephemeral texts, and were only later transcribed in academy proceedings. Although none of the poems presented in this chapter had the distinction of being framed in the Vatican museum like Monti's "Prosopopea," all were written for recitation at the same papally sponsored ceremony, the awarding of prizes to young artists by the Accademia di San Luca. This ceremony itself prescribed a rigid ideological frame, and it would be misleading to examine the poems apart from that context.

The Accademia di San Luca, founded in 1478, was the oldest artists' corporation in Europe. Greatly empowered by Clement XI (Albani) at the outset of the eighteenth century, the Academy remained closely allied to the papal court until the Napoleonic occupation and was one of the most active institutions in Rome in promoting the revival of interest in antiquity.[21]

At three-year intervals, the Academy sponsored a threefold competition in painting, sculpture, and architecture for all artists, regardless of their nationality, residing in Rome. The subjects in each division were prescribed in detail, and the prizes awarded after several stages of elimination in an elaborate ceremony in the Sala Senatoria on the Capitoline.

The volume of proceedings from 1775, the year of Gianangelo Braschi's accession to the papacy, describes the ceremony in some detail.[22] The hall, hung with velvet and damask, was brightly lit with banks of candelabra. At one end of the room, distributed by rank, were the seats of the cardinals, lesser ecclesiastics, and orators, along with the other members and officers of the Academy. These seats formed a semicircle facing the audience, from which it was divided by the orchestra. Swiss guards were stationed at intervals throughout the room. At the front of the hall, under a rich baldacchino, was displayed a portrait of Pius VI.

The elaborate setting, with its emphasis on hierarchy and decorum, was like many other expressions of papal ritual an image of the larger order and stability represented by the Church. The splendor of the setting and strict protocol of the ceremony were meant to impress both the contestants and the public with the high seriousness of the Church's renewed commitment to the arts. The ceremony was subject to few variations. It began with an address by the reigning "Principe" (here, Carlo Marchionni, architect of the monumental New Sacristy of St. Peter's). This was followed by a lengthy prose oration by the appointed speaker, the awarding of prizes individually by the cardinals, and the recitation of a series of poems by members of both the Accademia di San Luca and the Accademia dell'Arcadia. At established intervals there were musical interludes.

The poems we have been examining, then, were not isolated compositions but an integral part of a paraliturgical performance which dramatized the ideology of papal classicism. The ideal of a political and artistic *renovatio* through the conservation and emulation of classical antiquity was reflected not only in the poetry but in the unchanging forms of the ritual itself. It is not surprising that Napoleon, upon his occupation of Rome, chose to preserve the outward forms of the ceremony even as he substituted his own portrait at center stage for that of the deposed Pius VII; he recognized that the Academy was a crucial political arena and appropriated its rituals in the name of his own imperial program.

As De Gerando, member of Napoleon's Consulta Straordinaria, declared at the first of the Napoleonic *concorsi* in 1810, this day marked a transfer of power and patronage that would cause the arts to flourish as never before:

> Winners, come forward! . . . This is the first time that the crowns on the Capitoline are to be awarded in the name of NAPOLEON the Great; this is the first time that here the triumph of the arts concurs with the solemn day in which we celebrate both his august name and the felicity of the peoples under his protection! Oh glory! Oh hope! You may expect all things from your great Benefactor! Raise high on the Palatine a new palace to Caesar, raise new arches of triumph where Constantine entered, where another will enter who is greater than he! Paint on our palace walls his marvelous deeds, with which the whole world is resounding![23]

The archaeological genre that we have been examining was widely practiced in papal Rome and not limited to the occasion of the Capitoline competitions. Literary and artistic journals of the period such as the *Effemeridi letterarie di Roma* (1772–98), *Antologia romana* (1774–97), *Giornale delle Belle Arti* (1784–8), and *Memorie per le Belle Arti* (1785–8) are saturated with similar examples of this verse. Their conservative politics and antiquarian interests are closely related. Typically in these pages, excavation notices, monographs, reviews, poems and commentaries alternate with essays of miscellaneous erudition (mineralogy, botany, birds of Sardinia) and diatribes against Voltaire, Rousseau, the Encyclopedia, and the "idolatry of our philosophical age."[24]

Another active forum for archaeological oratory and verse was the Accademia dell'Arcadia, which in fact staged the celebration of Pius VI's *voti quinquennali* (1779) where Monti recited the first version of the "Prosopopea." His successive revisions, resulting in the version finally transcribed and mounted in the Pio-Clementine, were undoubtedly influenced by the example of other poems recited at this and related Academy ceremonies.

Archaeology is a dominant theme in the volume of verse from the *voti quinquennali*. The decision to revive such a celebration was itself, Gioacchino Pizzi declares in his opening oration, an archaeological move; for the tradition of renewing a ruler's vows to the people at five-year intervals began with Augustus, and was revived by the popes (Leo X, Sixtus V, and Benedict XIV) as a sign of deference to the classical tradition.[25]

In going on to list the achievements of Pius VI's "first term" in the Vatican, Pizzi stresses his public works, building programs, and archaeological patronage. The draining of the Pontine marshes, unsuccessfully attempted by the consuls, Caesar, and Augustus himself, promised to be one of the most spectacular *gesta* of the Braschi pope; but it was matched by the splendor of the New Sacristy at St. Peter's now under construction. (These two achievements also figure prominently in two fresco cycles later dedicated to Pius VI in the Vatican palace: that of Domenico De Angelis in the Sala Alessandrina of the library and the anonymous cycle in the apartments of Cardinal Zelada, now the Museo Gregoriano Etrusco. Monti himself began a poem on the draining of the Pontine marshes, "La Feroniade," which he continued to revise until shortly before his death.)

But the Pope's most impressive contribution, Pizzi claims, is his expansion of the Vatican museum and vigorous funding of fresh excavations in Rome. Praising Pius's plan to restore the Appian Way, he goes so far as to suggest that "this magnificent road . . . might well forget its original name and take from its benefactor another name more splendid and fitting."

Such hyperbole is of course endemic to the genre. The battery of odes, octaves, epigrams, sonnets, and *terzine* which follow all praise Pius's archaeology in similar terms, and point to the Vatican museum as a symbol of the revival of the ancient ideal of empire. As Giuseppe Manotti (pp. 67–73) proclaims, in pages of untiring *terzine:*

> Quanti marmi e colonne, e quanta gloria
> Chiudon quest'archi del possente Impero,
> Di cui fastosa và tanto l'Istoria!

(How many marbles and columns, and how much glory these arches
enclose of that powerful Empire, of which History is so proud!

Giovanni Kloz (pp. 19–25) finds an appropriate Dantesque allusion to
dramatize the recovery of the ancient marbles:

> Mira al favor de' suoi sovrani auspici
> Rifiorir le scienze e l'arti belle;
> Qua di Greco scalpel l'opre felici
> Tratte dal fango riveder le stelle,
> E de la rabbia Gotica vittrici
> Parlanti ripigliar forme novelle . . .

(See, by the favor of his sovereign protection, the sciences and fine arts
bloom again; here the fortunate works of Greek chisel, drawn from
the mud, return to see the stars and, victorious over the Gothic rage,
speaking return to their original forms . . .)

Like Dante's pilgrim, the Greek statues emerge from the underworld to
"riveder le stelle." Luigi Godard (pp. 25–34) in turn greets the renewed
"secol di Leon . . . folgoreggiando ne l'età futura" and applauds the Pope's
recovery of "urne, statue, e Museo d'Attico gusto / . . . / Care memorie de
l'età di Augusto."

The death of Mengs in the year of the Pope's *voti quinquennali* (1779) causes
the Arcadian poets to focus their attention again on the symbolism of the
Vatican museum. In an allegorical vision recounted in terza rima at an
assembly of the Arcadia in honor of Mengs, Felice Mariottini meets the
figure of Painting, disconsolate at the artist's death. To comfort her, he
takes her to the Vatican museum to "contemplar d'appresso / Della egregia
sua man la più bell'opra," and proceeds to explicate the entire program of
Mengs's Allegory of the Clementine in the Sala dei Papiri (Fig. 6):

> Ecco Mosè; guata in quel volto impresso
> Lo zelo, la pietà, l'umil sapere,
> L'alta virtude, e fino il Nume itesso.
> Piero è d'incontro, e il duplice potere
> Gliel vedi in fronte: e ognun ravvisa in lui
> Del popol santo il nuovo condottiere.
> Ma dove porti o Dea gli sguardi tui
> Più sereni, e più attenti? ah che la gloria
> Del felice pennel tu già ne frui.

55

Viva ti sembra la pensosa istoria,
  Che sul dorso del tempo, avvinto il piede,
  Registra degli eventi la memoria.
E il Dio bifronte, che il presente vede,
  E del passato l'ordine richiama,
  Vero argomento di sicura fede;
E l'agil Genio, e la volante Fama,
  Che della Tromba col fiato sonoro
  Al Museo di CLEMENTE invita, e chiama.[26]

(Here is Moses; see impressed in that face the zeal, the piety, the humble wisdom, the great virtue, and even the Divinity itself. Peter sits opposite, and you see on his brow the twofold power: and everyone can recognize in him the new leader of the holy people. But where, oh Goddess, do you turn your more serene and attentive gaze? Ah, already you are enjoying the glory of the skillful paintbrush. Thoughtful history seems alive to you, as on the back of time, his feet bound, she registers the memory of events. And the two-faced God, who sees the present, and calls back the order of the past, which is a true subject of certain faith; and the agile Genius, and flying Fame, who with the resonant sound of her Trumpet invites, and calls us to the Museum of CLEMENT.)

By revisiting the Vatican museum on the occasion of Mengs's death, and reexamining the iconography of this influential painting, the poets reinforce its importance as an expression of papal classicism. Both the poets and orators of the Arcadia stress the need to preserve the neoclassical tradition that he represented, and that arose from his study of the Roman antiquities. "From these ruins the arts came to rise again," Giovanni Cristoforo Amaduzzi warns (p. xli), "and it is only through them that the arts can continue to live among us; for as soon as we cease to study them, the arts too will cease, and we will lapse into barbarism and become dilettantes of Chinese painting, and the Longobardian taste."

Only through the imitation of classical models can standards in the arts be maintained, Amaduzzi argues; and the allegory of archaeology inscribed in Mengs's painting is elevated to a dogma after his death.

In much of this poetry of papal classicism there is a theatrical element, a tendency toward hyperbole, pageantry, and posturing; the prosopopea is itself a dramatic mode. We have seen too that music was frequently part of the ceremonies at which archaeological texts were performed. These two elements are combined in a cantata of 1842 dedicated to Gregory XVI's creation of the Etruscan and Egyptian museums in the Vatican. Written by Pietro Ercole Visconti ("Commissioner of Antiquities, Honorary President of the Capitoline Museum, Perpetual Secretary of the Pontifical Roman Academy of Archaeology, Honorary Member of the Academy of San Luca") with music by Giacomo Fontemaggi, this cantata was performed at the Capitoline competitions of 1842 and renders explicit the melodramatic potential present in many of the earlier poems.

Gregory XVI (1831–46), the hapless target of much of Belli's satirical verse, was at the same time the last great papal patron of classical archaeology. His active personal interest in the project is attested by Belli's famous sonnet, "Papa Grigorio a li Scavi" (1836), which records one of the Pope's visits to the ongoing excavations in the Forum.[27] Although the poem implies the Pope's ignorance of the subject ("Bèr bùcio! bella fossa! bèr grottino! / Belli sti sérci! tutto quanto bello!"), this is hardly fair; for Gregory XVI was an energetic and intelligent patron of archaeology, and sharply aware of its value as propaganda for the temporal power.

In the course of his thirteen-year reign, in fact, Gregory established three new museums of antiquities in Rome: the Museo Etrusco (1837) and Museo Egizio (1839), both in the Vatican, and the Museo Gregoriano Profano Lateranense, built to house recent finds from Rome, Cerveteri, Veii, and Ostia and conceived as a "national museum" of the papal states. Since the Pacca Edict of April 7, 1820, had guaranteed to the Church the right of preemption, storerooms at the Vatican had been rapidly filled; but as Gregory XVI argued, the need for more museum space was not merely practical but political as well. By expanding the network of its museums, he declared, the Church could spread the political message of the triumph of the Cross: "These images of false gods, these likenesses of consuls, of emperors, of men in togas [*togati*], who either did not know, or who persecuted the Christian religion . . . can be seen as the spoils of defeated enemies, as *trophies* of the victory won by the Cross over idolatry and idolators."[28]

As Commissioner of Antiquities Pietro Ercole Visconti, author of the 1842 cantata, was in large part responsible for planning both the Etruscan and Egyptian museums. Along with other members of a commission including the topographer Nibby, the painter Camuccini, the architect Valadier and the sculptor Thorwaldsen, he directed preemptions and purchases from the papal states and particularly from the spectacular excavations in southern Etruria that had brought to light both the Mars of Todi in 1835 and the Regolini-Galassi tomb in Cerveteri in 1836–9. Apart from its political implications, the discovery of these Etruscan sites brought with it a minor revolution in taste, recalling on a small scale the Pompeiian style of the previous century. In palace decoration and even jewelry design it now became fashionable to imitate the Etruscans.[29]

At the same time Champollion's pioneering work on Egyptian hiero-glyphs, based on the texts found on the Rosetta Stone, had generated new curiosity about Egyptian civilization throughout Europe. Invited to Rome by Angelo Mai, prefect of the Vatican Library, to study the Vatican papyri collection, Champollion there promoted a revival of scholarly interest in Egypt that led to the creation of Gregory's Egyptian museum.

Both the Etruscan museum, with its self-consciously sepulchral setting, and the Egyptian rooms, awash with exotic murals, may appear naïve by modern standards of museum design. But like the cantata that celebrates them, they reflect the sudden impact of these discoveries on the contemporary imagination and the century's enthusiasm for the ongoing drama of archaeology.

The Church's anxiety to stage that drama in its own ideological terms is clear from a reading of the cantata. As we have seen, poetry and painting of the previous century had established the *topos* of archaeology as an allegorical triumph over Time. In the form of a static tableau they had represented either the gesture of interdiction (Falconieri's "Arte, in atto di victar" and Pozzi's Minerva, standing poised in plumed helmet and breastplate over the figure of Time) or the moment of mastery (Mengs's History resting her book on his shoulders as she records the inauguration of the Clementine Museum). Visconti's cantata sets these tableaux in motion; in overtly melodramatic terms it rehearses every phase of the struggle, staging a heightened drama of sin and salvation at the Capitoline, the primal scene of archaeology itself.

Visconti's cantata is startling, grandiose, and even grotesque. The role of Time, the villain, is sung by a bass; we can imagine his swarthy complexion and drooping moustache. The Genius of Rome, the embattled heroine, is played by a soprano; she is rescued by a gallant tenor, the Genius of the Arts. Both in the Manicheistic structure of the moral universe that it postulates and the course of its highly predictable plot, the play conforms to the model of "classic" French melodrama proposed by Peter Brooks.[30] To enhance the inherent drama of archaeology it summons all the resources of the contemporary stage.

The "space of innocence" portrayed at the outset is that of the Capitoline, locus of the fiction as well as the performance. Before a neoclassical model of a Temple of Glory, the chorus of the Genius of the Arts wreathes garlands and verses in praise of Rome. In alternating stanzas the triple chorus

celebrates the return of the golden age under Gregory XVI. All unite in a
final hymn to the Pope:

> Di GREGORIO il nome suoni
> Quì sul colle degli eroi,
> Che di Pericle e d'Augusto,
> Che de' Giuli e de' Leoni
> Rende all'arti i fausti dì.[31]

(Let the name of GREGORY resound here on the hill of the heroes, he
who restores the arts to the fortunate days of Pericles and Augustus, of
Julius and Leo.)

But swiftly, inevitably, the villain intrudes. Time, having overheard part
of the festivities from his hiding place offstage, now stalks to the center and
announces his own evil plan:

> Che intesi! or qual baldanza
> Quest'arti a me nemiche
> Erge alla gloria de' primieri esempi?
> Indarno dunque i tempi
> Scossi dall'imo: i regii tetti stanza
> Resi a funesti augelli: e fu ruina
> Quanto splendea nella città latina!
> Non questo è il suolo, dove già difese
> Ebbero contro a me vane, o mal ferme,
> Colonne, archi, teatri, e circhi e terme?
> Non quì l'aratro agreste
> Frange di Paro i marmi e di Siene?
> Non son queste le arene,
> Dove fra l'auree volte e le prostese
> Sculture egregie il rettile serpeggia,
> E 'l gregge pasce ove sorgea la reggia? . . .
> Folle, chi pon sua speme
> In mura, in tele, in marmi!
> Spento con essi insieme
> Il nome suo cadrà. (31–2)

(What is this that I hear? now what impudence raises these arts, my
enemy, to the glory of their earliest examples? In vain then did I shake
the earth from the depths: and made kingly palaces the abode of
ominous birds: and left in ruin all that resplended in the Latin city! Is

this not the land where columns, arches, theaters, and circuses and baths had only vain, or feeble defenses against me? Is it not here that the farmer's plow breaks the marbles of Paros and Siena? Are not these the theaters, where amid the noble countenances and superb fallen sculptures the reptile slithers, and does not the flock graze where the palace once rose? Fool, who places his hope in palace walls, in paintings, in marbles! Destroyed together with them, his name will fall.)

Time delights in the "marble wilderness" that he has created. Like a true stage villain, he is not motivated so much as *inhabited* by evil, and speaks forth his identity upon his first traumatic entrance. With the completion of his opening recitative, the terms of the play's moral universe are established. The figure of Time, agent of darkness and damnation, stands profiled against the pastoral scene of the Capitoline. From his dark, subterranean lair ("dall'imo") he has emerged to interrupt the feast, to violate the space of innocence and drive out virtue.

Time's scorn for the ritual then being enacted, along with his contempt for all monuments, inscriptions, and representations ("Folle, chi pon sua speme / In mura, in tele, in marmi") identifies him as an enemy of the established order; for it is precisely through these that tradition, continuity, and hierarchy are preserved. This is of course the crux of the Church's polemic; for with the Manicheistic logic of melodrama it implies that the only alternative to the present order is the wilderness invoked by its primeval enemy. Like the beasts and monsters of fairy tale and myth, Time is an intruder into the space of innocence and a symbol of all the psychic (and political) forces that must be repressed.

By the end of the second scene, then, the stakes of the drama are clearly defined. As the Genius of the Arts and the Genius of Rome perform the idyllic duet which follows, we await the villain's return with increasing suspense. He is preceded by his chorus, who announce that "the earth already trembles at his step," and finally appears at the opening of the fourth scene ("Cessate, olà, cessate"), casting to the ground the laurel wreaths that Art and Rome are carrying toward the Temple of Glory to award to the winners of the Capitoline competition.

The Genius of the Arts is indignant; how dare Time cross the sacred threshold of the Capitoline, inscribed with the immortal glory of Rome? Time himself hesitates, his tyrant's heart softened by the sight of the Temple ("Nascer sento un'incognito affetto / Che nel petto – turbando mi va"). But after a moment's pause he only redoubles his rage ("Ah! trionfi la possa feroce / Di quell'ira, che nome non ha").

As in classical melodrama, the first act concludes with the apparent triumph of evil and expulsion of virtue. At Time's angry exit even the brave tenor despairs:

> Ah che a que' detti in seno
>   Pugnare io sento insieme
>   Con il timor la speme!
>   Chi vincerà non so.
> Parmi che 'l tempo sia
>   Possente troppo, e parmi
>   Che al suo furor, che all'armi,
>   Cedere, oh Dio, dovrò!   (42)

(Ah, at those words I feel fear and hope struggling together in my heart! Who will win I do not know. It seems that time is too powerful, and it seems that to his fury, to his arms, oh God! I shall have to yield.)

Yet it is the tenor who eventually will save the day, by extracting from his arsenal the one talisman capable of subduing the enemy. He begins by telling the tyrant of the two new Vatican museums, which stand as proof of Time's impotence to destroy the relics of Rome. The full exchange that follows is worth citing here:

> Tempo: Indarno dunque io spensi
>   L'egizio antico impero?
> Genio: Indarno, è vero.
> Tempo: È vero!
>   Oh acerbo mio rossor!
>   Dunque l'Etruria anch'essa
>   Scuote le sue ruine?
> Genio: Sì, leva il capo alfine
>   Dal lungo suo squallor.
> Tempo: Quanto nel suolo celai,
>   Quanto abbattei, dispersi
>   In lidi sì diversi,
>   Rivede il giorno ancor?
> Genio: Accolto in regie soglie
>   Splende del sole ai rai,
>   Pari all'opime spoglie
>   D'un genio vincitor.
>   Serbavi a noi tu stesso
>   Quel che bramasti estinto,
>   Se il suol ne rende adesso
>   Quanto coperse allor.   (49–50)

(In vain then did I extinguish the ancient Egyptian empire? – In vain, it is true. – It is true. Oh my bitter shame! Then Etruria too is awakening its ruins? – Yes, she raises her head at last from her long humiliation. – How much that I hid in the soil, how much that I cast down and scattered on such different shores, again sees the light of day? – Gathered in kingly palaces it resplends in the rays of the sun, like the rich spoils of a victorious genius. You yourself preserved for us that which you wished destroyed, for the soil now restores to us as much as it then covered.)

But Time's next question ("But who is it that challenges me / by reviving such ancient valor?") brings with it the *coup de théâtre:* for triumphantly the tenor replies:

> GREGORIO, il saggio, il giusto,
> Nostro e del mondo amor.
> Cessa la tua minaccia,
> L'ira al gran nome cedi . . .

(GREGORY, the wise, the just, beloved by us and by all the world. Cease your threat, yield your anger to the great name . . .)

With the enunciation of Gregory's *name,* the enemy is miraculously converted ("Sì, cedo alfin, m'abbraccia"). Not only does he admit his error, he even offers his services to the Genius of the Arts ("Or che 'l gran nome in noi / L'odio in amore cangiò"), promising henceforth to preserve rather than destroy.

The prodigy is celebrated in the tenor's next aria ("Or che 'l gran nome") and in the chorus that concludes the scene:

> Di GREGORIO il nome, il zelo,
> Fu cagion del lieto evento;
> Ah facciam con grato accento
> Il gran nome all'etra andar!   (52)

(The name, the zeal of GREGORY was the cause of the happy event; Ah, let us raise with grateful accents this great name to the skies!)

The drama of conversion, then, hinges on the enunciation of a name: a charm, a talisman with magical force that confounds the villain and brings him to his knees. This is the stuff of pure melodrama, as Brooks has shown;[32] and here clearly betrays the anxiety of the Church, intent to wrest its message from the archaeological drama and inscribe it forever in the memory of Rome.

The cantata concludes with an aria by the soprano, exulting at the tyrant's conversion and suggesting that the name be inscribed "in the temple, as it is in our hearts":

> Dunque del Tempo alfine
> È placato lo sdegno: e bastò solo,
> A far sue forze dome,
> Rammentar di GREGORIO i gesti, il nome!
> Deh! quel gran nome, alto di Roma amore,
> Suoni sui labbri ognor, com'è nel core!
> E per mia mano adesso
> Nel tempio sia, com'è ne' cuori, impresso.   (52–3)

(Then the anger of Time is at last placated: and it was sufficient, to subdue his forces, to remind him of the achievements and the name of GREGORY! Ah! let that great name, deeply beloved by Rome, be always on our lips and in our hearts! And now by my hand let it be engraved in the temple, as it is in our hearts.)

She writes the name of the Pope on the temple; and at a gesture from the tenor, Time falls into step and advances toward the Temple himself with a laurel wreath in hand. The curtain falls on a rousing chorus (*tutti*, "Vivan l'arti"). Time is safely integrated into the harmony which he had threatened. The society of innocence is providentially restored.

It is hard to imagine a more hyperbolic treatment of the themes that I have presented in this chapter. In the intensity of the moral claims that it associates with archaeology, and its consistently high rhetorical pitch, Visconti's cantata outdistances any of the examples we have considered before. But this should not be surprising, for it was written in 1842, and stands witness to the advanced political crisis of the papacy. It will be the purpose of the following chapter to review the events that contributed to that crisis, and to examine another group of texts that reflect the increasing rhetorical and ideological pressure that the Church brings to bear on the archaeological gesture in the maturing context of the Risorgimento.

3

THE RHETORIC OF RESTORATION:
ARCHAEOLOGY AND POWER, 1798–1840

THE ITALIAN BORDERS were still inviolate when on 31 August 1794 the Abbé Grégoire, a member of the Comité d'Instruction Publique, ominously announced: "Certainly, if our victorious armies penetrate into Italy, the removal of the Apollo Belvedere and the Farnese Hercules would be the most brilliant conquest."[1]

The French never managed to secure the Farnese Hercules, although at least once it stood in packing crates awaiting shipment to Paris.[2] But the Apollo Belvedere, along with eighty-two other masterpieces of antique sculpture, fell immediately into French hands upon Bonaparte's first invasion of the Papal States (18 June 1796). Article 8 of the Bologna armistice, signed only five days later, specified that one hundred art works were to be ceded to the French; and the Commission appointed to choose the works lost no time in stripping the Capitoline and Pio-Clementine of their most prized ancient marbles. Along with seventeen major paintings from the Vatican collections they requisitioned the Apollo Belvedere, the Torso, Cleopatra, and Laocoön, as well as the Spinario and Dying Gladiator from the Capitoline. A special status was reserved for the bronze bust of Lucius Junius Brutus, the legendary founder of the Roman Republic, and the marble head of Marcus Brutus the tyrannicide; these images, sacred to the Republic, were the only two to be demanded by name in the Bologna armistice and the first to be seized for shipment to Paris.[3]

Prominent French intellectuals, including Quatremère de Quincy, joined the aged Pope in protesting the sack of the Roman museums.[4] But Napoleon was adamant: "Nous aurons tout ce qu'il y a de beau en Italie," he declared after signing the Treaty of Tolentino (February 1797), which required that the works be sent to Paris without further delay. General Pommereul urged that the colossal Alexander and Bucephalus group from the Quirinal be added to the list; Trajan's Column itself, he argued, would show to better advantage in the Place Vendôme. Fortunately the project of dismantling Rome's museums presented sufficient practical difficulties to the Commission, and the general's suggestions were respectfully ignored. In April 1797 the first of four convoys left Rome; and in July 1798 the sculptures, still in their packing cases, were paraded through the streets of Paris to commemorate the fourth anniversary of the fall of Robespierre.

Meanwhile, on the pretext of avenging the murder of the French general Duphot (28 December 1797), the Directory had ordered a march on Rome. Unlike the death of Bassville, commemorated in Monti's infamous "Bassvilliana" of 1793, this insult to French honor and republican principles would be swiftly punished. On the morning of 11 February the French troops entered Rome; by early afternoon Roman crowds watched in amazement as liberty trees rose in the Piazza di Spagna and Piazza del Popolo. On 15 February the Roman Republic was proclaimed and the temporal power abolished. Five days later the Pope himself was seized and sent into exile in Siena, pulled down from his pedestal like the statues he prized and himself shipped off as a hostage of the Revolution. From Siena and finally from Valence, where he died six months later, Pius VI watched the progress of the republican experiment in Rome.[5]

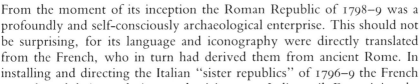

From the moment of its inception the Roman Republic of 1798–9 was a profoundly and self-consciously archaeological enterprise. This should not be surprising, for its language and iconography were directly translated from the French, who in turn had derived them from ancient Rome. In installing and directing the Italian "sister republics" of 1796–9 the French transplanted their revolutionary classicism onto Italian soil. By reviving the ideal of the Roman Republic *in situ* they reintroduced into Italy a domestic iconography that had long been suppressed. The rhetorical dangers of such an experiment in Italy were of course immense; but like Cola di Rienzo, braving all anachronism, the self-styled senators, tribunes, and consuls of 1798 sought to fashion a republic in the resurrected image of ancient Rome.

Ennio Quirino Visconti, one of five consuls appointed in 1798, was not the first revolutionary philologist in Roman history. Cola himself had enlisted archaeological evidence to support his conversion to republican ideals. One of his most spectacular political gestures was in fact the unveiling of Vespasian's *Lex de imperio* tablet (long hidden behind an altar in St. John Lateran) to demonstrate the inalienable sovereignty of the Roman people.[6] But like Cola, Visconti saw his archaeological utopia collapse; and upon the fall of the Republic he prudently took refuge in Paris, where he became director of the Louvre sculpture collections recently confiscated from Rome.

Unlike their counterparts a decade earlier in Paris, the pageant masters of the Roman revolution found their classical sets and props ready-made. For a performance of Voltaire's *La mort de César* at the Apollo Theater on 22

September 1798, they borrowed both the Capitoline Wolf and the Palazzo Spada statue of Pompey, at the foot of which Caesar was said to have been assassinated. The text of the play may have remained obscure to the audience – one wonders why no one bothered to translate it into Italian – but the icons, at least, were familiar. It is impossible to gauge the extent to which such images succeeded in reviving a collective memory of republican tradition, but official reports of the occasion were enthusiastic. In a letter to the Directory, the commissioners Bertolio and Duport especially praised the incorporation of authentic classical props into a live performance. "Ce rapprochement," they declared, "est peut-être unique dans l'histoire."[7]

But it was not only the formal Jacobin theater that exploited the archaeological resources of Rome. In street pageants and festivals designed to represent the new government to its bewildered constituency, classical monuments and sites were programmatically used to provide a visual and rhetorical frame for the political message.

Not surprisingly, the first act of the revolutionary drama was staged in the Forum. On the morning of 15 February 1798, the *Monitore di Roma* reports, "a great multitude of educated and highly respected citizens" gathered in the Campo Vaccino. After centuries of disarray and neglect the site thus recovered its original civic function as a gathering place for "the People, and the Senate, when it became necessary to deliberate on the gravest concerns of the Republic."[8]

Among the buried arches and fallen columns of the Forum, the citizens erect a liberty tree – painted in the Roman tricolor (white, red, and black), decorated with garlands of flowers, and crowned with a Phrygian cap. After an introductory address urging them to overthrow the papacy and "abolish all emblems of oppression and despotism," accompanied by a military band they march in triumphal procession to the Capitoline, bearing the liberty tree and twin banners of the French Republic and Roman people. The climax on the Capitoline is predictable: after installing the tree on a special pedestal facing the city (and not accidentally upstaging the statue of Marcus Aurelius), they join in "infinite applause" and rejoicing. The ceremonial distribution of tricolor cockades gives way to the solemn declaration of the Act of the Sovereign People and nomination of the consuls. Shortly past noon, the flag of the new republic is raised on the tower of the Campidoglio.

It would be easy to deride such an archaeological charade, hastily improvised on the example of the more elaborate French festivals of the revolutionary decade. But it would be naïve to underestimate its importance as an expression of the political ideals that the governing Jacobin élite wished to project to the community. Like the revolutionary festivals of France, only recently given serious critical attention,[9] the archaeological pageantry of the Roman Republic was an integral part of its political practice. Along with the classicizing imagery everywhere adopted to displace Christian symbols – in its oratory, edicts, coins, seals, and standards – the political festivals attempted to re-present papal Rome in republican guise.

It is true that the ceremony of the Republic's foundation, like many other festivals in the twenty months to follow, was largely conceived and orchestrated by the French. The ritual that I have just described presents a curious pastiche of indigenous Roman forms (the quasi-military "triumph," designation of the consuls, and strategic scenography of the Campo Vaccino and Capitoline) with others of more recent vintage imported directly from France (the liberty tree and tricolor cockade).[10] Within weeks of the proclamation of the Republic, Rome may have bristled with liberty trees – contemporaries remarked that the city seemed a "vero boschetto" – but these emblems of insurrection were not native to Rome; and skeptics predicted that these trees without roots would be easily felled:

> Alberi senza radica?
> Berretti senza testa?
> Roma, in ver, Repubblica
> Non resta, no, non resta![11]

(Trees without roots? Caps without heads? Rome, surely, will not remain a republic!)

Years later Napoleon, wishing to embellish his imperial city of Rome with trees as Augustus had faced its brick palaces in marble, impatiently asked Canova why so few trees had ever been planted in Rome. "Maestà," Canova is said to have replied with dignity, "a Roma non piantano alberi, piantano obelischi."[12]

But if Romans were accustomed by years of papal domination to a language of power unfamiliar to the French, this brief experiment in republican government served to reintroduce a secular and classicizing iconography that they could eventually make their own. In many respects the Republic itself was a sham, but the legacy it left to Rome was not. Despite their systematic pillage and economic exploitation of Italy, the French left an arsenal of rhetorical weapons that would prove useful to the discourse of the Risorgimento. In the speech read by the occupying general Berthier on the Capitoline after the founding ceremony of the Republic, we can recognize many of the *topoi* of democratic oratory of the 1830s and 1840s:

Shades of Pompey, of Cato, of Brutus, Cicero, and Hortensius . . .
here on the Capitoline, so renowned through your efforts, where you
so often defended the rights of the People, accept the homage of the
free French. These sons of the Gauls come with olive branch in hand
to this very same place to restore the Altars of Liberty which the first
Brutus erected. And you, Roman People, revived at last by the blood
which runs in your veins, with your eyes fixed on the glorious monuments that surround you, have recovered your rights, and with them
have recovered your ancient grandeur, and your ancestral virtues.[13]

The Republic of 1798–9 established the polemical precedent of seculariz-
ing the monuments and landscape of papal Rome. This process began by
displacing the center of political authority from the Vatican palace to the
ancient Forum; quite literally, the ceremony on the Capitoline upstaged a
ceremony simultaneously scheduled at St. Peter's, the celebration of the
twenty-third anniversary of Pius VI's election as Pope. Most of the cardinals, warned of the insurrection planned on the Capitoline, judged it
prudent that morning not to attend; Pius himself was absent, allegedly due
to illness. The ecclesiastical procession planned to accompany the event was
suspended as well; but the ceremony took place, in the presence of seven
cardinals, who were arrested immediately at its conclusion.

These first steps were dramatic; but in order to extend and consolidate its
power the new regime had to penetrate the entire city, destroying all physical signs of the previous order while disseminating republican monuments
and symbols. To join in this work the government enlisted the services of
the Roman mob, who responded so enthusiastically to its official order to
"erase, cast down and demolish . . . all Arms and Insignia of every description" that the same order was revoked only five days later with a note that
henceforth the consuls would attend to such matters. The initial phase of
destruction gave way to a more moderate stage; sculpted pontifical and
heraldic arms occasionally were spared by being transformed into Jacobin
images. Cardinal Sala, whose journal is one of the richest contemporary
chronicles of such events, reports in disgust on the metamorphosis of the
shield of Clement XII on the palace of the Consulta at the Quirinal: "The
Tiara has become a liberty cap, the keys are consular *fasces,* and in the
middle of the shield they have carved the statue of the Republic."[14]
    Republican symbols similarly displaced Christian emblems in the Piazza
del Quirinale, where a bronze liberty tree and fasces substituted the cross
atop Pius VI's obelisk; and in the Piazza Colonna, where a statue of liberty
was secured to the top of the Antonine column by a cord tied around the
neck of the statue of St. Paul the Apostle.

But along with its campaign of antipapal burlesque and *damnatio memoriae,* the Republican government made a wide-ranging attempt to map out a new political and administrative order in the city. By suppressing the convents, suspending the right of legal immunity in the churches, replacing papal scaffolds with liberty trees, and releasing the Jews from the Ghetto, the new regime mapped out a revisionary topography of Rome, redefining the spaces associated with privilege and punishment under papal government. At the same time it reorganized the fourteen *rioni* into twelve *sezioni* with appropriately classicizing names. Even the piazzas acquired new republican names: the Piazza di Spagna became "Piazza della Libertà," Piazza Venezia the "Piazza dell'Eguaglianza," and Campo dei Fiori the "Campo di Flora."

Along with these reforms – some, obviously, more substantial than others – came a series of festivals intended to educate the people in the ideals of the revolution and instill in them patriotic and antipapal sentiment. These festivals were the most important arm of the Republic's cultural and ideological offensive. Although it is not possible to review and describe them all here, it is important to consider their chief representational strategies, for they constituted both a precedent and a provocation to the restored papacy and greatly influenced its own manipulation of archaeological imagery in the early nineteenth century.

The first of such festivals, held in the Piazza San Pietro on 23 February 1798, commemorated the death of General Duphot. Ephemeral architecture had long been an instrument of political propaganda in Baroque Rome, as artists vied to create ever more spectacular "macchine," illusionistic devices, and fireworks displays to glorify their royal patrons seeking greater influence with the Pope.[15] In sharp contrast to these elaborate designs is the monument erected by Paolo Bargigli in the Piazza San Pietro. Consisting of a simple pyramid on a rectangular base flanked by a column bearing an ancient urn (containing the ashes of Duphot), this monument shares the austerity of Ledoux's designs of the 1780s and reflects in the pure geometrical vocabulary of its forms the moral severity of the ideals represented by the Republic. Like the goddess Liberty strangling the bronze statue of San Paolo, this pyramid must have been a startling apparition among Bernini's colonnades; and it marks the Republic's first official attempt to occupy the consecrated ground of Saint Peter's with signs of its new secular and visionary order.

Bargigli remained the principal architect of the revolutionary festivals, and throughout was responsible for its most innovative designs. His "Altare della Patria," built in collaboration with Giuseppe Camporese and Andrea Vici for the Festa della Federazione on 20 March 1798, was a gigantic circular staircase set down in the middle of St. Peter's Square. Halfway up the staircase, on rectangular bases, rose four columns of imitation porphyry wreathed with garlands. Each was surmounted by a "bronze" figure of Fame resting on a "gold" globe and proclaiming with her trumpet the act of the federation. At the summit of the staircase rose a circular platform decorated with trompe-l'oeil bas-reliefs representing the allegorical triumphs of Paris and Rome. On this platform stood the three colossal figures of Rome, Equality, and Liberty. In front of the platform was a tripod burning with the sacred flame of the Republic.[16]

To judge from contemporary illustrations of this scene, such as Felice Giani's painting in the Museo di Roma (Fig. 8), the visual and rhetorical effect of this "macchina" must have been dramatic. The gigantic altar aimed to do no less than displace the great basilica, overwhelming even Michelangelo's dome with its bold scale and the variety and ingenuity of its ornament. Giani's painting reflects this distortion of perspective, as the elaborate altar rises in the foreground to block our view of the receding façade of St. Peter's. With this monument the Republic sought to occupy the sacred center of Rome. Even its architectural frame, the elliptical colonnade of Bernini, was draped in republican dress; the new insignia of the Republic covered each of the papal arms on the entablature and the columns were decked with military trophies, banners, and garlands of flowers.

Yet some of the artists collaborating in the republican festivals returned to more traditional architectural forms, appealing to the archaeological memory of Rome through explicit reconstructions of classical monuments. Such is the case of Giuseppe Barberi, whose arch of triumph erected for the same Festa della Federazione at the foot of the Ponte Sant'Angelo (now Ponte della Repubblica) was clearly inspired by the Arch of Constantine, imitating both its proportions and the distribution of its sculptural ornament (here, approximated in trompe-l'oeil bas-reliefs narrating Bonaparte's victorious Italian campaign). It is possible that this ephemeral arch itself inspired Percier and Fontaine in their Arc du Carrousel, for a number of reproductions of it quickly circulated in France. In any case this monument was consciously paraphrased – and parodied – by the arches constructed in both 1800 and 1814 to celebrate Pius VII's triumphal entry into Rome and the restoration of the temporal power.[17]

One of the most popular republican festivals was the burning of the "Libro d'Oro" of the nobility in the Piazza di Spagna (now Piazza della Libertà) on 17 July 1798. Bargigli collaborated with Pietro Guerrini in devising an elaborate "macchina" to be placed on the Fontana della Barcaccia, at center stage at the foot of the Spanish Steps. In a parody of the Christian symbolism of the Trinity, a huge pyramid of wood and painted canvas was built to enclose this "macchina," which consisted of a triangular base bearing inscriptions denouncing the three "monsters" of Superstition, Pride, and Tyranny surmounted by a statue of Truth raising a torch in her right arm. At a signal from the drums, three youths dressed as Philosophy,

8. Felice Giani, "*Altare patrio* in Saint Peter's Square for the Feast of the Federation," 1798 (Rome, Museo di Roma).

Reason, and Humanity were to emerge from opposite ends of the piazza and light three bonfires connected by fuses to the central pyramid, which would then collapse in flames, revealing the nude figure of Truth.

Opponents of the regime were delighted when gusts of wind and driving rain felled the pyramid before the ceremony began, severing the right arm of Truth and reducing the cast of the pageant to confusion; but the bonfire was lit, and the ceremony completed when the young princes Santacroce and Borghese, among others, trampled and threw into the fire their heraldic shields and family trees and joined the crowd in dancing a *carmagnola*. Henceforth, they declared, all signs of aristocracy and privilege would be abolished. The only true ancestors worthy of memory were those common to all: Brutus, Cassius, and the other heroes of the ancient Republic.

Along with the "Libro d'Oro" this same bonfire destroyed all papal records of the trials against the patriots in the months preceding the proclamation of the Republic. The choice of the setting for the festival was then itself polemical: for the elder Bernini's "Barcaccia" rose opposite the Palazzo de Propaganda Fide, the emblematic center of the Church's missionary activities throughout the world.

The round of patriotic festivals continued, interrupted only by Ferdinand IV's brief occupation of the city in November 1798. But it came full circle at the Forum again, where the Festa della Rigenerazione was held on 15 February 1799 to honor the first (and only) anniversary of the Republic.

Along with the imagery of regeneration went a good deal of wishful thinking; for Rome's financial and moral resources were by now nearly exhausted. Food of all kinds was scarce, even on the black market, and riots had already begun to break out to protest the lack of bread. But Bargigli seems to have spared no expense on the "macchina" he erected in front of the church of S. Lorenzo in Miranda, in the center of the Forum. Lavishly decorated with the usual figurative apparatus of such festivals – Roman eagles, garlands, banners, friezes, flaming altars, and the twin busts of Brutus and Cassius – it featured a single Doric column, "simbolo della solidità," to be crowned with a colossal statue of liberty (shown in the artist's design, Fig. 9). The choice of a Doric column may reflect a nostalgia for origins even deeper and more sustaining than many to be glimpsed in the surrounding Forum. In any case bad weather again disrupted the plan, and on the day before the festival the fresh plaster figure of liberty was knocked down and shattered by the *tramontana* wind. In its place Bargigli mounted a simple sphere.

To celebrate Rome's resurrection of its republican origins Bargigli exploited the entire available space of the Forum, erecting an altar and sarcophagus to the martyrs of the Republic in front of the Basilica of Maxentius and decorating the arches of Titus and Septimius Severus with flowers "a seconda del costume degli antichi."[18]

9. P. D. Humbert de Superville, " 'To the Perpetuity of the Republic.' A moment of the patriotic festival on the first anniversary of the Roman Republic," 1799 (engraving by T. Piroli on the design of Humbert de Superville, Rome, Museo Napoleonico).

The ceremony itself seems to have been endless. At intervals between the speeches, pageants in Roman costume were performed for the consuls. At one point a child, an adolescent, and an old man, all dressed in togas and representing the three ages of man, offered laurel and oak wreaths to the consuls, and were rewarded each with a silver coin specially minted for the occasion. Later, twenty-four young women, bareheaded and dressed in white robes, repeated the same gesture, followed by twenty-four young men, also in Roman dress. The dramatic repertory seemed to be growing thin; or perhaps the redundancy was deliberate, an exaggerated display of the government's control over an external situation that had almost hopelessly deteriorated. In any case, after the consuls and French ambassador join the performers in hanging wreaths on the altar in front of the Basilica, they proceed briefly to the Capitoline to view the column to the fallen General Duphot (erected there a year earlier after his funeral ceremony at St. Peter's) and move on to consume "democratic refreshment," enlivened by tales of Brutus, Marcus Aurelius, Mucius Scaevola, and Camillus, while the crowds watch a fireworks display in the Forum.[19]

The last republican festival, held five months later – again in the Forum – was a perfunctory affair, with a "macchina" built by Bargigli in a single day. The crisis of the Republic now seemed irreversible. When in September the Neapolitans invaded Rome, they rushed to destroy all reminders of the twenty-month republican regime – liberty trees, statues, insignia, and of course the insolent column to General Duphot. They restored the cross to the Quirinal obelisk, the scaffold to the Corso, and the Jews to the Ghetto. But the real work of restoring the ruined prestige of the papacy was left to Pius VII, newly elected in Venice.

It was a desolate prospect that met Pius VII upon his arrival at the Vatican on 3 July 1800 after a triumphant procession through the Porta del Popolo and the streets of Rome. The palace of which he reclaimed possession was stripped of its most prestigious icons; and the museum that his predecessor had worked for a quarter-century to create had been quickly dismantled. In the place of its marbles transported to Paris stood some copies roughly cast in plaster; elsewhere, empty pedestals still inscribed with Pius VI's name and arms marked the place of sculptures that had been removed. Meanwhile, Visconti himself was at work in the Louvre arranging those same statues in an order more pleasing to Napoleon. He would remain in Paris until his death, turning his philological talents to the two major works commissioned by Napoleon to trace his own imperial genealogy – *L'ico-nografie grecque* and its logical successor, *L'iconografie romaine*.[20]

Napoleon had decimated the papal collections; but even the private collections throughout Rome were severely reduced. Prominent families such as the Albani and Braschi had been forced to sell many of their ancient sculptures to pay the high taxes imposed by the republican government; as a special favor to his impoverished brother-in-law, Camillo Borghese, Napoleon would acquire almost his entire family collection. In addition to the works claimed by the Treaty of Tolentino, and the many treasures later confiscated from the churches (including pieces such as Legros's colossal statue of St. Ignatius, taken from the Gesù and melted down to make silver coin, along with countless reliquaries, candelabra, crosses, and ex votos), Rome had lost hundreds of paintings and sculptures to the private market. Intercepted by agents shrewd enough to see the profits in store, these were resold at vastly higher prices to collectors throughout Europe.

Never before had the city been so thoroughly plundered. But instead of abandoning his predecessor's program of archaeological patronage, Pius VII redoubled his efforts to promote and sustain archaeological research, and prevent the exportation of antiquities from Rome. Restoration remained a

VETERIBVS · ARTIVM · MONVMENTIS ·
SERVANDIS. COMPARANDISQVE · DATA · LEX

10. Vincenzo Ferreri, "Pius VII issues the Edict of 1802, protecting the Roman Antiquities," 1818 (Vatican, Galleria Chiaramonti).

controlling metaphor throughout the Chiaramonti papacy (1800–23); and clearly the archaeological restoration he promoted was a figure for the larger political and religious restoration made necessary by the deteriorating position of the Church.

The most dramatic statement of the Pope's renewed commitment to archaeology was the Chirografo of 2 October 1802, later celebrated as the founding act of Pius VII's papacy in a fresco cycle commissioned by Canova for the Galleria Chiaramonti in the Vatican (Fig. 10).[21] Composed primarily by Carlo Fea, who already in 1799 had been appointed Commissioner of Antiquities by the occupying Neapolitan general Naselli, the edict represented the papacy's most systematic and concerted attempt to prevent the destruction and exportation of antiquities and protect the cultural patrimony of Rome.

> In the vortex of recent events, immense has been the damage suffered by our beloved City, due to the loss of its finest monuments and most illustrious works of Antiquity. Far from being discouraged by this, however, our Paternal Solicitude has assumed the responsibility of establishing measures both to assure that such losses will not be repeated, and to replace the old monuments by the excavation of the new. These have been the considerations which, following the illustrious example of His Majesty Leo X toward the great Raphael of Urbino, led us recently to appoint the incomparable sculptor Canova . . . Inspector General of the Fine Arts.[22]

The mature period of Canova's career as a sculptor coincides almost exactly with the years of the Chiaramonti papacy. From his appointment for life as Inspector of the Fine Arts to his death in 1822 (only a year before Pius himself), Canova would enjoy extraordinary prestige and power at Pius's court. As a sculptor he symbolized the revival of the arts after the sack of Tolentino; as a patron he provided commissions to a new generation of artists, most notably in the series of sculpture busts for the Pantheon and the fresco cycle in the Galleria Chiaramonti; and as Inspector of the Arts he shared with Carlo Fea the responsibility of regulating illegal excavation and traffic in antiquities.

It would be naïve to exaggerate the practical effects of this law; since the Renaissance, like Manzoni's litany in *I promessi sposi,* such edicts had in fact proliferated, and often the popes were the first to ignore them.[23] The humanist Pius II, whose memorandum of 1462 prohibiting the destruction of ancient monuments is explicitly recalled in Article 8 (p. 117), was himself one of the worst offenders. Despite Canova's vigilance and Fea's frequently apopleptic crusade, the law could not be uniformly enforced, due in part to the inadequacy of administrative structures and in part to explicit diplomatic pressures (as in the celebrated case of the Barberini Faun, which Pius VII's secretary of state, Cardinal Consalvi, finally permitted Ludwig of Bavaria to export at the request of Ludwig's sister, the Empress of Austria).[24] But the edict is considered a landmark in protective legislation for the vigor of its language and the force of its attempt to fill all gaps in previous regulation – so that *no* individual ("di qualunque privilegio fornite, e di qualunque dignità decorate, compresi anche li R.mi Cardinali benchè Titolari, Protettori di Chiese, ed altri privilegiatissimi," p. 114) could secure or concede an exemption from its conditions.

The inventory of antiquities prohibited for export is almost incantatory in its insistence, and provides a striking example of the rhetoric of restoration under Pius VII:

> In the first place we declare that it is absolutely forbidden to remove from Rome or from the Papal States any Statue, Bas-Relief, or other similar work representing Human figures, or Animals, in Marble, in Ivory, or in any other material, and also any ancient Paintings, whether Greek or Roman, cut or otherwise removed from the walls, Mosaics, Etruscan vases, Glass objects, and other colored artifacts, and also any inlaid object, antique Vases, Gems, and engraved Stones, Cameos, Medals, works executed in Lead, Bronze, and in general all those works, whether large or small in format, which are identified as "antiquities" [antichità], public or private, Sacred or Profane, with no exceptions, even in the case of simple Fragments . . . and in addition any ancient Monument, i.e., Tablets or Inscriptions, Grave-markers,

Urns, Candelabra, Lamps, Sarcophaghi, Cinerary Urns, and other ancient objects of a similar nature, regardless of the material of which they are composed, including even the simplest Ceramics. Furthermore, we wish this prohibition to extend to the movable elements of Architecture, i.e., Columns, Capitals, Bases, Architraves, Friezes, sculpted Cornices, and all other ornaments of ancient Buildings, and in addition to Terracotta Figures, Precious Stones, Lapis Lazuli, Green, Red, and Yellow marbles, Oriental Alabasters, even those which have not been carved, Porphyry, Granite, Basalt, Serpentine, and other marbles, apart from simple white Marble. (113)

No previous document had shown such determination to "say it all"; but the catalogue continues, with an insistence to which I cannot do justice here (the above paragraph is one of seventeen articles). Particularly relevant to the Pope's larger program of restoration are the provisions regarding the destruction (as well as export) of ancient monuments. No structure, however fragmentary, is to be molested; every ancient building, where possible, is to be "cleared, restored, and preserved with the greatest possible exactitude" (p. 117); no site, however fortuitously discovered, is to be looted for building materials, and no excavations undertaken even on private property except by the express consent and in attendance of the inspector, the commissioner, or one of his deputies (pp. 119–20). In addition, any laborer, farmer, or mason who in the act of plowing or digging up the earth should discover a statue, coin, or gem, or the remains of an ancient structure, whatever its condition, must report his discovery within ten days at the risk of a fine to be determined according to the severity of the case; and *all* persons, native or foreign, whether permanent residents or visitors, must report every ancient artifact or fragment in their possession to the inspector, who will make an annual inspection to verify that the object has not been damaged, lost, or removed from Rome (p. 118).

Clearly such provisions defied enforcement; but they give a fair indication of the utopian nature of Pius VII's archaeological campaign. Along with explorations at Ostia and other outlying sites, he ordered Carlo Fea to begin a vast plan of excavations in the Forum (later continued by Antonio Nibby) from the slopes of the Capitoline to the Temple of Castor and Pollux. These excavations were still far from scientific – they were mainly an organized treasure hunt – but the Pope obviously expected them to yield spectacular results, for in 1805 he commissioned the architect Raffaele Stern to design a new wing at the Vatican to *extend* the already depleted Pio-Clementine galleries.[25]

In addition to ordering fresh excavations, Pius VII worked to replenish the Vatican collections through a vigorous campaign of purchases from private collectors in Rome; required by the Edict of 1802 to declare all the antiquities in their possession, these individuals found themselves barred from the profitable international market and forced to accept the less favorable prices offered by the Holy See. At the same time the Pope encouraged new work in the classical manner to replace the works transported to Paris; he bought Canova's Perseus in 1801 to occupy the empty pedestal of the Apollo Belvedere, and the Creugas (1801) and Damoxenas (1806) shortly thereafter.[26]

Unlike his predecessor, Pius VII did not limit himself to collecting the removable trophies of classical Rome. He also began an ambitious program of restoring the most prominent monuments *in situ;* in addition to work on Trajan's Column and the Colosseum, he began to restore the arches of Constantine and Septimius Severus (and later, the Arch of Titus).[27] The polemical thrust of this project was clear. Unlike the precarious republican regime, forced to celebrate its triumphs in ephemeral arches of wood and painted canvas (imitating Rome's richest polychrome marbles in an economical trompe-l'oeil pastiche),[28] the papacy still guarded the resources of Rome and boasted the wealth and leisure to reconstruct its original emblems of empire with an accuracy that would dismay the lovers of the picturesque (Stendhal was to complain of Valadier's antiseptic reconstruction of the Arch of Titus in his *Promenades dans Rome* of 1829).[29]

Of the Pope's various projects of restoration, not the least important was the restoration of the remains of Pius VI, made possible by the 1801 Concordat. The return of Pius's body to Rome and his funeral at St. Peter's are illustrated in countless prints of the period, as well as in the 1818 Biblioteca frescoes. Canova's own last work of monumental sculpture was the Braschi pope's tomb (completed a year after his death by Adamo Tadolini in 1823) for the sunken *confessio* under the main papal altar of St. Peter's. It is fitting that Canova's last work should have symbolically restored to the Vatican a pope who died in exile, and that this statue should have marked the spot later to become the focus of unprecedented archaeological scrutiny throughout the Second World War – when the Roman Church, finally reconciled to the loss of the temporal power by Mussolini's Concordat of 1929, in imitation of lay archaeology undertook to identify beneath the *confessio* and crypt the site of its own objective origins – the actual tomb and remains of Saint Peter.[30]

Canova's monumental representation of Pius VI presided over the site claimed most precious to Christianity – encircled by ninety-five gilded lamps perpetually burning and canopied by Bernini's *baldacchino* and the Michelangelo dome with its revolving inscription of the words with which Christ is said to have instituted the Church: "TU ES PETRUS ET SUPER

HANC PETRAM AEDIFICABO ECCLESIAM MEAM ET TIBI DABO CLAVES REGNI CAELORUM" (Matthew 16:18). No more spectacularly overdetermined setting could have been desired by any pope for his tomb; and the official twentieth-century archaeological sanction of the site would have particularly gratified a pope who himself skillfully manipulated archaeological imagery for rhetorical effect.

Pius VII's contemporaries appreciated and quickly acknowledged the political significance of his archaeological effort. As early as 1801 the reigning Prince of the Accademia di San Luca, the sculptor Vincenzo Pacetti, praised Pius's patronage of archaeology in his opening address at the restored Capitoline competitions:

> As the three sister Arts of Painting, Sculpture, and Architecture lay despondent in Rome, lamenting the disasters they had recently suffered, they saw, Blessed Father, a glad new dawn (presage of a brighter day) in the exaltation to the Pontifical Throne of Your Sacred Person: they recognized in you that beneficent Patron, and provident Sovereign, who would protect them . . . and who, to compensate for their well-known misfortunes, would resurrect the remains of the Greek and Roman schools, and build museums and new sanctuaries for the conservation of artistic monuments.[31]

Pacetti's pious concern for the preservation of Rome's artistic patrimony seems ironic in view of his own involvement in the ongoing scandal of the Barberini Faun. Having acquired the sculpture from the Barberini family in 1799, he had extensively restored it and offered it for sale to a series of French and English clients. The profits he stood to gain were tremendous; in the legal battle that ensued when the Barberini attempted to reclaim the sculpture, Pacetti's restoration alone was assessed at a value of two thousand *zecchini,* two-thirds of the price Pius VII had paid for Canova's Perseus. Despite all his efforts to retain the statue, Pacetti was obliged to return it in 1804.[32]

However questionable the politics of his private activity as a restorer and dealer of antiquities, in his public role as Prince of the Accademia di San Luca, Pacetti praises the Church's program without reservation. He urges that the Pope continue his campaign to excavate new statues to replace the old and ensure them permanent sanctuary in Rome, safe from the threat of expropriation by the French.

The poems recited at the 1801 *concorsi* join in praising the Pope's renewed excavations, and insist that even Napoleon can not permanently deface the heroic landscape of Rome. In an elegy on the sack of Tolentino, Giuseppe Alborghetti points to Bernini's Fountain of the Four Rivers as an emblem of the artistic legacy remaining to the Pope:

> Or che la spada di Bellona ha vinto,
> E alla Cittade ha tolto
> Tutto il più bel, che scolto
> Già fosse in marmo, o da pennel dipinto,
> Sol mi conforta, che un trofeo de l'arte,
> Il gran Berninio Fonte
> Sul Tebro alza la fronte,
> Nè teme la rapace ira di Marte.[33]

(Now that the sword of Bellona has triumphed, and taken from the City all the most beautiful works that ever were sculpted in marble, or painted by a brush, it is my sole consolation that one trophy of art, the great Fountain of Bernini, raises its head on the Tiber and fears not the rapacious anger of Mars.)

Monuments like Bernini's fountain acquire "gloria maggior" in the present crisis and console the Romans for the trophies they have lost, just as Canova's statues come to substitute the ancient marbles removed to Paris. The 1801 competitions include four poems commenting on the rise of Canova, including three *ecphrases* of the Perseus recently purchased for the Vatican. In a sonnet dedicated to Canova, the papal architect Giuseppe Antinori (who had raised Pius VI's three obelisks at the Quirinal, Trinità dei Monti, and Montecitorio) expresses the shared hope that Canova will repair the damage inflicted by the French:

> Roma t'applaude, o Prometeo novello,
> E riparar di sue perdite il duolo
> Pel vital spera tuo divin scarpello:
> Che, come il fior d'ogni beltà raccolto
> Fu già ne l'Apellea Cipri, in te solo
> Tutto è il miglior de' prischi geni accolto.[34]

(Rome applauds you, oh new Prometheus, and hopes that your divine and life-giving chisel will assuage the grief of its losses: for, just as the flower of all beauty was once gathered in the Cypris of Apelles, in you alone is gathered all the greatness of ancient genius.)

Canova would of course be instrumental in negotiating the return of the papal collections after the Congress of Vienna; but for the moment his

contemporaries perceived his role as that of catalyzing a revival of the arts in
Rome. The 1805 *concorsi* testify to the growing myth of Canova; the seven
poems dedicated to his recent works include a Latin epigram by Giuseppe
Capogrossi praising Canova's displacement of the Apollo Belvedere by the
work of his own "Daedalian" hand:

> Heic ubi Phoebus erat (magnum hoc manus Attica saxum
>   Ferro olim potuit sculpere Daedaleo)
> Stat Perseus; (nuper magnum hoc manus Itala saxum
>   Ferro ipso potuit sculpere Daedaleo).
> Haec PIUS Ausonio dat praemia digna Canovae,
>   Auspice quo, Romae est Graecia facta soror.[35]

(Here where Phoebus was [an Attic hand once sculpted this great
stone with a Daedalian chisel] stands Perseus [an Italian hand now has
sculpted this great stone with a Daedalian chisel]. PIUS gives these
rewards to the Ausonian Canova; under his auspices Greece has been
made a sister of Rome.)

As the century progressed the myth of Canova would become increasingly important to the Risorgimento cause. Democrats and liberals
alike adopted him as a symbol of the regeneration of the arts that they hoped
would contribute to political unification; his tomb of Vittorio Alfieri, completed at Santa Croce in 1810 (three years after the publication of Foscolo's
Sepolcri), became a primary landmark of the Risorgimento movement (Fig.
16).[36] But for the moment the myth of Canova was contained within the
ideological coordinates imposed by the Church; and as they celebrated the
young sculptor's rising prestige the poets and orators of the Chiaramonti
court inevitably concluded with praise of his patron.

Pius's commitment to archaeology was meant to promote not only an
artistic but a political renewal. Ercole Dandini's oration of 1805 makes
explicit the nexus between archaeology and power. Addressing the young
winners of the Capitoline competitions, he explains:

> Valorous youths . . . the memory of men is like a monument, which
> resists the ravage of the centuries, and the force of revolutions . . .
> Your school is Rome, and you live under the auspices of the glorious
> Pius VII . . . His subtle and discerning spirit has fully appreciated this
> important maxim: that *in Rome the arts must constitute one of the principal
> objects of politics* . . . The ruins of Ostia stand as eloquent and eternal
> proof of his sublime providence, and it seems that the famous shades
> of our ancient ancestors give reverent thanks to the arm which was
> able to vindicate these works from the ravage of time and the outrage

of barbarians. Our age lacks nothing to rival the greatest days of Pericles, Leo X, Julius II, and Louis XVI; and our August Protector of the arts lacks nothing to merit, like these, the name of greatness. (Emphasis added)[37]

Yet by reconstructing an imperial image of Rome, Pius VII was inviting the fresh trespass of Napoleon. Anxious to appropriate the city itself as part of his expanding empire, Napoleon finally occupied Rome in May 1809 and proclaimed the end of the temporal power, entrusting the city's administration to a temporary Consulta and deporting Pius VII to exile in France.

From its very inception the Consulta proclaimed the importance of archaeology to its political program. Article 3 of the institution of the Consulta Straordinaria (17 May 1809) specified: "The monuments of the ancient grandeur of Rome will be protected and maintained at the expense of our Treasury," and already on 21 June the Consulta appointed a special Commission to fulfill this function.[38]

Officially it was Napoleon's claim that the Church had neglected the classical landscape of Rome, and that his intervention alone could restore its "ancient grandeur"; but in fact he assumed most of Pius VII's appointees in his new administration (including Fea, Valadier, Camporese, Camuccini, Filippo Aurelio Visconti, and Canova himself), and privately he confessed to Canova in Paris a certain anxiety regarding the Pope's formidable precedent. Was he allocating enough money to fund profitable excavations, he inquired; and how had the Pope and private patrons like the Borghese determined the amount to be spent on archaeology?[39]

Canova used his considerable influence with the Emperor to flatter his archaeological ambitions;[40] and shortly after the sculptor's return from Paris the excavations, now directed by the prefect De Tournon, began in earnest. In order to make Rome worthy of its new title as "Seconde Ville de l'Empire" and to prepare for the anticipated visit of the imperial couple (which never took place; Napoleon in fact would never set foot in Rome), Tournon turned the Forum into an immense *cantiere,* hiring over two thousand workers to clear the rubble from the monuments of imperial Rome. He directed his first efforts at the Tabularium, freeing the three buried columns of the Temple of Vespasian (then believed to be that of Jupiter) with their weighty entablature, inscribed [R] ESTITUER [UNT] (Fig. 11). Hoping to stage the new emperor's triumphal procession through the arches of Titus and Septimius Severus, he dug through to the original stones of the Via Sacra (an event much acclaimed in the *Journal du Capitole* and the Parisian press)[41] and began the long work of its excavation. At the same time he cleared the three columns of the Basilica of Constantine and Maxentius. From the temples of Vesta and Fortuna Virile on the Tiber to the Colosseum, the Baths of Titus, and Trajan's Forum, the French team inau-

ESTITVER

11. Luigi Rossini, "View of the Three Columns of Jupiter Tonans," 1817 (Rome, GCS).

gurated a program of excavations that were soon interrupted by Napoleon's fall and even today are far from completion.

Perhaps no one learned more from Napoleon than Mussolini; the Via dei Fori Imperiali and Via della Conciliazione from St. Peter's to the Tiber are both based on projects first conceived by the French. Napoleon himself intended to demolish the façade of St. Peter's; despite their scorn for the Baroque, the Fascist architects never went that far. But Napoleon and Mussolini shared the goal of isolating the existing monuments in grand rhetorical spaces. We can be thankful that neither accomplished his plan of opening up the piazzas of the Pantheon and the Trevi fountain.[42]

But Napoleon's most ambitious plan for transforming Rome exceeded even those of Mussolini. The French historian Madelin describes his project for a colossal imperial palace to extend from the Piazza Colonna to the Colosseum; the Palazzo Venezia was to have been its administrative wing, the Aracoeli its chapel, and the Forum its inner courtyard.[43]

Although this architectural folly, proposed by Scipione Perosini, was quickly abandoned in favor of a more realistic renovation of the Quirinal (entrusted to Raffaele Stern), the image of the *palazzone mancato* survives as an hallucinatory emblem of Napoleonic classicism.[44] The enclosure of the Roman Forum as a private courtyard would have been a gesture surpassing all papal precedent. Not even the Vatican museum complex had so dramatically exploited Rome's archaeological resources, and no pope had proposed a comparable manipulation of its landscape.

Madelin notes the irony of the Pope's repossession of the Quirinal palace – newly redecorated at Napoleon's expense – upon his return to the city in 1814. Along with the Sèvres porcelain, Gobelins tapestries, and freshly painted allegorical frescoes intended to celebrate the triumphs of Napoleon, Pius VII inherited a city substantially improved and embellished during his five-year absence.

Certain of the imperial spaces he appropriated with pleasure; he approved Valadier's design of the Pincio (enjoying the commanding view prepared for Napoleon), and in an archetypal assertion of papal ascendancy planted his own obelisk along its main axis, unaware that Mazzini would one day seed the same ground with the busts of Italian patriots.[45]

But the Pope refused to tolerate certain archaeological initiatives of the French. Most dramatically he filled in Tournon's excavations in the Colosseum and restored the Stations of the Cross first placed there by Benedict XIV, thus reclaiming the Colosseum as a strictly religious symbol and site consecrated to the Christian martyrs (Figs. 12 and 13).

It is significant however that the Pope directed Valadier to proceed with the restoration of the Arch of Titus – a symbol particularly offensive to the Jews, whom he sent back to the Ghetto even as he reinstated the Jesuit order and the Inquisition.[46]

12. Luigi Rossini, "Interior of the Colosseum excavated in 1813 and refilled in 1814," 1820 (Rome, GCS).

13. Luigi Rossini, "View of the grand interior of the Flavian Amphitheatre, called the Colosseum," 1822 (Rome, GCS).

85

CLARIORA · ARTIFICVM · EXCELLENTIVM · OPERA · AD · EXTEROS · AVECTA
VRBI · RECVPERATA

14. Francesco Hayez, "The Restoration of the Art Works to Rome," 1816 (Vatican, Galleria Chiaramonti).

Restoration remained a dominant metaphor throughout the second phase of the Chiaramonti papacy (1814–13), and gained new resonance from its generalized use as a political metaphor following the Congress of Vienna. Like the other European monarchs reinstated in Vienna, the Pope demanded the immediate return of his territories and possessions. On 28 August 1815 Canova arrived in Paris to negotiate the return of the art works from the Louvre. With the help of the English diplomat William Richard Hamilton, he persuaded the French to release most of the statues taken from the papal collections; and on 4 January 1816 the convoys arrived in Rome. Six months later Francesco Hayez had already commemorated this event in a lunette painted for the new Museo Chiaramonti (Fig. 14). In this scene, two *putti* and the reclining Tiber (flanked on the extreme right by a bas-relief of Romulus and Remus) look from their position in front of the Castel Sant'Angelo toward Monte Mario, where the carts are arriving laden with the Vatican treasures. In the foreground at left is a portrait bust of William Richard Hamilton, to acknowledge his role in negotiating the release of the sculptures from Paris.

This lunette is part of a larger fresco cycle to which I have already had occasion to refer; and the entire program deserves a brief description here, for it significantly develops the theme of restoration under Pius VII. Commissioned in 1818 to a group of German Nazarene and Italian neoclassical painters by Canova (who personally paid for the project with the income from his appointment as Marchese d'Istria), the lunettes represent the many phases of Pius VII's restoration of the arts from his accession to the foundation of the Braccio Nuovo.[47] Chronologically the series begins with Vincenzo Ferreri's representation of the signing of the Chirografo of 1802 (Fig. 10). As Heisinger notes, this is also the physical center of the program; it is the only scene to include a portrait of the Pope, and is located in a privileged position opposite the original entrance to the gallery from the Cortile della Pigna.[48]

The cycle thus establishes the 1802 edict as the founding act of the Chiaramonti papacy. By issuing a law protecting the antiquities, the Pope had symbolically proclaimed the restoration of the temporal power. The fifteen remaining scenes illustrate individual episodes from his papacy which I have already mentioned in this chapter, including the restoration of the Colosseum (Philippe Veit); the excavation of the arches of Constantine and Septimius Severus (Luigi Durantini); the donation of Egyptian and Attic art to the Vatican museums (Giuseppe Caponeri); and the foundation of the Museo Chiaramonti (Filippo Agricola). Veit's representation of the Colosseum is perhaps the most interesting in view of the recent vicissitudes of the monument; himself a recent convert to Catholicism, Veit depicts the Colosseum as a strictly religious arena, occupied by the central figure of Religion enthroned. Veit omits any reference to the work of Tournon, and instead shows a view of the buttress built by Raffaele Stern (1807) on a tablet held by an angel at the right of Religion's throne.

The cycle thematizes the politics of restoration in the scenes represented in its individual lunettes; but it also enacts a larger restoration of the art of fresco painting, to which Canova's contemporaries attributed an equally political significance. During the Napoleonic period the art of fresco painting had rapidly declined; and critics such as Giuseppe Tambroni urged its revival in explicitly nationalistic terms. In a book published in 1816 and dedicated to Canova, Tambroni declared that fresco painting, traditionally dominated by the Italians, should be promoted to rehabilitate the country's cultural prestige.[49] It was no accident that Pius's papacy saw the systematic restoration of many of the Vatican frescoes (including Michelangelo's *Last Judgment* in 1824–5), along with the restoration of many deteriorating frescoes, oil paintings, and mosaics in the churches of Rome.[50]

Another encomiastic cycle in the Vatican complex, painted by Domenico De Angelis in 1818, portrays the restoration of antiquity as a central theme of the Braschi and Chiaramonti papacies.[51] Among the political vicissitudes of his reign, the biography of Pius VI in the Sala Alessandrina depicts the three obelisks that he erected in Rome, along with his inauguration of the Pio-Clementine Museum and King Gustav III's visit to the museum in 1784. The parallel narrative of Pius VII's life places even greater strategic emphasis on the archaeological gesture; separate scenes commemorate his restoration of the Colosseum, his order to begin excavations at Ostia, the founding of the Galleria Lapidaria, excavation of the Imperial Fora, donation of Etruscan vases to the Vatican library, and construction of the Braccio Nuovo. Clearly the rhetoric of restoration is as central to the visual documents of the papal court as it is to its legislation, poetry, and oratory.

Admired as an artist, diplomat, and patron, Canova was only an indifferent orator; but his 1816 address on the reopening of the Roman Academy of Archaeology is of considerable interest as an illustration of the evolving strategies of archaeological encomium under the Restoration.[52] Where Monti had celebrated the restoration of a single emblematic *artifact* in order to trace a fantastic "linea aurea" from fifth-century Athens to Settecento Rome, Canova here commemorates the restoration of a public *institution* itself dedicated to archaeological inquiry and allegedly dependent for its survival on the continuity of the *pax cristiana*. As if archaeological activity had been suspended during the Napoleonic regime – rather than promoted and personally conducted by many of the members of this audience – Canova portrays the reorganization of the Academy and the return to peaceful and productive research as one of the most urgent political concerns of the Pope:

> An institution so useful and distinguished could not escape the paternal solicitude of our revered Pontiff and hence became one of his first concerns. Therefore, as soon as Providence with unprecedented prodigies reordered the reign entrusted to him, with his benign consent he deigned to approve the reestablishment of this most interesting Institute, under the name of the Accademia Archeologica.
>
> (34)

Papal propaganda of the Restoration increasingly resembles that of the Counter-Reformation in its dramatization of the dangers of heresy and of the precarious nature of the *pax cristiana*. Hence the antithetical images of ruins and reconstruction are central. In Canova's address the Napoleonic interlude is implicitly compared to the barbarian invasions. The restored Chiaramonti papacy represents the era of rebuilding; hence the strategic emphasis on Pius VII's projected extension of the Vatican, all the more courageous in view of the recent depredations:

> And in truth, whoever remembers with tears of gratitude and consolation the travailed era of his reign, will have no choice but to admire that generous spirit, who enriched the Museum with such an extensive addition . . . and who opened up an immense accumulation of riches to the science of epigraphy with inscriptions so numerous, and so care-

fully ordered and displayed, that they gave even greater splendor to the halls and vestibules of this magnificent palace of Minerva.

(32)

Pius VII's additions to the Vatican link him not only to his immediate predecessors but to the great architect popes of the Renaissance, Julius II and Leo X, who "vied to surpass each other in munificence by dedicating in the Vatican the most august temple that ever was consecrated to the Arts" (32). In addition, his reorganization of the Accademia Romana di Archaeologia relates him to another prestigious precursor – Benedict XIV, who had revived this body in the mid-Settecento, widely promoted antiquarian studies, and founded the Museo dei Conservatori on the Capitoline.

Commending Pius VII's insatiable desire to distinguish himself as patron of the arts and rebuilder of Rome, Canova continues:

Our glorious Pontiff Pius VII, not content to be remembered by future generations for his virtues both public and private, and for the disastrous and prosperous turns of fortune which agitated and distinguished his pontifical reign, wished that in this respect too his name would be remembered, and blessed, and highly commended.

(32)

Among the Pope's many accomplishments, which Canova proceeds to list in a formulaic *praeteritio* ("Lascio le escavazioni . . . e tante altre illustre sue imprese") are the repairs to the Colosseum, the excavations of the arches of Constantine and Septimus Severus, the recovery of the art works from Paris, and the reinstatement of the academies themselves. Each of these individual acts of restoration Canova represents as emblematic of the broader political restoration on which the progress of the arts depends. And since archaeology involves the retrieval and description of finite material objects, its center can only be in Rome, where the majority of those objects are once again located:

It is the destiny of works of art to be bound to a fixed location. Nor can the whole world be traversed by us all; and the desires of the majority would be frustrated if the scholar did not intervene to provide his learned analyses, accounts, and comparisons. This kind of study, though appropriate in any well-ordered state which desires to distinguish itself through the patronage of the Arts and Letters, becomes absolutely necessary in Rome, in this immense depository of the works of the greatest Artists, in this seat of the grandeur of human genius. Every stone, so to speak, of this capital solicits the scrutiny, the study, and the attention of the scholar and antiquarian. Through his efforts we examine the infinite number of objects addressed by his research, and through him we are transported into ancient times, we observe its customs, wander through its streets, admire its temples, and become citizens of the centuries.

(33–34)

Canova's oration clarifies the politically conservative function assigned to archaeology under the Restoration. It is in the name of a generic humanism ("cittadini de' Secoli") and cautious curatorship of the ecclesiastical landscape that he invites scholars to resume their inspection of Rome's "every stone."

In the period following the Pope's reinstatement, scholars throughout Europe responded to this invitation, and Rome again became a center for philological and antiquarian studies. But the conservative ideology of papal classicism could not contain the revolution in historical scholarship inaugurated by the work of scholars such as Niebuhr, who arrived in Rome in 1816 as Prussian minister to the Holy See and remained there until 1823 to complete his revisionary history of ancient Rome.

Massimo D'Azeglio, who himself first visited Rome in 1814, accompanying his father on a diplomatic mission to the papal court, remembers the excitement attending the Pope's return; as he approached the city, he saw triumphal arches of wood and plaster still standing on the outskirts of Rome, where the Pope had arrived only days before.[53] But like Leopardi – who after his initial appeal to the Vatican philologist Angelo Mai grew rapidly disillusioned with the intellectual climate of papal Rome[54] – D'Azeglio ridiculed the *mania antiquaria* of the Restoration, and observed: "Antiquarianism was and is one of the few studies possible under the government of priests. It would require real ingenuity to discover in it any subversive tendencies."[55]

D'Azeglio is naïve or inconsistent here, for he was well aware of the subversive potential of philological studies, and in fact complained that his first guide to the monuments of ancient Rome, Filippo Aurelio Visconti, showed no interest in the "bei moderni lavori" of Niebuhr and other contemporary scholars:

> Roman history was accepted in those days just as the ancients had handed it down to us, without inquiring any further. The fine new studies of Niebuhr and the other Germans, of Thierry, Ampère, Micali and many others on Italic origins had not yet . . . shown us how carefully we ought to reconsider the complex fabric of those histories. The teachings of Sig. Visconti served then simply to *confirm those facts which we already knew* ["la conferma de' fatti da noi già conosciuti"] . . . We rehearsed the whole inventory of antiquities without missing a

single stone, accepting Romulus and Clelia, Scevola and Horace at the Sublician Bridge, etc., etc., the complete cast of that great drama with the fanatical faith of Moslems.

(115)

For his own part D'Azeglio concludes that "those venerable relics, which inspired the minds of Gibbon and Goethe, produced no great impression on my poor little brain"; dismissing Visconti, he found a more compatible and amusing guide in the young painter Malvotti, who showed him the galleries and churches of Rome. D'Azeglio presents his indifference to the antiquities as a measure of his own modernity; but the papal antiquarians could not so easily dismiss the implications of the work of scholars such as Niebuhr, and campaigned vigorously against his deconstruction of the Roman myths that they had long adapted to the service of the Church. The irascible Carlo Fea, as Commissioner of Antiquities, led this campaign; his address to the Accademia dei Sabini in 1832 was a vehement defense of the historicity of Romulus.[56]

Resistance to Niebuhr in Rome was widespread and crossed ideological boundaries; Leopardi himself, in the famous "patriotic" stanzas of the *Paralipomeni della Batracomiomachia,* heaped fresh insults on the grave of the Prussian philologist who by virtue of his "molti e belli ragionamenti" and "bel diploma" had presumed to rewrite the history of Rome.[57] Nevertheless the motives of the Church are clear. Ecclesiastical archaeology was intended as custodial rather than critical, and was dedicated to the apology of power through the preservation and reinforcement of an established hermeneutic tradition – the "conferma de' fatti da noi già conosciuti." This tradition of the providential continuity between classical and Christian Rome had symbolically rehabilitated the pagan city by consecrating it to the service of the Church: and the *cicerone* Visconti with his patient litany of erudite misinformation was more properly a sacristan shuffling through the streets and *scavi* of Rome, revealing its treasures upon request.

The Vatican philologist Angelo Mai is still remembered today for the *canzone* dedicated to him by the young Leopardi. The poet's fervent tribute to this "Italo ardito" could not have been less appropriate, for in resurrecting the text of *De republica* Mai had no intention of contributing to any larger revolution; in fact he was one of the more submissive members of the papal bureaucracy, and protective of his privileged access to the archives of power. Nonetheless the *canzone* enjoyed widespread influence, and Leopardi's idealistic misprision of the philologist's motives was passed on to a generation of Italian patriots long after Leopardi realized and regretted his error.[58]

We can get a more accurate picture of Mai's politics from his own writings, such as the anniversary oration on the founding of Rome (21 April 1837).[59] Like Canova's oration of 1816, this address was delivered to the Pontificia Accademia Romana di Archeologia; but rhetorically it is considerably more sophisticated, and invites analysis as a document of the mature phase of Restoration classicism with which to conclude this chapter.

Mai begins by characterizing his discourse as an extended *ecphrasis* modeled on Virgil's famous description of the shield of Aeneas (itself an imitation of the Homeric motif):

> Inspired by your invitation, oh valorous scholars, to speak about the glories of Rome on the anniversary of its foundation, I am immediately reminded of that solemn episode in the greatest epic, that is the description of the shield of Aeneas, on which with superb skill was represented the celebrated history of the eternal city. But instead of rehearsing those facts, worthy of admiration and indeed magnificent, but already familiar and known to all, I wish to imitate, rather than comment on, that heroic shield: and I believe that a brief picture [*quadro*] of our modern Rome, rapidly sketched and compared with ancient Rome, will fulfill both your desire, gentlemen, and my duty, to celebrate on this day with appropriate praise the common homeland of all peoples, the immortal mistress of the universe.
>
> (188–9)

Ecphrasis had traditionally served in epic poetry as a device permitting the proleptic narration of events outside the time frame of the poem. But beyond its telescopic narrative function, the figure also encouraged close descriptive focus (from Aeneas's shield we remember not only the panoramic Battle of Actium but also the necklaces fastened about the "fair-skinned throats" of the invading Gauls). By thematizing the technical virtuosity of an artist in a plastic and visual medium (e.g., on Vulcan's shield, "Among these scenes stretched a wide sea; it was carved in gold but seemed blue water crested with foam," *Aeneid* VIII, 671–2), the poet could conveniently display his own verbal artistry. *Ecphrasis* tended then to transcend its thematic function and stand alone as a rhetorical set-piece, a tour de force dramatizing the paradox of representation itself.

By invoking the figure of *ecphrasis* Mai not only implies an epic context for his discourse – the ongoing epic of the Church militant – but declares that he will demonstrate the superiority of papal Rome to even the Rome of Augustus and Virgil, pictured on Aeneas's shield. He asks only for permission to substitute the symbolic language of the Church for that of the Roman Empire:

I ask then to transmute pagan Rome into Christian Rome: I ask to substitute Saint Peter the apostle for the Trojan Aeneas, and for the laurel of the Caesars the pontifical tiara: I ask to raise in place of the Capitoline eagles the life-giving banner of the cross of the Redeemer: I ask finally to lead out to the conquest of the world not the consular legions, but the evangelical armies of the missions.

(389)

This premise granted, he claims, "I will be able to demonstrate that the authority of modern Rome not only is not inferior to, but exceeds that of ancient Rome, which merited the noble epic of Virgil."

Once we accept Mai's fiction of the extended *ecphrasis,* it becomes clear that the "quadro" which he sets out to evoke is not (as one might expect to be the nineteenth-century counterpart of a shield, terrace, or tapestry) an heroic cycle of history painting. In fact the temporal dimension is almost completely absent from his representation of "magna Roma" – it is a purely spatial model that he chooses, without depth, dimension, or overt incident – it is the *map,* a favorite encomiastic image of the Church militant at least since Gregory XIII commissioned the Vatican's colossal Galleria delle Carte Geografiche in 1580.[60]

Mai's object is to illustrate the extent of the papal dominion by mapping out its missionary conquests throughout the world. He echoes the geographer Pomponius Mela in warning at the outset: "Orbis situm dicere adgredior, impeditum opus, et facundiae minime capax; constat enim fere gentium locorumque nominibus" (I am preparing to discuss the subject of topography, which is a difficult task, and unsuited to eloquence, because it deals almost exclusively with the nomenclature of places and peoples).

Yet there is a contrived eloquence precisely in the catalogue of names that follows. Because he has resolved to omit, "per amore di brevità," the list of the orthodox Catholic nations in order to concentrate on the "heterodox and infidel" nations at the periphery of the Empire, Mai is able to assemble an exotic geographical index with its own incantatory effect.

Like a general diagramming military strategy, placing a flag to designate each new stronghold, Mai lists the seemingly endless outposts of the Catholic Church, from the Adriatic through northern Europe to Greece and northwest Africa. Here in an unexpected maneuver he returns to the text of Virgil:

Once Mauritania was the farthest border of the empire of the Caesars in Africa; but it is certainly not that of the Popes. "His ego" (says Christ and not Jupiter)

His ego nec metas rerum nec tempora pono;
imperium sine fine dedi . . . [I, 278–9]
. . . iacet extra sidera tellus,
extra anni solisque vias, ubi caelifer Atlas
axem humero torquet stellis ardentibus aptum   [VI, 795–7]

(To these I set no boundary in space or time; I have granted them
dominion, and it has no end . . . there lies beyond the stars, beyond
the paths of the years and sun, a land where on his shoulders heaven-
bearing Atlas turns the axis set with blazing stars.)

Mai freely splices citations from the first and sixth books of the *Aeneid,*
and from two different speakers and contexts (Jupiter's prophecy to Venus,
I, 278–9; Anchises's exhortation to Aeneas, VI, 795–7) to dramatize Virgil's
territorial claims for the Roman Empire and his prophecy of its indefinite
expansion. Since he believes the Church to have inherited Rome's imperial
destiny – of *spiritual* rather than political conquest – Angelo Mai, the *retore*
and representative of the Propaganda Fide, presses tirelessly on ("Adunque
passiamo oltre . . .") through inner Africa to the Cape of Good Hope, and
north along the coast to the Red Sea and the Orient.

Again reaching an area described by Virgil (but with an encomiastic
intent!) as one of the outer limits of the empire of Augustus, Mai points out
that the legions of the Church have penetrated still further:

I have already said that the Roman pontificate exceeds every boundary
prescribed by the enthusiastic poet, where he wrote:

. . . super et Garamantas et Indos
proferet imperium.

(He will extend his rule beyond the Garamantes and the
Indians).

In fact we have on the Indus, where Augustus never arrived, and where
the mythical god Bacchus and Alexander of Macedon were forced to
stop; we have, as I was saying, the pontifical vicar of Bombay . . .

He goes on, with increasingly insistent anaphora, to list the papal emissaries
at work in this land uncharted in Roman times:

We have another in Verapoli in Malabar; we have a third in Taprobana
or Ceylon, who nourishes on that small island a flock of one hundred
and eighty-three Catholics. Here is the fourth prelate in the French
colony of Pontischery; here is the fifth already decreed in the Mediterranean kingdom of Maduré; here is the sixth in wealthy Madras; the

seventh in populous Calcutta on the Ganges; and finally the eighth on the edge of Tibet.

(393)

It would be unkind to quote much more of this. My main concern is to point out, beyond such rosters of papal personnel, the overall centrifugal impulse of the narrative – the insistent movement *outward* from the center that will lead us as far as China, New Zealand, and even the Sandwich Islands.

"The Roman Church is then truly catholic – that is, universal – and the universe, with all of its lands, islands, and seas, pays homage to the most holy father of Rome . . ." (p. 396). By dramatizing the supranational and "universal" authority of the Church such rhetoric implicitly suppresses the idea of an Italian nation. The roving aerial views systematically *prevent* such an image from coming into focus. By training our eyes toward the ever-widening horizon of Catholic missionary activity, the author strategically blurs objects in the foreground; and by concentrating on a common enemy (the classic epithet of "infidel" now applying to Protestants as well as Moslems and Jews), he blurs any suggestion of dissension at home.

"Per amore di brevità" Mai had passed over the entire Italian peninsula at the outset. He will return to Rome only as from the circumference of a circle to its center – to celebrate the city's role as the base of Catholic missionary operations and seat of the Collegio de Propaganda Fide, which trains missionaries of all nationalities in the Roman art of conquest proclaimed by Virgil's Anchises:

And now within the walls of Rome we see a school and a refuge . . . open to every nation to train its apostles as the conquerors of new peoples and realms for the Vatican. Here the Englishman, the Scot, the German, the Batavian, the Greek, the Illyrian, the Thracian, the Armenian, the Syrian, the Persian, the Egyptian, the Abyssinian, the American, and the Chinese come to learn the Roman art of conquest. Because to the eternal city it was said:

> Tu regere imperio populos, romane, memento;
> haec tibi erunt artes.   [VI, 851–2]

> (Remember, oh Roman, the rulership of nations: these will be your arts.)

The claim that Rome's destiny transcends all local and national politics is sealed by the following peroration, which culminates in a final quotation from Anchises's exhortation to Aeneas:

Then if this is true we indeed have good reason, oh illustrious scholars, to rejoice as we celebrate this anniversary of the foundation . . .
for if the Roman Empire, instead of diminishing after the fall of the
Caesars, on the contrary grew beyond measure under the Pontiffs;
who will not judge more favorably the new state of affairs than the
old? Who will not take greater pleasure in the *pax cristiana* than in the
bloody arms of empire? *Who will not desire the increase of the reign of
virtue, rather than that of politics?* Who finally with every means in his
power will not join in this enterprise of extending the holy pontifical
empire?

> Et dubitamus adhuc virtutem extendere factis?
> (And do we still hesitate, then, to extend our power by our
> deeds?)
>
> (397, emphasis added)

Having confirmed Rome's privileged exemption from national politics
through this extraordinary Virgilian pastiche (three quotes from the *Geor-
gics* appear in the final pages), Mai finally presents in the form of a dénoue-
ment a vision of Italy as a whole. It is a pastoral landscape, an "hortus
conclusus" in perpetual spring, free from conflict and change:

> Verdi pianure e delicati colli
> d'alberi ingombri e di vivaci erbette
> amenissime valli e prati molli,
> ove scherzan tra i fior soave aurette;
> e frutti mille d'ambrosia satolli,
> e bei cipressi, e olive pallidette;
> dove stagnan le fonti, ivi son laghi,
> lucidi specchi ed a vedersi vaghi.

(Green plains and gentle hills laden with trees and lively grasses, gentle
valleys and soft meadows, where tender breezes play among the
flowers; and a thousand fruits bursting with ambrosia, and beautiful
cypresses, and pale olives; where the fountains lie still there are lakes,
shining mirrors which delight in contemplating themselves.)

In the "laghi" of the penultimate line one could maliciously find an
emblem of papal encomiastic discourse itself, narcissistically contemplating
its own image in the literature of Augustan Rome and in the stagnant pools
of its Academies. We must assume that this irony did not occur to Angelo
Mai as he concluded, "Hail then, oh Latium, the delightful refuge [*ricetto*] of
mysterious Saturn and of the archaeologists his sons!"

In reviewing the literature of papal encomium we have encountered a number of genealogical fantasies; but this affiliation with Saturn is particularly striking, for it dramatizes the complicity between archaeology and myth in the larger rhetoric of Restoration Rome. Just as Latium provided a refuge for Saturn from the political intrigues of the gods upon his expulsion from Mount Olympus, Rome continues to serve as a sanctuary (*ricetto*) from the political turmoil of nineteenth-century Europe. The function of papal archaeology, then, is to fortify the city against the vicissitudes of human history – restoring a legendary golden age beyond all historical corruption and trespass.

Like Venus revealing to the bewildered Aeneas the genealogy of the empire that he was to found, Angelo Mai raises on the shoulders of the papal archaeologists the ingenious device he has fashioned in imitation of Virgil. The Saturnian ancestry is his own invention, but the sentiments animating his argument are the same as those we have seen in all the texts in this chapter. In a period that witnessed the rapid disintegration of the ancien régime, these texts continued to advance the claim that the Church's restoration of Rome's ancient monuments might signify a permanent restoration of the temporal power.

4

ARCHAEOLOGY IN BELLI'S ROMAN
SONNETS

O NE OF THE MOST INTRIGUING WITNESSES to the
contradictions of Restoration Rome is the poet Giuseppe Gioacchino Belli. A founding member of the Accademia Tiberina in
1813 (along with Mauro Cappellari, the future Gregory XVI), Belli was in
the front ranks to welcome the return of Pius VII in 1814.[1] Throughout his
life he occupied various posts in the papal bureaucracy, culminating in his
appointment as papal censor in 1850.[2] Yet his verse production in Roman
dialect, largely unpublished during his lifetime, remains the most vivid
critique of papal authority to emerge in the literature of the nineteenth
century.

Belli's lifelong ambivalence toward the papacy is a problem of undeniable
interest to his biographers, but my concern in this chapter is more specific:
to review his satire of papal archaeology in the Roman sonnets of 1831–6.[3]
Written from the point of view of the *popolano,* these poems provide a
useful corrective to the encomiastic literature of the papacy itself, abruptly
deflating its fundamental claims. In a period that witnessed the revival of
antithetical myths of Rome by the Church and its democratic opposition,
these texts remind us of popular distrust of both schools of political rhetoric. One of the limits of the Italian revolution was in fact the exclusion of
the lower classes from the political process of unification; and Belli's poetry
helps us to measure the rift between popular discourse and the ideological
debate of the Risorgimento.

Behind Belli's sonnets lies a long literary tradition satirizing the figure of
the antiquary. Thoroughly to trace this tradition, and to provide a historical
typology of the figure, is impossible here. Larrabee points out that as early
as 1628, with the post-Renaissance vogue of collecting, the antiquary appeared as a character in English satire in Earle's *Micro-cosmografie.*[4] Certainly
with the discovery of Herculaneum and Pompeii and the ensuing *mania
antiquaria,* the antiquary became a favorite target of Italian Settecento satire,
conflating the traditional figures of charlatan, pedant, and buffoon. Two
obvious examples are Goldoni's *La famiglia dell'antiquario* and Verri's prose
sketch "L'antiquario fanatico," intended as the introduction for his *Notti*

romane. Belli himself reworked this stereotype in several of his Italian poems.[5]

What sets the dialect sonnets apart from the tradition of Settecento satire is the representation of this figure from a novel perspective, that of the Roman *popolano*. "I have resolved to leave a monument to the common people [*plebe*] of Rome, as it exists today," Belli explains in his introduction.[6] Yet this monument is antiheroic and resolutely fragmentary in nature. The 2,279 sonnets succeed in random order; Belli's *canzoniere* presents neither development nor synthesis ("Every page is the beginning of the book; every page is its end," he declares, again in the introduction, p. 101).

Rather than a single monolithic image of the Roman *popolano*, Belli provides a shifting and kaleidoscopic view of the range of sentiments and sympathies characteristic of a population long repressed by papal rule but instinctively protective of a status quo to which it had successfully adapted for centuries – and deeply ambivalent toward the glimpses of social and political change afforded by the Napoleonic occupation.

Like his contemporary, the engraver Luigi Rossini,[7] Belli assembles in these sonnets an ambitious range of Roman *vedute* which document archaeological activity in Restoration Rome. The sites and protagonists are familiar – the arches of Titus and Septimius Severus, Trajan's Column and the Capitoline, Fea, Thorwaldsen, and Gregory XVI himself – but the ironic and irreverent perspective is new, and alerts us to the practical limits of the archaeological propaganda of the nineteenth-century papacy.

Of all the sonnets in the series, the most famous is undoubtedly "Papa Grigorio a li scavi" (V, 1744). The poem documents a visit actually made by the Pope to the Forum to resolve a dispute that had arisen between the archaeologists Fea and Nibby and the architect Valadier. Such controversies aroused considerable attention in academic circles; Leopardi, as we have seen in Chapter 3, note 52, refers to them with scorn, and contemporary caricatures show the embattled Fea defending his theses from the assaults of his enemies, who hurl quadrants, compasses, architectural plans, and marble tablets at his dwarflike figure (Fig. 15). In this poem Belli directs his satire at the Pope himself, who upon his arrival at the Forum praises the archaeologists' efforts in a series of remarks as jovial as they are inane:

> "Bene!", diceva er Papa in quer macello
> De li du' scavi de Campo-vaccino:
> "Ber bucio! bella fossa! ber grottino!
> Belli sti serci! tutto quanto bello!"
> E guardate un po' lì quer capitello
> Si mejo lo pò ffà uno scarpellino!

15. Anonymous caricature, "Savage Battle among the Antiquarians of Rome," 1813
(Rome, GCS).

> E guardate un po' qui sto peperino
> Si nun pare una pietra de fornello!"
> E ttratanto ch'er Papa in mezzo a cento
> Archidetti[8] e antiquari de la corte
> Asternava er zu' savio sintimento,
> La turba, mezzo piano e mezzo forte,
> Diceva: "Ah! sto sant'omo ha un gran talento!
> Ah! un Papa de sto tajo è una gran zorte!"

("Nice job!" said the Pope in the middle of that mess where they're
digging up the Campo Vaccino: "Nice hole! nice ditch! nice little cave
you've got here! Nice paving-stones! All of it, very nice! And take a
look at that capital, see if any of our stone-cutters could do better! And
look at this tufa, tell me if it doesn't look just like a stone we'd use in
our ovens!" And while the Pope, surrounded by a hundred architects
and antiquarians of his court, went on making his shrewd observa-
tions, the crowd half whispered and half said aloud, "Ah! This holy
man is really a genius! What luck to have a Pope like this one!")

As Commissioner of Antiquities, Fea gets his share in a pair of sonnets on
the statue of Marcus Aurelius. In "Campidojo" (I, 33), the speaker im-
presses a friend by explaining why the statue is only partially gilded (it will
turn completely gold, he says, at the Last Judgment), and refers to "sor
abbate Fea" as his source. "Er caval de bronzo" pictures Fea himself astride
the horse, demanding its immediate restoration (a job soon completed in
fact by Thorwaldsen):

> Er zor don Carlo Fea, jeri, e nun celio,
>   Ce stava sopra a cianche larghe in groppa,
>   E strillava: "Si qua nun z'arittoppa
>   Se va a ffà buggerà com'un Vangelio."
> L'abbate aveva in mano un negroscopico
>   E sseguitava a urlà ppien de cordojo:
>   "Qua c'è acqua, per dio! questo è ritropico."
> Dice inzomma che l'unica speranza
>   De sarvà Marc'Urelio in Campidojo
>   È er faje una parèntisi a la panza.   (IV, 1694)

(Mr. Carlo Fea [and I'm not kidding] was sitting there yesterday with
his legs spread wide in the saddle, and he was yelling, "If they don't
patch up this horse it'll go all to hell, and that's the God's truth!" The
abbot had a negroscope [microscope] in his hand, and he kept on
bawling, "Goddammit, there's water here! It's got the dropsy!"
That's it – he says the only hope of saving Marcus Aurelius on the
Capitoline is to make a parenthesis in his belly.)

In a third sonnet, "San Pietr'in Carcere," the speaker takes his friend on a
tour of the Mamertine prison. After a garbled account of its history (inevitably attributing the construction of any prison to Nero), he refers his friend
to Fea for further information:

> La mejo cosa che a Campo-Vaccino
>   Se facessi a li tempi de Nerone
>   Fu a ppied'a Campidojo una priggione,
>   Che ttutti ce parlaveno latino.
> Quer logo se chiamava er Mammerdino;
>   E nun credete a me che ssò un cojone,
>   Ma ffatevene fà la spiegazzione
>   Da un certo avocatuccio piccinino.   (III, 873)

(The best thing they built in the Campo Vaccino in Nero's time was a
prison at the foot of the Campidoglio, and everybody spoke Latin

there. They called that place the Mammerdine; and don't take my word for it because I'm a numbskull, but get that funny little lawyer to tell you all about it.)

Belli shows a particular antipathy for Luigi Biondi, who as president of the Pontifical Academy of Archaeology was also engaged in excavations for Maria Cristina of Savoy at her villa, La Rufinella, on the site of ancient Tusculum.[9] Biondi published a number of reports on these excavations; and Belli has his servant give a layman's view of the project:

> L'avocato marchese mi' padrone
>   Dice che a giorni vò stampà in un puscolo
>   Che all'ombra de le cerque de l'Attuscolo
>   Ce spasseggeno Marco e Cicerone.
> Se dà un spropositone ppiù majuscolo
>   Compaggn'a sto su' gran spropositone?
>   Volemo dì er calor de la staggione
>   Che j'abbi fatto dà de vorta ar muscolo?
> Io sò stato co lui pe ppiù d'un mese
>   Fisso a la Rufinella, e, amico caro,
>   Ortr'a ppochi villani e quarch'ingrese,
> Ecco quelli che ciò ssempre incontrati:
>   L'arciprete e la serva, e quer zomaro
>   Der maestro de scòla de Frascati.   (IV, 1421)

(My boss, the lawyer Marchese [Luigi Biondi], says he's going to publish a book any day now saying that Marcus and Cicero are up there in Tuscolo walking around in the shade of the oak trees. Have you ever heard anything more ridiculous? If you ask me, it's the heat that's gone to his head. I was with him for a month straight at the Rufinella and, my friend, except for a few country folks and the odd Englishman I'll tell you the only people I ran into – the priest, the servant-girl, and that ass of a schoolteacher from Frascati.)

To the servant, Marcus and Cicero are two separate people – hallucinations, in any case, which he attributes to the heat. Belli's satire is clearly directed here not only at Biondi but at the entire tradition of sepulchral scholarship that had made a game of resurrecting shades from the ruins of Rome since the publication of Verri's *Notti romane.*

Belli knew the world of the Academies well; and he attacks them specifically in two sonnets of April 1834, both written on the occasion of the anniver-

sary of Rome (a holiday sacred to antiquarian circles, as we have seen from
Mai's oration of 1837). The first, "La compaggnia de Santi-Petti," is staged
as a dialogue between a servant and the owner of a tavern where the "Caccardians" and "Argeologists" are holding a banquet in honor of Rome.
Hearing the commotion, the servant rushes in:

> Mattia! chi bestie ciai nell'osteria
>   Che sse senteno urlà come li cani?
>   – Ciò l'Arcàdichi e Argòlighi, romani,
>   Che un po' ppiaggneno, e un po' ffanno alegria.
>   – E che vò dì Arzigoghili, Mattia?
>   – Vò dì gente che ssa: boni cristiani,
>   Che ssull'arco dell'Arco-de-Pantani
>   Te ce ponno stampà una libbraria.
>   – Ma qui che ce sta a ffà ttutta sta soma
>   De Cacàrdichi o d'antro che je dichi?
>   – Fa una maggnata perch'è nata Roma.
>   – Ahà, ho capito: sò li Santi-Petti,
>   Che ttra loro se gratteno, e l'antichi
>   Li suffragheno a ffuria de fiaschetti.   (III, 1206)

("Mattia! what are these animals you've got in your tavern? you can
hear them howling like dogs!" – "They're the Roman Arcadians and
Argeologists; they spend half their time whining and half living it
up." – "But what does that mean, Arzigogilists, Mattia?" – "It
means: people in the know, good Christian folks who could write a
whole store full of books just on the arch-of-the-Arch-of-Pantani."[10]
– "But what are they doing here, all these Caccardians or whatever
you call them?" – "They're having a banquet, because it's Rome's
birthday." – "Ah, I get it: they're the Santi-Petti: they scratch each
other's backs and pray for the ancient Romans by boozing it up.")

The second sonnet, written only a day later ("La nasscita de Roma"), is
more pointed in its criticism of the empty pageantry of the Academies and
the parasitism of the papal court. A servant of one of the cardinals calls his
fellow servants together to report the scene he witnessed at the Collegio dei
Sabini on the anniversary of Rome:

> Oh Farzacappa, oh Gazzoli, oh Dandini,
>   Vedéssivo li nostri Cardinali
>   Come staveno attenti co l'occhiali
>   A guardà l'improvisi a li Sabbini?
>   E quanno inciafrujorno certi tali

> Quelli lòro ingergacci de latini,
>   Li vedévio a dà ssotto co l'inchini
>   Pe nun fàsse conosce pe stivali?
> E quanno quer povèta scarzacane
>   Strillava *evviva Roma,* eh? come allora
>   S'ammazaveno a sbátteje le mane!
> Pe lòro infatti benedetta l'ora
>   C'è nata Roma a rigalaje un pane
>   Arrubbato a chi ppena e a chi lavora.   (IV, 1208)

(Oh Farzacappa, oh Gazzoli, oh Dandini, you should have seen those Cardinals of ours watching the show up at the Sabini! And when some of those guys got going with their Latin, you should have seen how they bowed and scraped so nobody would take them for imbeciles! And when that blockhead called out "Long live Rome!", did they ever clap till their hands fell off! No wonder – they ought to be glad Rome was born, so they could live off the rest of us who do all the work.)

If the Academies – like the entire political edifice of the Church – are maintained at the expense of the people's labor, this is nowhere more evident than at the Forum itself, where Fea and his colleagues direct the ongoing excavations. In a sonnet of 3 January 1834 ("Er cariolante de la Bonificenza"), Belli offers the unusual perspective of one of the workers employed by the Istituto di Beneficenza, founded by Napoleon's prefect De Tournon and maintained by Consalvi and Pacca after the restoration of Pius VII. Excavations have been ordered to resume at the Capitoline; but, this worker declares, they can go on without him:

> Mo ss'ariscava a Campidojo; e, amico,
>   Già ssò du' vorte o ttre che cianno provo.
>   Ma io, pe pparte mia, poco me movo,
>   Perch'io nun zò ppiù io quanno fatico.
> E lo sapete voi cosa ve dico
>   De tutti sti sfrantumi c'hanno trovo?
>   Che mànneno a ffà fotte er monno novo
>   Pe le cojonerie der monno antico.
> Ve pare un ber procede da cristiani
>   D'empì de ste pietracce oggni cantone
>   Perché addosso ce piscino li cani?
> Inzomma er Zanto-padre è un gran cojone
>   A dà retta a st'arcòggioli romani
>   C'arinegheno Cristo pe Nerone.   (V, 2023)

(They're digging again at the Campidoglio; and my friend, they've already tried it two or three times. But me, I'm not moving – I'm not myself when I have to work. And you know what I tell you about all these ruins they've found? That they're sending this world all to hell for that old rubbish. Does it sound like what a good Christian ought to do? – fill up every corner with old rocks just so dogs can piss on them? If you ask me the Holy Father is an ass to listen to these Roman arcoggolists that give up Christ and go worship Nero.)

The sonnet reminds us of the sheer physical labor required to implement the archaeological politics of the papacy. To the uncomprehending *popolano* this work is particularly demeaning because it is pointless. In his irritation the speaker suggests that archaeology is in fact the work of the devil; and this suspicion was actually widespread among the lower classes in Rome. Since medieval times, pagan statues retrieved from the earth had been believed to possess demonic powers.[11] Dread of such archaeological images only focused a more general fear of the underworld that persisted in Rome well into the nineteenth century. Remembering Hugo's extraordinary description of the sewer system of Paris in *Les misérables* (1862), it is hard not to imagine a comparable fear of Rome's intricate subsoil, laced with catacombs long believed to have been the clandestine refuge as well as the cemetery of Christian martyrs.

In the popular mind, archaeologists were grave-robbers, raiding the sacred precincts of the dead. It was not easy to reconcile a pope's interest in archaeology with this persistent prejudice. Popular fears were confirmed when Gregory XVI's successor, Pius IX, was nearly killed in a bizarre accident at the church of S. Agnese in 1855, as he returned from a visit to the new excavations at the basilica and cemetery of S. Alessandro; as he addressed a group of cardinals assembled in the bapistry, the floor suddenly gave way and he fell through to the foundations. The Pope's miraculous survival was commemorated in a fresco at the site by Domenico Toetti, but to the popular imagination this episode was clearly an omen from the devil, warning the Church to desist from its exploration of the underworld.[12]

Superstition and skepticism alternate in Belli's characters as they reflect on the phenomenon of archaeology. Their reports of papal discoveries are frequently cynical: telling a friend of the excavation of Raphael's tomb at the Pantheon (an event widely discussed in antiquarian circles),[13] Belli's speaker finds the entire operation absurd:

> È una scena, per dio, propio una scena.
> Ma ttutte ar tempo mio s'ha da vedelle!

> Pe quattr'ossacce senza carn'e ppelle
> S'ha da pijà la gente tanta pena!
> E ttutti fanno sta cantasilèna:
> *È lui: nun è: sò quelle: nun zò quelle:*
> *È Raffaele: nun è Raffaelle . . .*
> E ttutt'er giorno la Ritonna è ppiena.
> Certo, nun dibbità, sò casi seri!
>   Come c'a Roma ciamancassin'ossa
>   Tramezz'a un venti o un trenta cimiteri!
> Trovi uno schertro in de la terra smossa?
>   Ebbè, senza de fà ttanti misteri,
>   Aribbuttelo drento in de la fossa.   (III, 983)

(It's a scene, by God, a scene you wouldn't believe. And I have to live to see things like this! For a couple of bones without skin and flesh on them people have to go to all this trouble. And everybody keeps on jabbering, "It's him: no, it's not: these are the bones: no, they're not: it's Raphael: it's not Raphael . . ." and every day the Pantheon is full of them. Don't get me wrong, this is serious business! As if we didn't have enough bones in Rome, with twenty or thirty cemeteries already! So you find a skeleton in the ground? Don't make such a big deal about it – throw it back in the ditch.)

Belli's characters are often shrewd in their assessment of the Pope's political motives in promoting archaeology. The significance of Valadier's reconstruction of the Arch of Titus is not lost on one Gregorio, who tells his friend Gaetano the history of Titus's persecution of the Jews as they stand together admiring the arch ("Campo Vaccino III," I, 27). Titus humiliated the Jews, Gregorio explains, by forcing them to walk through the arch, which commemorated the destruction of Jerusalem: but Roman Jews today, "prima de passace sotto, / Se farìano ferrà dar maniscarco" (before walking under it, would sooner be shod by the blacksmith; lines 13–14).[14]

Quick to recognize the political malice of the Pope in restoring this symbol so offensive to the Jews, Belli's characters are more naïve in their remarks on the Vatican museums. Impressed by the colossal scale of the Pope's sculpture collection, one character compares it favorably to the Christmas fair of crèche figures at the Piazza Sant'Eustachio. Urged by his friend, a Swiss guard, to visit the museum on one of the days when it is open to the public, he returns with this enthusiastic report:

> Ah! quer Museo è un gran ber gruppo, cacchio!
> Quante filare de pupazzi in piede!
> Antro che li casotti a Ssant'Ustacchio!
>
>   ("Er museo," IV, 1381)

(Oh! that museum is one hell of a lineup: all those dolls up there, standing in a row! It makes S. Eustachio look like peanuts!)

This speaker's naïve admiration for the antiquities is shared by many of the characters in Belli's sonnets. Despite their distrust of the "arzigolighi" and professed indifference to archaeological speculation, Belli's *popolani* inevitably share their fascination for all that is Roman, and their impulse to account for both the prodigies and flaws in its landscape. Throughout the sonnets they rehearse an unwitting parody of the papal archaeologists – taking turns playing *cicerone*, improvising explanations for puzzling iconography, trading tireless harangues on the antiquities. "Guarda, Ghitano mia: eh? di', te piace?" demands Gregorio, in the first of the four-part sonnet series documenting their tour of the Campo Vaccino (to conclude at the Arch of Titus, above). Together they admire the Basilica of Maxentius, awesome if only as a heap of masonry:

> Nun fuss'antro la carcia! – Buggiarona!
> E li mattoni? Sai quante fornace! (I, 25)

(Just the lime would be a job! – You're not kidding! And the bricks! – think of all those ovens!)

Dodging Gaetano's question as to who inhabited the temple ("Eh! tanta gente: e ttutti ricchi sai?"), Gregorio adds that "before the Turks came along" the temple was even bigger, stretching all the way to the Capitoline. Moving on to the three columns of Castor and Pollux that dominate all views of the Forum, in a fantastic, quasi-oneiric reconstruction of the imperial city he explains that these three columns are all that remain of the three-hundred-column bridge of Caligula, which once extended from the Colosseum to the Campidoglio.

In their role as *cicerone*, Belli's characters invent a number of ingenious theories about the monuments and ruins of Rome. Often these ideas are based on folk etymologies; a character in "Li battesimi de l'anticaje" (IV, 1286) objects to the name "Teatro di Marcello" recently affixed to a structure he confidently recognizes as a "Culiseo" ("Sti cosi tonni com'er culo, a Roma / Se sò ssempre chiamati Culisei"). Another character, lecturing a companion on the proper pronunciation of "Colonna Trojana," insists that the name shows the column was brought from Troy: to call it anything else (his friend had pronounced it "Trogliana") is a violation of all common sense:

> Ebbè, si viè da *Troja* sta colonna,
> S'ha da dì, si tte piaceno li fichi,

> *Trojana,* pe l'amor de la Madonna!
> Ché a chiamalla sinnò come tu dichi,
> Sarebbe com'a dì che nun è ttonna,
> E volenne sapé ppiù de l'antichi.   (I, 196)

(So listen – if this column comes from *Troy,* if you don't mind, you have to call it *Trojan,* for God's sake! To call it anything else, like you're doing, is like saying that it's not round, and that you're smarter than the ancient Romans.)

Such a "dialogo tra sordi" is a fine parody of the degraded forms of archaeological debate that Belli surely had witnessed at the papal court. A similarly futile conversation, in "La Dogana de Terra a Piazza-de-Pietra," goes on for thirty-eight lines (I, 199). In "La salara de l'antichi" one character goes so far as to speculate, on the basis of a confusion between "il sale" and "le sale" (the Sette Sale of Titus, as Belli explains in a note), that a cistern at that site, currently used for storing salt, probably doubled as a warehouse of tobacco for the ancient Romans (I, 150); for both were controlled by the same monopoly in papal Rome.

Roman pride in the antiquities is allied with anti-French polemic in the sonnet "Roma Capomunni." Conducting a French visitor on a tour of the monuments of Rome, the speaker boasts that archaeology was a thriving industry in Rome until the French invaded and occupied the city:

> Nun fuss'antro pe ttante antichità
> Bisognerebbe nasce tutti qui,
> Perché a la robba che ciavemo qua
> C'è, sor friccica mio, poco da dì.
> Te giri, e vedi buggere de lì:
> Te svorti, e vedi buggere de là:
> E a vive l'anni che campò un zocchì
> Nun ze n'arriva a vede la mità.
> Sto paese, da sì che sse creò,
> Poteva fà cor monno a ttu pper tu,
> Sin che nun venne er general Cacò.
> Ecchevel'er motivo, sor Monzù,
> Che Roma ha perzo l'erre, e che pperò
> De st'anticaje nun ne pò ffà ppiù.   (I, 157)

(If only for all the old monuments everybody should have the luck to be born here, because there's not much you can find anyplace, my

friend, to top what we've got here. Everywhere you look you see the
stuff: turn around, and you see it again: and even if you lived to be as
old as who-knows-who, you'd never get to see half of it. From the
day they founded it, this town didn't have to look up to any other
town in the world – that is, until General Cacò came along. That's
why, Monsieur, Rome has gone downhill [lost its "R"] and just can't
make these old monuments any more.)

The conclusion implies a notion that is elsewhere made explicit – that the
"anticaje" are actually manufactured by the Pope to exploit a rich international market. One character cashes in on the profits himself; in the sonnet
"L'innustria" he brags to a friend:

> Un giorno che arrestai propio a la fetta,
>   Senz'avé manco l'arma d'un quadrino,
>   Senti che cosa fo: curro ar cammino
>   E roppo in quattro pezzi la paletta.
> Poi me l'invorto sott'a la giacchetta,
>   E vado a spasso pe Campovaccino
>   A aspettà quarche ingrese milordino
>   Da daje una corcata co l'accetta.
> De fatti, ecco che viè quer c'aspettavo.
>   "Siggnore, guardi un po' quest'anticaja
>   C'avemo trovo jeri in de lo scavo?"
> Lui se ficca l'occhiali, la scannaja,
>   Me mette in mano un scudo, e dice: "Bravo!"
>   E accusì a Roma se pela la quaja.   (II, 623)

(One day when I was really broke, not a cent in my pocket, listen
what I did: I run to the fireplace and break the shovel. Then I wrap it
up in my jacket and go for a stroll in the Campo Vaccino to look for
some sissy little Englishman and play him a trick. Sure enough, here
he comes along, just like I thought: "Signore," I say, "have a look at
this antiquity we found yesterday at the excavation." He puts on his
glasses, looks it over, gives me a scudo, and says, "Good work!" And
that's how a man gets ahead here in Rome.)

But the cynical hypothesis of the "finte antichità" masks a genuine ontological perplexity regarding the origin and function of the ruins themselves. "Subbito che nun zò ssane né ttonne / e doverebbeno èsse tonne e
ssane, / c'era bisoggno qua de la colonne?" Nino asks, pointing out the
twelve crumbling columns in the façade of the Dogana (I, 199). Another
character, guardedly identifying "L'arco de Campovaccino, quello in qua"

as "l'arco de Sittimio s'è vero" ("ché pò èsse che ssii 'na buggiarata"), concludes in obvious exasperation:

> Oh vedi che crapiccio de penziero,
>   Vedi si ch'idea matta sconzagrata,
> De nun annallo a ffrabbicallo intiero,
>   Ma co una parte mezza sotterrata!   (I, 151)

(Just look what an asinine idea this is, what a damned screwy thing not to build it in one piece, but with half of it buried underground!)

Living in a city whose ruins represent two millennia of historical change, Belli's characters have no conception of history. For them the city of Rome has always existed in its present form (Campidoglio, Vatican, Piazza del Popolo, and all) since the day it was built by Romulus and Remus:

> Chi ha ffrabbicato Roma, er Vaticano,
>   Er Campidojo, er Popolo, er Castello?
> Furno Romolo e Remolo, Marcello,
>   Che gnisun de li dua era romano . . .
> Di li sfrìzzoli oggnuno ebbe li sui:
>   E Roma, quelli dua la liticorno,
> Ma venne er Papa e sse la prese lui.   (III, 1002)

(Who built Rome, the Vatican, the Campidoglio, Piazza del Popolo, the Castel Sant'Angelo? It was Romulus and Remus, Marcello – and neither of them was a Roman . . . They both got their share of bruises too, and those two guys fought it out to see who would get Rome – but the Pope came along and took it himself.)

This comically foreshortened view of Roman history caricatures the basic papal claim of the continuity of the "two Romes." For Belli's *popolano,* classical and Christian Rome are not merely complementary; they are quite literally identical, and merge into that single, spontaneous, and phantasmagoric vision of the city which alone responds to his direct experience. The very idea of a distinction between ancient and modern Rome is ludicrous to Belli's Romans: with characteristic emphasis, one rejects the idea:

> Rom'antich'e moderna! Oh quest'è bella!
> Mo adesso Roma s'è ffatt'un'amica!
> Ma ss'una è questa qua, l'antra indov'ella?
> Bravi! Roma moderna, e Rom'antica!

Sarebbe com'a dì: "Vostra sorella
Lo pija ne la freggna e ne la fica." (III, 1107)

(Ancient and modern Rome! Oh, that's a good one! So now Rome has
made itself a friend! But if one of them is this one here, where's the
other? Very smart! Modern and ancient Rome! That's like saying,
"Stick it to your sister – and screw her while you're at it.")

Small wonder that the archaeologists find so little sympathy in Belli's
world: the very premises of their activity are absurd. Belli's characters are
hostile toward any show of erudition; one character, annoyed by rumors
that he is a "know-it-all," insists that he is as ignorant as the next man, and
proud of it too:

Che cosa m'ho da intenne io si er Messia
È nato prima o doppo de Maometto,
Oppuro de Mosè? Vadino in Ghetto,
A ffà ste ciarle: vadino in Turchia.
Sò impicci da sbrojà doppo tant'anni?
L'omo nun pò ssapè che quer c'ha visto:
Ma eh? nun dico bene, sor Giuvanni?
Prima o doppo, chi vòi che je n'importi?
Basta, o Mosè, o Maometto, o Gesucristo,
Quello ch'è certo è che ssò ttutti morti. (III, 1006)

(What do I know if the Messiah was born before or after Mohammed,
or Moses, for that matter? Go to the Ghetto if you want to waste your
breath that way – go to Turkey. Is that stuff to be worrying about
after all these years? A man can only know what he sees with his own
eyes: Am I right, sor Giovanni? Earlier or later, what do I care? It
doesn't matter if it's Moses, or Mohammed, or Jesus Christ – the one
thing that's certain is that they're all dead.)

The same sentiments are echoed by another character, who interrupts his
companion's long-winded account of "L'istoria romana" by saying:

Che me ne preme un cazzo de l'istoria:
A me me piace de vive a la broccola . . .
Bast'a ssapé c'oggni donna è pputtana,
E l'ommini una manica de ladri,
Ecco imparata l'istoria romana. (III, 880)

III

(I don't give a Goddamn about history myself: I just like to live my own life as I see it . . . All you need to know is that every woman is a whore, and that men are all just a gang of thieves – and there! you've learned all there is to know about Roman history.)

Belli achieves some of his most comic effects by exploiting his characters' tendency to anachronism. In the sequence of sonnets devoted to the Old Testament, his characters constantly interpolate familiar Roman landmarks into their accounts of the Biblical stories. God orders Noah to build an ark "like the ferry at the Port of Ripetta" and warns that the flood he is preparing "will make the waterfall at Tivoli look like piss in a urinal" ("Er diluvio univerzale," III, 900). Before God destroys Sodom, the angel warns Lot and his wife to run "all the way down the [Via] Lungara without ever looking back at the Hospital [of Santo Spirito]" ("Sara de Lotte," I, 331).

Rome is ubiquitous and universal; Belli's *plebe* can conceive of no other point of reference. Asking a friend about his travels to Paris (which he imagines to be in Spain), one character demands, "Chi Papa c'è?" (Who have they got as Pope?) and "Giri pe Roma là tutta la robba?" (I, 273). In this comic inversion of the antonomasia traditionally identifying Rome as *l'Urbe*, "Rome" becomes a name inevitably applicable, by extension, to any city. In Belli's world, Paris can exist only as "Roma là."

Belli's characters were evidently not readers of Byron; but Belli does not miss the chance to parody the Byronic posture toward Rome in his "Rifressione immorale [sic] sur Culiseo." Just as he had ridiculed the literature of the papal academies in "La nasscita de Roma" and "La compaggnia de Santi-Petti," he pokes fun at the romantics in this mock elegy staged in the Colosseum:

> St'arcate rotte c'oggi li pittori
>   Viengheno a diseggnà co li pennelli,
>   Tra l'arberetti, le croce, li fiori,
>   Le farfalle e li canti de l'ucelli,
> A ttempo de l'antichi imperatori
>   Ereno un fiteatro, indove quelli
>   Curreveno a vedé li gradiatori
>   Sfracassasse le coste e li cervelli.
> Qua loro se pijaveno piacere
>   De sentì l'urli de tanti cristiani
>   Carpestetati e sbranati da le fiere.
> Allora tante stragge e ttanto lutto,

E adesso tanta pace! Oh avventi umani!
Cos'e stò monno! Come cammia tutto!   (IV, 1588)

(These broken arches, that the painters come to draw today with their
paintbrushes among the shrubs, the crosses, flowers, butterflies, and
songs of birds, at the time of the ancient emperors formed an amphi-
theater, where they ran to see the gladiators smash their ribs and
skulls. They had a good time too, listening to the Christians yell as
they were trampled and torn to pieces by the wild beasts. Such violence then, all that grief, and such peace today! Oh human events!
What a world! How things change!)

The elevated statements of elegiac poetry are subverted by their trans-
position into Roman dialect. Already in the title the dialect works to under-
mine the pretenses of the genre, refracting its philosophical "refrections" in
comically garbled form. Such ruin-sentiment, Belli implies, resists translation into *romanesco* because it is alien to the nature of the Romans themselves; a far more authentic response on their part to the spectacle of ruin is
the pragmatic suggestion made in another sonnet on the Colosseum:

Co' un po' de sassi e un po' de carcia e gesso,
Lassa che je se dii quarche arittoppo
e un'imbiancata, e pò servì anch'adesso.   (I, 145)

(With a few more stones and a bit of lime and plaster, give it a patch-
up and a paint job and you can still get some use out of it.)

The Colosseum was turned to unexpected use in 1849 as a tribune for the
orators of the Roman Republic. Given the radical anticlericalism of the
sonnets, one might have expected Belli to sympathize; but Belli was no
friend of the democrats – least of all in the final years of his life, when his
reactionary politics embarrassed even the restored Pius IX. Mazzini admired Belli's sonnets, but the poet did not return the favor; among his
poems in Italian composed for the Pope's reinstatement after the fall of the
Republic was a sonnet ("Al Signor Giuseppe Mazzini") pledging the undy-
ing loyalty of the Roman *plebe* to their Pope.[15]
    The Roman sonnets in fact were profoundly subversive; and perhaps no
one was more alarmed by their implications than Belli himself. Although
Belli ordered that the dialect sonnets be destroyed at his death, they survive
as an eloquent and paradoxical critique of the authority of the nineteenth-
century papacy. Divided between his deeply conservative alligiance and the
revolutionary insights of his dialect poetry, Belli occupies a central position

in this book; for he embodies the very contradiction we have witnessed between papal and secular uses of archaeology in the nineteenth century. As a civiliarn officer in the papal court he underwrites the rhetoric of the Restoration papacy; but his dialect poetry exposes the very power he is serving, and points toward the radical discourse of the Risorgimento.

PART II

RISORGIMENTO ARCHAEOLOGY: THE EXHORTATORY MODE

5

DEI SEPOLCRI AND THE DEMOCRATIC TRADITION

P ROBABLY NO SINGLE TEXT did more to adapt the archae-ological metaphor to the service of Italian nationalism than Foscolo's *Dei Sepolcri* of 1807. Conceived as a protest against Napoleon's ex-tension of the Edict of St.-Cloud to the Italian Cisalpine state,[1] the poem began as a meditation on tombs and their function in every community as a means of cultural and political survival; but transcending its immediate polemical purpose, the poem freely modulated from contemporary Milan to the tombs of Renaissance heroes in Florence's Saint Croce and through an archaeological voyage in the Aegean to the graves of ancient Greece and the still buried site of the city of Troy (to be excavated by Schliemann a half-century later).[2]

Later the character in his own novel, Jacopo Ortis, significantly denied a passport to Rome,[3] Foscolo elides in this poem any reference to the city. Still stigmatized in many Italian democratic circles as the seat of the papacy and more recently associated with Napoleonic imperialism, Rome was an emblem not widely trusted in the early years of the Risorgimento. Leopar-di's own patriotic canzone "All'Italia" (1818), conceived in imitation of Foscolo, similarly elided all reference to Rome, projecting the reader into a philological fantasy of Greece in its exhortation to resurrect the ruined landscape of Italy.[4] As the following chapter will show, it was largely due to the efforts of Mazzini and Gioberti that Rome moved into the foreground of Italian nationalist discourse by the mid-nineteenth century, displacing the rival iconographies of Florence and Greece. But Foscolo's poem served to establish the decisive precedent of politicizing Italy's monuments as icons of the Risorgimento movement – symbolic "props" and images to aid the rediscovery of a national identity without which political unity would be meaningless.

By challenging an elegiac tradition of representation – the sepulchral poetry of Hervey, Young, and Gray – and investing its object with a new political significance, Foscolo contributed to the larger project of reclaiming the Italian landscape from the tyranny of the picturesque. At the same time his poem suggested that the surest way to reinvent a political idiom in contemporary poetry was through the archaeological appeal to Italian origins – a lesson that proved central to the cultural politics of the Risorgimento.

——— ——

Foscolo's poem provoked sharp debate among contemporary readers; criticized for its apparent lack of unity, it was nonetheless appreciated and widely distributed, surpassing even the historical novel in the number of copies sold.[5] Bettoni, Foscolo's publisher, capitalized on its success by issuing a series of iconographical catalogues directly inspired by the Santa Croce section of the poem: *Vite e ritratti di illustri italiani,* begun in 1812 in Padova and completed in Milan in 1820; *Vite e ritratti di cento uomini illustri,* Padova, 1815; *Ritratti di illustri italiani viventi,* Padova, 1815; *Le Tombe ed i Monumenti illustri d'Italia descritti e delineati con tavole in rame,* Milan, 1822; *Cento ritratti di illustri italiani,* Milan, 1825; *Pantheon italiano con tavole in rame e con vite scritte dal Professore Arici,* Milan, 1827.[6] Such catalogues, offered at low cost on a subscription basis, propagated the images of the Italian heroes and monuments celebrated in Foscolo's poem by exploiting the new techniques of mechanical reproduction that had already revolutionized archaeological illustration in the early nineteenth century. To a bourgeois public unable to afford either the sumptuously engraved catalogues of the Pio-Clementine era or the gallery paintings and *capricci* of a Pannini or Piranesi, these volumes made accessible a gallery of Italian portraits and images that would assume increasing political significance in the decades to come.

Foscolo's considerations on the nature and function of tombs were in no way original or distinctively Italian; though they appeal to Vico's theory of history, they reflect even more closely the contemporary debate in France. As Lionello Sozzi has pointed out, at least thirty separate publications during the years of the Directory (1795–9) and the Consulate (1799–1804) addressed the problem of tombs in terms closely resembling Foscolo's own.[7] Certainly Foscolo must have been influenced by the work of Volney.[8] But the context that Foscolo explicitly invokes in his poem is the tradition of English sepulchral poetry represented by Hervey, Young, and Gray. Both the covert references to Gray's "Elegy" that frame the opening section of the *Sepolcri* and the overt criticism of Gray made in Foscolo's famous "Letter to Monsieur Guillon" clarify Foscolo's intention to inaugurate a modern school of political poetry by inverting the premises of the sepulchral tradition. In revisiting the tombs of Santa Croce and Marathon, he invites readers not to melancholy reflection but to vigorous emulation of the deeds of their ancestors: "A egregie cose il forte animo accendono / L'urne de' forti" (to mighty deeds the tombs of the great move great souls).[9]

"All'ombra de' cipressi e dentro l'urne / Confortate di pianto è forse il sonno / Della morte men duro?" the poem begins (in the shadow of cypresses and within the urns comforted by tears is the sleep of death perhaps any softer?). Editors acknowledge the echo of Gray's "Elegy" ("Can storied urn or animated bust / Back to its mansions call the fleeting breath?"),[10] but the irony implicit in Foscolo's reference to Gray becomes clear only when we examine the intricate argument that follows.

The rhetorical function of the question ("Can storied urn . . . ?") in the "Elegy" is to assert the legitimacy of a poetry devoted to a humble milieu ("the short and simple annals of the poor"), by *denying* the privileged status of an heroic idiom serving the wealthy and powerful:

> The boast of heraldry, the pomp of power,
> And all that beauty, all that wealth e'er gave,
> Await alike the inevitable hour.
> The paths of glory lead but to the grave.
>
> Nor you, ye Proud, impute to these the fault,
> If memory o'er their tomb no trophies raise,
> When through the long-drawn aisle and fretted vault
> The pealing anthem swells the note of praise.

$$(33-40)$$

In this lofty Gothic cathedral, rejected by Gray as both a figure and setting for his poetry, the reader recognizes Foscolo's Santa Croce, celebrated at the center of the *Sepolcri* and traversed there in solemn procession; as each station of a civic *via crucis* is revisited, the "pealing anthem" of Foscolo's Latinate and erudite verse "swells the note of praise."

In the *Sepolcri,* then, the question ("All'ombra de' cipressi e dentro l'urno . . . ?") serves an entirely different rhetorical function from that in Gray's text. By introducing a discussion of the objective futility of tombs (which passes from the double interrogative of lines 1–3 and 3–15 to the declarative "conclusion" of lines 16–22), it generates a radically pessimistic proposition ("Vero è ben, Pindemonte! anche la Speme, Ultima Dea, fugge i sepolcri . . ."), which it becomes the business of the poem to refute. The heroic scale of the poet's eventual claims for the subjective value of tomb worship to the community is dialectically implicit in the apparently ineluctable pessimism of its premise. In both poems, then, the question is part of a complex argumentative strategy; but the "Elegy" argues in praise of obscurity, whereas the *Sepolcri* defends the praise of famous men.

Thematically, of course, neither of these arguments is new. In fact, the "Elegy" and *Sepolcri* might be said to represent two ancient and perennially opposed literary genres: the pastoral "retirement poem" and the militant *poema civile* (which is in turn a structural descendant of the exhortatory oration, the classical *genus deliberativum*). Gray's idealization of the secluded rural life, "far from the madding crowd's ignoble strife," is a topos of the pastoral tradition – as are the praise of a life close to nature and conforming to its rhythms (lines 16–20),[11] description of the joys of family life (21–4),[12] and the praise of manual labor (25–8).[13]

The regret for talents undiscovered (45–8)[14] and beauties unrevealed (53–6)[15] is countered by gratitude for the freedom from corruption in a community both deprived and protected by its "destiny obscure" (65–9).[16] The communal ideal of the golden mean displaces the cult of individual distinction; and fear of the corruption inherent in public, political life leads the poet to idealize a sheltering prospect of anonymity ("Along the cool sequestered vale of life / They kept the noiseless tenor of their way," 75–6).

Foscolo's challenge to this ideological position is immediately clear. The *sepolcri* thematized in his poem are those of famous men, who have made unique contributions to literature (Dante, Petrarch, Alfieri), science (Galileo), art (Michelangelo), political theory (Machiavelli), and warfare (the Greeks at the Battle of Marathon, Achilles, Ajax, Hector). Hence the importance in his text of proper names, which occur in Gray's poem only to signify an absence, a destiny unfulfilled: "Some mute inglorious Milton here may rest, / Some Cromwell guiltless of his country's blood," (59–60).

"Me ad evocar gli eroi chiamin le Muse" (228), writes Foscolo, urged on by his own poetic ambition, his "desio d'onore." Furthermore, the function of the *sepolcri* themselves is to generate emulation of the heroic acts they commemorate, just as the contemplation of one tomb (for example, that of Michelangelo, "che nuovo Olimpo / alzò in Roma a' Celesti") seems within the text to generate analogically the vision of another (that of Galileo, "chi vide / sotto l'etereo padiglion rotarsi / più mondi, e il sole irradiarli immoto"), and still another ("onde all'Anglo che tanta ala vi stese / sgombrò primo le vie del firmamento," i.e., Newton, born in the year of Galileo's death).

Foscolo's appeal to individual heroism is motivated by an immediate political concern: "Pur nuova legge impone oggi i sepolcri / Fuor de' guardi pietosi, e il nome a' morti / Contende" (yet a new law bans tombs from the eyes of mourners, and denies the dead their name, 51–2). To those who might respond to his exhortation he implies the reward of posthumous fame: "A' generosi / Giusta di glorie dispensiera è Morte" (to brave spirits Death gives their due portion of glory, 220–1). All these themes place the *Sepolcri* squarely in the tradition of the Italian *poesia civile* most conspicuously inaugurated by Petrarch's canzone 128, "Italia mia." Foscolo's text represents a concrete attempt to emulate Petrarch's achievement – to inaugurate a modern school of political poetry by uniting Petrarch's own legacy with modern tradition polemically revised.

Foscolo rejects Gray's characterization of the role of the poet in society as well as the symbolic valence of the central image of his text (Foscolo's *sepolcri* are portrayed as continually generating life rather than elegiac meditations on death). For the figure of the poet in the "Elegy" stands in an ambivalent and curiously passive relationship to the society that he portrays; he is a sympathetic observer but necessarily, and somewhat complacently, *apart*. Foscolo too characterizes himself as an exile; this is a major autobiographical theme in all his writings.[17] But at the time of writing the *Sepolcri* he considers his exile a rational political choice which will enable him to represent the Italian people more effectively and which will therefore be compensated by posthumous fame – and an epitaph clearly writ in marble.

Gray's poet, however, in fantasizing his own death and final, peaceful absorption into the community he has described (with the actual moment of his death gracefully elided and observed by no one), reveals that a vital "difference" remains: both in the perceptions of the "hoary-headed swain" who tells his story to the passerby, and in the words of his own epitaph: "And Melancholy marked him for her own."

The implication is that the poet can never be fully integrated into the community, in life or in death. He leads a marginal, strange, and solitary life, "muttering his wayward fancies" on his "customed hill."

The opening movement of Foscolo's poem concludes, as mentioned earlier, with a second direct intertextual reference to the "Elegy": "Nè passeggier solingo oda il sospiro / Che dal tumulo a noi manda Natura" (49–50; cf. Gray's "Ev'n from the tomb the voice of Nature cries," 91). This citation itself has a complicated genealogy within Foscolo's earlier work. As editors point out, an Italian version of the phrase appears in the *Ultime lettere di Jacopo Ortis* ("Geme la Natura perfin nella tomba . . .").[18] A Latin version, taken from Costa's translation of the "Elegy," enjoys the strategic position of epigraph in that text: "Naturae clamat ab ipso / vox tumulo."

In the various metamorphoses of Gray's phrase we note its slight alteration in lines 49–50 of the *Sepolcri,* where "sospiro" is substituted for the English "cries," the Italian verb "gemere," and the Latin verb "clamare."

The effect of this substitution is clearly ironic. As he prepares to move from the general philosophical meditation of the first section (lines 1–50) – which deals mainly with the private, subjective needs of individuals and does not yet substantially question Gray's orientation – to the body of his political argument, introduced by the references to the Edict of St.-Cloud, Foscolo takes leave of Gray's text with one slightly sentimental look back (cf. Gray's own "lingering look behind" of line 88). His "sospiro" attenuates the one truly fervent moment in the "Elegy" ("Ev'n in our ashes live their wonted fires"), and reserves for his own poetic climax of line 283 the expressive violence of the verb "gemere": "Gemeranno gli antri / Secreti, e tutta narrerà la tomba." It is not the voice of an unspecified "Nature" that interests Foscolo but the historical narrative of a fallen nation that has again been found.

Foscolo defends his project of policitizing the sepulchral tradition in the famous "Letter to Monsieur Guillon," written in response to an attack on the poem by a French reviewer in the *Giornale italiano*.[19] Before examining Foscolo's response it is worth considering the charges made by Guillon. The French reviewer, in any case an unsympathetic reader of Foscolo, is particularly critical of the second half of the poem (lines 151–end), which passes from Santa Croce to the plains of Troy in a series of rapid and even baffling transitions. Guillon gives this summary of the poem's abruptly shifting plot:

> [First] we find [the poet] in that Florentine cathedral which contains the tombs of N. Machiavelli, Michelangelo, Galileo, etc. And the urn of Alfieri receives his most tender and respectful homage. Then, suddenly, he retreats to the sepulchers of the Athenians on the battlefield of Marathon . . . Retreating ever more rapidly, he moves into the mythical ages of Greece. He visits the tombs of Achilles and Patroclus; then moves on to that of Ajax on the Rhetian promontory; then to the plains of Troy and the tomb of Ilus, the descendant of Dardanus. Young, Hervey, and Gray never traveled so far; they were satisfied to meditate on the tombs which they and their countrymen found close at hand: and their words were more eloquent, and far more consoling, for all their poems are sustained by the hope of that future resurrection to which Signor Foscolo never refers.
>
> (507)

Guillon's paraphrase comes to rest on a highly serious point: the accusation of paganism. This was of course a standard charge in the ongoing polemic against literary classicisms; but it betrays particular anxiety here, since the critic correctly perceives that the only "resurrection" in which Foscolo has faith is the political resurrection of Italy.

Hence the "voyage" metaphor, derived from the literal voyage mapped out in the text (an itinerary which is in fact difficult even for sympathetic readers to follow). For Guillon the voyage signifies poetic and ideological deviance; it is literally a departure from acceptable precedent and a violation of the boundaries clearly set up by a Christian and elegiac tradition. Guillon's repeated complaints about useless "erudition" and complicated itineraries through the Aegean mask a real fear of Foscolo's ideological trespass.

What is most interesting in Foscolo's response to this charge is his emphasis on the theme of the voyage:

> If one is to find fault with the means of a book one must first understand its end. Young and Hervey meditated on sepulchers as Christians: the object of their books is resignation in the face of death and the reassurance of another life: Protestant preachers, therefore, were content to reflect on Protestant tombs. Gray wrote as a philosopher: the object of his elegy is to persuade us of the obscurity of life and tranquillity of death; hence he is satisfied with a country churchyard. The author [Foscolo himself] considers sepulchers politically; and intends to animate the political emulation of Italians with the examples of nations who honor the memory and sepulchers of great men: therefore he has had to *travel farther than Young, Hervey, and Gray,* and preach not the resurrection of bodies but that of virtues.
>
> (518, emphasis in original)

Clearly the poet's italics are significant.[20] Foscolo's strategy here is that of the *décadent* who defiantly adopts the language of his critics, converting a term of opprobrium into a positive metaphor of his own activity.[21] For Guillon the voyage had signified moral digression, aberration, error, and trespass; it compromised the poem's unity; it was a departure from acceptable precedent, a wandering away from the center.

Yet in the act of clarifying the political intent of the poem – surely the crux of his defense of the *Sepolcri* – Foscolo meets and accepts the metaphor of the voyage, not as an image of evasion or digression but as necessary *exile* and *search* for a political poetry adequate to Italy's historical circumstances. The new law literally made obsolete the privileged, central spaces in which communities had honored their dead and preserved continuity with the past – spaces out of which a vatic poet might speak. Neither the village *camposanto* nor the cathedral, its urban equivalent, was to be allowed to retain its function as civil shrine and burial ground. With this decree it seemed that Italy's humiliation was complete. The dispersion of bodies in unmarked communal graves reflected Italy's own geographic and political dismemberment, its loss of an identity and a name. A writer could no longer remain at home; he must risk a voyage, ranging far in search of exemplary historical and mythical sites long consecrated to a community and guarded with the filial *pietas* that Italy had forgotten.

It is thus that Foscolo's search for *sepolcri* becomes archaeological. In imaginative response to the real constraints of contemporary Italy, the "fugitive" poet reaches back into a heroic and mythical past hoping to demonstrate its essential truth. If the setting of the poem shifts rapidly, it is because the moral basis on which Italy rests is itself continually shifting, and the poet must look farther to find a stable and secure ground for his poem, a plot of "pious earth" once designated as sacred, long cultivated as a shrine, and now perhaps overgrown.

Commentators generally note that Foscolo's account of the origin and function of tombs as a social institution ("Dal dì che nozze e tribunali ed are . . . ," lines 91–103) is derived from Vico's *Scienza nuova*. The reader is reminded of Vico's theory of *corsi e ricorsi* in human history by Foscolo's suggestion of the periodic rediscovery of "lost" civilizations – which is in part inevitable and wholly fortuitous, predestined yet disbelieved (as illustrated by the archaeological fantasy of Homer's discovery of Troy, which Foscolo not accidentally attributes in the poem to Cassandra), and in part a measure of human perspicacity rather than blindness – a reward for deliberate exploration and research.

Troy surfaces significantly in the poem as the primary archaeological scene, continually and ritually rediscovered: "E oggi nella Troade inseminata / Eterno splende a' peregrin un loco" (and even today in Troy's sterile plain a site shines forth to travelers forever, 235–6). The reference, as Foscolo's own notes show, is to Lechevalier's recent expedition to Troy.[22] Foscolo not only credits Lechevalier's claim to have identified the ruins of the tomb of Ilus, legendary ancestor of the Trojans, but celebrates this discovery with great ceremony in his poem, finally staging his own rhetorical climax on that same multilayered and historically overdetermined site.

As the final Homeric fantasy shows, if Troy is the primary scene of archaeology, it is at the same time the primary scene of poetry itself; and specifically, of the heroic, political poetry that Foscolo wishes to write. The metaphor of archaeology provides access to heroic argument unavailable in a contemporary context; at the same time it concretely *represents* the search for that political content, distant, submerged, and hidden from public view.

Thus the archaeological itinerary of the second half of the poem is fully justified, in Foscolo's view, by the political constraints to which he is subjected. The poet's departure from Santa Croce marks the beginning of an exile that is itself a quest for a poetic idiom adequate to its historical context.

Before leaving Santa Croce to retrace that voyage, several remarks on Foscolo's representation of Florence may help clarify the function of that site in the poem. In contrast to the "bello italo regno" of Napoleon's Milan, Santa Croce appears a welcome and sanctified enclosure. It preserves the tombs of Italian heroes from violation by the invaders who have despoiled Italy of all but its memories:

> Ma più beata [Firenze] che in un tempio accolte
> Serbi l'itale glorie, uniche forse,
> Dacchè le mal vietate Alpi e l'alterna

Onnipotenza delle umane sorti
Armi e sostanze t'invadeano ed are
E patria, e, tranne la memoria, tutto.   (180–5)

(But even more blessed art thou, Florence, for preserving together in one temple the Italian trophies – perhaps the only ones left to us, since the ill-defended Alps and the vicissitudes of human fate robbed you of arms and possessions, altars and homeland, and everything save memory alone.)

Yet even Santa Croce is vulnerable to trespass, as we are reminded in the celebrated passage from *Ortis* that is recalled by this reference to the "mal vietate Alpi." In that passage, which began as a topographical "prospect" sketch from a vantage point among the "mal vietate Alpi" themselves, Jacopo Ortis imagined Italy's own worst political prospects in a fantasy of the violation of the tombs of her heroes:

At last I am in peace! – but what peace is this? exhaustion, the lethargy of the tomb. I have wandered throughout these mountains. There is not a tree, not a hut, not a blade of grass – only stumps and jagged discolored rocks; and many scattered crosses to mark the site where wayfarers were murdered. Below is the Roja . . . the *tramontana* wind descends from the divided ridges of the Alps, through their jaws it invades the Mediterranean . . . .
These, Oh Italy, are your boundaries! but every day they are violated by the avarice of nations. Where are your sons? You lack nothing but the force of unity . . . Even as we invoke the magnanimous shades [of our ancestors], our enemies trample their sepulchers underfoot. And the day will come when, losing our possessions and our dignity and even our voice to cry out in protest, we will be reduced to the condition of slaves, or bought and sold like Negroes, and we will see our masters open the tombs and empty them and scatter to the winds the ashes of those Heroes to annihilate their memory . . . .

(259–60)

The relevance of this passage to the topography of the *Sepolcri* and larger iconography of the Risorgimento is clear. Destined in European romanticism to become a prototypical symbol of the sublime, the Alps retain a distinct political connotation in Italian literature. Since Petrarch's canzone "Italia mia" had grounded Italy's identity in the natural border provided by the Alps ("Ben provide Natura al nostra stato, / Quando de l'Alpi schermo / pose fra noi et la tedesca rabbia"), this had become a topos of the Pe-

trarchan tradition;[23] and for Foscolo the political significance of this privileged landscape is never lost. His fashionably oleographic description of the
desolate mountain pass, complete with crashing waterfall, cliffs, and the
crosses of "viandanti assassinati" (à la Salvator Rosa) in turn generates a
political meditation; just as the topographic studies commissioned by
Napoleon to document his first Italian campaign entered into the iconography of the Risorgimento, as images of the borders henceforth to be defended from all foreign trespass.[24]

If Florence is the true center – geographic, political, linguistic, cultural – of
Italy, Santa Croce, temple of the "itale glorie," is the true center of Florence. The focus on the cathedral as a symbolic expression of a nation's
history reminds us inevitably, in a nineteenth-century context, of Hugo's
Notre-Dame de Paris of 1831.[25] Hugo describes the cathedral as a "chronicle
in stone," a concrete, collective representation of a nation's history to be
"read" in three dimensions, along the slow axes of its construction and
gradual interment by the rising tide of the city's pavement. He compares the
great cathedrals to organic, geological formations: "le dépôt que laisse une
nation; les entassements que font les siècles; le résidu des évaporations suc-
cessives de la société humaine . . . Chaque flot du temps superpose son
alluvion, chaque race dépose sa couche sur le monument, chaque individu
apporte sa pierre."[26]

The novel is perhaps the genre best suited to developing the analogy
between architecture and history. Hugo's sprawling text brings the cathedral to life, perversely animating it through a swarm of descriptive detail (all
authenticated through the author's consultation with archaeological experts
in Paris), and the hunchback Quasimodo, ranging freely over the façade and
through the city, seems a gargoyle detached from that structure. Foscolo's
chosen form of the *poemetto* does not permit such elaboration. The constraints of the genre require him to condense his description of the cathedral
of Santa Croce into a few strategic lines. Foscolo's panorama of the surrounding landscape of Florence thus seems schematic when compared to
Hugo's aerial reconstruction of fifteenth-century Paris from the towers of
Notre Dame, but within the poem it fulfills the same polemical function.
Santa Croce, last temple of the "itale glorie" left standing in a land de-
spoiled by the enemy, provides a visual focus comparable to Hugo's Notre
Dame, and dramatizes the need to guard the monuments of Italy from
Napoleon's law.

In the *Sepolcri* Santa Croce is the symbol of a cultural edifice and collective identity that must be preserved. Each of its tombs commemorates an
individual whose contribution is an inalienable part of Italy's heritage.
These tombs personalize the concept of history and make it accessible to the

common man who comes to the cathedral to worship, just as its frescoes traditionally taught Biblical stories to the illiterate. None of the niches provided in the church must be left empty. Hence Foscolo's protest against Parini's anonymous burial in Milan, and his approval of Alfieri's prompt burial in Santa Croce with full ceremony and the promise of a tomb sculpted by Antonio Canova (Fig. 16).[27] These measures assured that his memory would be honored and his effigy installed in its proper place among the marbles where he himself had often sought inspiration.

Yet the image of Alfieri's death mask — its features frozen between hope and certain knowledge of death, as if an emblem of the oxymoron informing the entire text — leads to the poem's rapid dislocation:

> Qui posava l'austero, e avea sul volto
> Il pallor della morte e la speranza.
> Con questi grandi abita eterno, e l'ossa
> Fremono amor di patria. Ah sì! da quella
> Religiosa pace un Nume parla,
> E nutria contro a' Persi in Maratona,
> Ove Atene sacrò tombe a' suoi prodi,
> La virtù greca e l'ira.   (194–201)

(Here he would stand austere, with death's pallor and hope both stamped on his brow. With these great souls now he dwells forever; and his bones tremble with love for his homeland. Yes! – from that devout peace a godhead speaks: as at Marathon, where Athens raised tombs to its heroes, it aroused Greek virtue and wrath against the Persians.)

We are transported in mid-line from the Gothic interior of Santa Croce to a phantom reenactment of the Battle of Marathon (lines 201–12). This is one of the many abrupt transitions that prompted Guillon's charge of obscurity, and in fact caused difficulty for many readers. Foscolo's transition implies that Santa Croce is a necessary but not a sufficient center for a modern political poetry. The poet's departure from this scene concretely marks the beginning of his search for an alternative "plot" in which to ground his text. Turning from the death mask of his precursors, as if to demonstrate the risks inherent in any emulation of the "forti," he embarks on his own poetic journey.

We discover by the reference to the *navigante* (line 201) that it is a voyage by sea. The tombs described along the way are like the points along a coast that aid a navigator to orient his ship. But the waters are basically familiar, both to the poet and to the intended recipient of his poem, Ippolito Pindemonte – both Hellenists and translators, Foscolo of the *Iliad* (his "Esperi-

16. Antonio Canova, Detail of Monument to Vittorio Alfieri, 1806–1810
(Florence, Santa Croce).

menti di traduzione della *Iliade* di Omero" was printed contemporaneously
with the *Sepolcri* by Bettoni in Brescia), and Pindemonte of the *Odyssey*.
Foscolo's knowledge of Homeric topography provides a map upon which
to trace his poetry of exile.

"Veleggiando quel mar sotto l'Eubea," the first tomb sighted – and the

first episode in this nineteenth-century odyssey – is that of the Greek soldiers who died in the Battle of Marathon in 490 B.C. From the aisles and
chapels of Santa Croce, with their catalogue of individual tombs to Italian
cultural heroes, we have moved to one massive memorial of war (a mound
of earth built fifty feet high, filled with weapons and relics that were retrieved during its excavation, which began in 1890). This tomb preserves a
collective memory of its dead by promoting the illusion of a nightly reenactment of that battle (the popular legend of such a spectacle at Marathon
was reported by Pausanias in his *Voyage in Attica*).

From this vision the poet maneuvers, via the invocation of Pindemonte,
into the Aegean and toward the sites of the Trojan War:

> Felice te che il regno ampio de' venti,
> Ippolito, a' tuoi verdi anni correvi!
> E se il piloto ti drizzò l'antenna
> Oltre l'isole Egee, d'antichi fatti
> Certo udisti suonar dell'Ellesponto
> I liti, e la marea mugghiar portando
> Alle prode Retee l'armi d'Achille
> Sovra l'ossa d'Ajace. A' generosi
> Giusta di glorie dispensiera è Morte:
> Nè senno astuto nè favor di regi
> All'Itaco le spoglie ardue serbava,
> Chè alla poppa raminga le ritolse
> L'onda incitata dagl'inferni Dei.   (213–25)

(Oh happy Ippolito, who in your youth freely ranged the ample realm
of the winds! And if your pilot steered beyond the Aegean islands, you
surely heard the shores of the Hellespont echo with ancient memories,
and the surf roar as it brought Achilles's arms to the bones of Ajax on
the Rhetian shore: to brave spirits Death gives their due portion of
glory; neither his craftiness nor the favor of kings could reserve the
coveted trophy to Ulysses, for the waves incited by the gods of the
underworld wrested it from his wandering ship.)

The tribute to Pindemonte is highly ambiguous. First, Pindemonte's own
literal "odyssey" – actually a leisured eighteenth-century European tour –
is set up in potential opposition to Foscolo's own political exile and pilgrimage ("E me che i tempi ed il desio d'onore / Fan per diversa gente ir
fuggitivo . . . ," 226 ff.). More deviously, Pindemonte's chosen Homeric
protagonist, Ulysses, is portrayed in the moment of losing Achilles's armor
to Ajax, who would become the hero of Foscolo's 1811 tragedy.

"A' generosi / Giusta di glorie dispensiera è Morte . . ." If it is legitimate to read in this episode an allusion to the rivalry between Foscolo and Pindemonte for the "arduous spoils" of literary success, we can not expect the gift of the *Sepolcri* to have much assuaged the previous affronts to Pindemonte to which Foscolo refers in a letter to Isabella Teotochi Albrizzi.[28]

The fact that the two poets shared an interest in the theme of *sepolcri*, and that Foscolo's text actually displaced Pindemonte's own intended treatment of that theme, increases the probability of the allusions that I have just suggested. In any case Pindemonte's response to the poem, with its elegiac tone and resolutely Christian climax, well illustrated the genre of sepulchral poetry that Foscolo intended to overturn.[29]

To return to Foscolo's archaeological itinerary: the tomb of Achilles and Patroclus on the shores of the Hellespont does not appear directly in the poem, as Foscolo explains with some irritation to Guillon, "bensì in una nota per incidenza." In the text it is present only through the aural suggestion (which follows the visual hallucination of the Battle of Marathon) of lines 216–18 ("d'antichi fatti / Certo udisti suonar dell'Ellesponto / I liti"). This "suonar" is analogically related to the "mugghiar" of the "marea" that brings the arms of Achilles to the "ossa d'Ajace" (a reference that is "archaeologically" accurate since, according to Homer, Ajax as a suicide was denied cremation). This passage has led us through some rough waters ("l'onda incitata dagl'inferni Dei"!), but with the tide that washes the trophy ashore the poet too steps onto solid ground and invokes the Muses:

> E me che i tempi ed il desio d'onore
> Fan per diversa gente ir fuggitivo,
> Me ad evocar gli eroi chiamin le Muse
> Del mortale pensiero animatrici.
> Siedon custodi de' sepolcri; e quando
> Il Tempo con sue fredde ale vi spazza
> Fin le rovine, le Pimplèe fan lieti
> Di lor canto i deserti, e l'armonia
> Vince di mille secoli il silenzio.   (226–34)

(And let the Muses call me – whom the times and the desire for honor cause to flee through foreign nations – to evoke the heroes, for the Muses breathe life into human thought. They stand guard over the sepulchers, and when Time with its cold wings sweeps away even the ruins, the Pierian sisters cheer the deserts with their song, and its harmony overcomes the silence of a thousand centuries.)

Foscolo's own explication of this passage emphasizes its portrayal of the complicity between archaeology and poetry, which arises from their shared responsibility to preserve a nation's memories. The Muses keep watch over the sepulchers and continue to guard the monument throughout the phases of its physical decay, perpetuating the memory of a sacred place eventually lost to view . . . until "l'amor delle lettere" leads to its rediscovery as in the case of the recent expedition to Troy. To cite Foscolo's own gloss on this passage in the "Letter to Monsieur Guillon":

> The very sites where the tombs of heroes were located, even if no trace of them remains, inflame the hearts of generous men. Though men of great virtue be persecuted in life, and time destroy their monuments, the memory of their virtues and monuments lives on immortal in writers and is renewed in those spirits who cultivate the Muses. We find proof of this principle in the sepulcher of Ilus, discovered after so many years by travelers whom the love of literature brought on a pilgrimage to Troy; a sepulcher privileged by the fates so that it might protect the body of Electra, mother of Dardanus and of the Trojan line, whose progeny founded Rome and the empire of the Caesars. The author concludes with an episode on this sepulcher itself . . .
>
> (510–11)

Here Foscolo quotes, and paraphrases in impassioned detail, the last forty-one lines of the poem. He argues that far from representing a digression, a falling off from the central interests of the poem (as charged by Guillon), these lines release its greatest power.

The strength of this section lies, according to the author, in the unifying image of the tomb of Ilus ("a monument which survived the ravages of the centuries"), which as mausoleum of the Trojan princes is a particularly rich rhetorical focus because of its multiple literary and historical associations. By superimposing in rapid succession on the original image the diverse characters and narratives associated with the site ("Here rested Erichthonius . . . here the Trojan women . . . here Cassandra . . ."), Foscolo claims that he was building a deliberate rhetorical climax:

> The Trojan women who pray . . . the virgin Cassandra . . . the prayer to the palms and cypresses . . . the shades . . . Homer . . . so many characters, so many passions, so many contrasting attitudes, and all of them assembled round a single sepulcher: do these seem to you lacking in spirit and invention?
>
> (512)

Defending with equal vehemence the logic of his conclusion, Foscolo explains that he chose to end the poem with the words of Cassandra because she, like the Trojan tombsite from which she speaks, is at the same time a locus of many conflicting emotions – sorrow, pride, solicitude, despair. As a virgin prophetess she embodies too the fundamental contradiction between innocence and experience. Her relationship to the question of genealogies, central to this multiple tombsite and to Foscolo's entire poem, is highly ambiguous and her role as counselor to the young on their filial duties is particularly poignant (lines 261–2).

The condensation of so many contradictory figures and affects, Foscolo concludes, is an appropriate vehicle to achieve effects of the sublime, and redeems the apparent obscurity of the poem. His text is "archaeological" not only in theme but in its profoundest poetic strategies; at the Trojan tombsite where his text comes to rest, the conflicting emotions of the characters are dramatically superimposed, like the layers of history in any vertical section of soil.

In a poem that enacts a search for collective origins, the theme of genealogy is obviously central. I have mentioned the importance of genealogies in reference to Cassandra. Actually the issue first explicitly arises in lines 235– 40, where the poet proclaims his arrival at the "eternal site" of Troy by the ritual recitation of the genealogy of the *Giulia gente,* descended from Electra:

> Ed oggi nella Troade inseminata
> Eterno splende a' peregrini un loco;
> Eterno per la Ninfa a cui fu sposo
> Giove, ed a Giove diè Dárdano figlio,
> Onde fu Troja e Assáraco e i cinquanta
> Talami e il regno della Giulia gente. (235–40)

(And even today in Troy's sterile plain a site shines forth to travelers forever, ever sacred to the nymph beloved by Jove who bore him Dardanus, whence sprang the Trojan line, Assaracus, the fifty sons of Priam and the Julian clan.)

The elaborate genealogical periphrasis serves to identify the nymph who lies buried at this site (who is then named in the next line). More importantly, it proleptically clarifies the significance of the site to Italian readers. From the union of Electra and Jupiter can be traced the legendary ancestry of the Italians themselves, through Dardanus, Erichthonius, Tros, Assaracus, Capys, Anchises, and Aeneas. The pathos of the poem's final focus on Hector, last adult survivor of Ilus's branch of the house of Troy (Hector's son Astyanax, according to the *Iliad,* was thrown by the victorious Greeks from the walls of the city) is mitigated by this proleptic vision of *survival,* pointing directly toward the Italian race.

From this dramatically foreshortened view the poet retreats to an orderly narrative of the death of Electra and Jupiter's consecration of the site (lines 241–53). The rapid passage of time is conveyed spatially now, as the layers of history rise to bury the spot, and it is transformed by new human action:

> Ivi posò Erittonio, e dorme il giusto
> Cenere d'Ilo; ivi l'Iliache donne
> Sciogliean le chiome, indarno ahi! deprecando
> Da' lor mariti l'imminente fato;
> Ivi Cassandra, allor che il nume in petto
> Le fea parlar di Troja il dì mortale,
> Venne; e all'ombre cantò carme amoroso . . .   (254–60)

(There rested Erichthonius, and there sleep the just ashes of Ilus; there the Trojan women loosened their hair; in vain – alas! – praying fate to spare their husbands; there Cassandra, moved by the god in her heart to proclaim the last day of Troy, came and sang a song of love to the shades . . .)

Cassandra's prophecy elides the day of Troy's destruction, pointing instead toward the survivors' eventual return from slavery in Greece to find the city of their childhood gone:

> . . . "O, se mai d'Argo,
> Ove al Tidide e di Laerte al figlio
> Pascerete i cavalli, a voi permetta
> Ritorno il cielo, invan la patria vostra
> Cercherete! le mura, opra di Febo,
> Sotto le lor reliquie fumeranno . . ."   (263–8)

(Oh, if heaven ever grant you return from Argos, where you will tend the herds of Diomed and of the son of Laertes, you will search for your homeland in vain! The walls built by Apollo will lie smoking beneath their rubble . . .)

But this vision is redeemed by the final archaeological fantasy of Homer's rediscovery of Troy and the depths of its legend:

> . . . Un dì vedrete
> Mendico un cieco errar sotto le vostre
> Antichissime ombre, e brancolando
> Penetrar negli avelli, e abbracciar l'urne,
> E interrogarle. Gemeranno gli antri
> secreti, e tutta narrerà la tomba

Ilio raso due volte e due risorto
Splendidamente su le mute vie
Per far più bello l'ultimo trofeo
Ai fatati Pelidi . . .   (279–88)

(One day you will see a blind beggar wander beneath your ancient
shade and grope his way into the burial vaults, and embrace the urns,
and interrogate them. The secret depths will groan, and the tomb will
tell all the story of Ilion twice razed and twice resurrected, its silent
streets splendidly rebuilt to redouble its glory as a last trophy destined
to the children of Peleus . . .)

Troy's history of survival enhances its value to the Greeks as a military
trophy. And like Achilles's armor, the memory of Troy outlasts all historical vicissitudes; preserved underground and inarticulate in the images of the
Penates, it surfaces again to be cast in permanent literary form by Homer:

. . . Il sacro vate,
Placando quelle afflitte alme col canto,
I Prenci Argivi eternerà per quante
Abbraccia terre il gran padre Oceano.
E tu onore di pianti, Ettore, avrai
Ove fia santo e lagrimato il sangue
Per la patria versato, e finchè il Sole
risplenderà su le sciagure umane.   (288–95)

(The sacred bard, placating those afflicted souls with his song, will
make the Greek princes immortal throughout all the lands embraced
by the great father Ocean. And you, Hector, will be honored by tears
wherever blood shed for the fatherland is mourned and revered, and
for as long as the Sun continues to shine upon human misfortunes.)

The labyrinth of classical allusions ends here. With the funeral honors
granted to Hector ("E tu onore di pianti, Ettore, avrai"), we have reached
the end of the *Iliad;* but it is also the end of an odyssey for the figure of the
poet in the *Sepolcri*. It is a difficult path that Foscolo traces in this poem; but
it served to propel the sepulchral genre into an exhortatory political dimension that would prove central to the rhetoric of the Risorgimento.

On the restoration of Lombardy to Austrian rule in 1815, Foscolo left Italy
for Switzerland and final exile in England. From a distance his example
continued to inspire the new generation of Italian patriots, including

Mazzini, who himself arrived an exile in London in 1837, ten years after Foscolo's death.

"Foscolo was one of my first enthusiasms in life," Mazzini recalls, in an essay of 1871.[30] "From my earliest years, when I began to study and feel pride in my identity as an Italian, my study of his works was persistent, assiduous, unrelenting . . ." Upon his arrival in London years later, Mazzini explains, he gave himself over to the archaeological search for Foscolo's unpublished manuscripts: "I rushed to collect every lost fragment and relic of Foscolo and unearthed both his notes for an edition of Dante and part of the *Lettera apologetica.*"

In recalling his lifelong admiration for Foscolo only months after Italy's unification was completed, Mazzini had a distinct polemical purpose. For the revolutionary ideals that Foscolo represented had been betrayed, in his view, by Italy's acceptance of the Savoy monarchy; unification had been achieved only by sacrificing the idea of the republic. Mazzini argued that the Italian revolution was still incomplete and that the new regime had no right to appropriate the memory of its martyrs until it had accomplished the goals for which they had died.

Mazzini's essay was prompted by the new government's proposal to transfer the ashes of Foscolo from the English churchyard of Chiswick, where they had lain since 1827, to the cathedral of Santa Croce celebrated in his poem. It was a gesture calculated to gratify public opinion and integrate Foscolo's memory into the edifice of the new regime. Mazzini argued that the repatriation of the poet's remains would be an act of *hubris* on the part of the monarchy, which had not proved itself worthy of Foscolo's memory; but his rebuke was not sufficient to prevent the move, and with due ceremony Foscolo's ashes were transferred to Santa Croce.[31]

From Foscolo Mazzini had inherited an archaeological ideal, a dream of resurrecting Italian origins that lay buried beneath the edifice of the ancien régime. In his vision of a "Third Rome," to rise on the ruins of the papacy, Mazzini transmitted this ideal to the democratic tradition: and with his adversary Gioberti brought the idea of Rome to the foreground of the debate on Italian nationalism.

6

THE RISORGIMENTO DEBATE:
MAZZINI AND GIOBERTI

IF THE PRIMARY STRATEGY of Pio-Clementine and Restoration classicism was to create vast ceremonial spaces in which to display the spoils of recent excavations and proclaim the Pope's exclusive title to the complex legacy of Rome, Mazzini and other writers of the left dreamed of reclaiming the "marble wilderness" itself as a common ground for the democratic opposition.

In the works of Mazzini and other writers of the "scuola democratica,"[1] and in the works of other European writers sympathetic to the cause of Italian nationalism, the ruins of Rome are repeatedly invoked as a setting for revolutionary action – a transitional topos or "common place" in which to mobilize the scattered forces for Italian unity in preparation for the overthrow of the temporal power.

Recalling the archaeological experiment of the Roman Republic of 1798–9, writers such as Charles Didier – whose novel *Rome souterraine,* published in 1833, was much admired by Mazzini and is a text to which I will return later in this chapter[2] – represent the ruins as the literal rallying point of the people and the site from which to move their assault on the Vatican. In Didier's fictionalized account of a *carbonaro* uprising, the church of San Lorenzo in Miranda, layered into the ruins of the Temple of Antoninus and Faustina at the edge of the Forum, is chosen as the rendezvous and base of operations of the *carbonari;* and it is to this site that the insurgents, having won an abandoned Vatican only to be routed from the Castel Sant'Angelo, retreat for the final siege in which all but one of them will die, martyrs to the cause of a united Italy.

It is easy to understand why Mazzini, in a review of *Rome souterraine* published in the *Giovine Italia,*[3] applauded the metamorphosis of the ruins into barricades. By reclaiming the ruins as political symbols and deploying them in an "epic" narrative that promised wide popular appeal, Didier's text helped to counter an increasingly mannered "poetry of ruins" which throughout Europe had found in Rome its privileged setting.

Just as Foscolo in the *Sepolcri* had resisted the elegiac tendency of the

English sepulchral tradition, both as political orator and literary critic Mazzini tirelessly campaigned against the shallow despair over Italy's fortunes made fashionable by Lamartine – declaring with Giusti to the alleged "terre des morts": "fin le vostre ruine / sono un'apoteosi."[4] It is characteristic of Mazzini's apocalyptically distended vision to move from the focus on the individual sculptural monument (increasingly delicate in Foscolo as he approached *Le grazie*) toward a wide-angle view of the entire monumental complex of Rome; but however that city is transfigured through Mazzini's myth of the "Terza Roma," as an ideal everywhere present in his writings it supplies a unifying image and *center* that had been lacking in Foscolo – whose exploratory archaeological odyssey I traced in the previous chapter.

Where Mazzini, in the tradition of David and other artists of the French Revolution, exploits the full subversive potential of the classical landscape by reclaiming it as the stage for the austere trials of republican virtue – polemically overturning broken bas-reliefs, urns, and sarcophagi and aligning them as improvised barricades, introducing a new and severe visionary order into the picturesque disarray prized by the romantics – Gioberti is far less radical in his representation of Rome.

Although he too strategically exploits the archaeological metaphor, his emphasis is not on the actual elaboration of the site but on the hallucinatory display of the *artifact* – that fragile and priceless Italian *primato* lost through centuries of foreign domination.[5]

Where Mazzini develops the imagery of excavation – the search for civic and spiritual ideals long buried under the débris of the ancien régime, the patient shared work of *undermining* the remaining vestiges of that authority through the labyrinth of clandestine organization – Gioberti remains more consistently on the surface, denying the need to "break ground" at all, miraculously resurrecting an object of dubious authenticity from the depths of his own imagination.

In this chapter, devoted to the role of archaeology in the Risorgimento debate, I have chosen to focus on Mazzini and Gioberti because in the period leading up to the events of 1848 they represent the two rival forces most influential in shaping public opinion and enlisting widespread sympathy for the goal of a united Italy. Certainly some measure of their influence is due to the common strategy that I have pointed out here – an archaeological revival of the idea of Rome.

In his *Storia della politica estera italiana dal 1870 al 1896*, Federico Chabod has shown that the idea of Rome was not widely trusted by the left during the early years of the Risorgimento, precisely because of its imperial, papal, and Napoleonic associations.[6] It was largely due to the contribution of Gioberti and Mazzini that by mid-century the idea of Rome had gained sufficient popular appeal to displace its main rival iconography, that of the medieval communes (and signally of Florence), which had been used by writers as diverse as Cattaneo, Sismondi, and D'Azeglio implicitly to illustrate the advantage of a federalist system of government over those of a strongly centralized state.

That even then the question was not fully resolved is clear from Chabod's account of the continued debate during the 1860s on the choice of a capital city for the new Kingdom of Italy. Nonetheless, with the events of 1848–9 – and especially Garibaldi's epic defense of the Roman Republic from the Janiculum – the image of Rome, with its rich landscape of *rovine esortatrici,* moved increasingly toward the foreground of nationalist discourse in Italy.

Italian archaeological inquiry was of course not limited to Rome during the first half of the nineteenth century. During the Napoleonic period, the success of such works as Vincenzo Cuoco's *Platone in Italia* (1804–6) and Micali's *L'Italia avanti il dominio dei Romani* (1810)[7] attests to a polemical revival of interest in pre-Roman civilizations, which like the cult of the medieval communes attempted to divert attention from the centralizing image of Rome by reconstructing the annals of previous civilizations assimilated by Rome during its conquest of the peninsula.

Where Cuoco's novel, in the tradition of Barthelemy's *Voyage du jeune Anarcharsis en Grèce,* was a freewheeling archaeologico-political fantasy whose only claim to historical authenticity was the purely formal conceit of the "found manuscript,"[8] Micali's study, despite the paucity of empirical evidence to support his theory, presented itself as a serious scientific treatise, complete with an erudite apparatus largely improvised to support his premise of a network of highly developed and differentiated autochthonous civilizations anterior to the Roman conquest.

That Micali himself did not fully anticipate or intend the politically subversive impact of his *Storia* as the century progressed does not alter its effective status as a prototypical narrative of resistance to Rome and an early attempt to rewrite the history of Italy from the perspective of the *vinti.* Although he notes Mazzini's distrust of this "letteratura pelasgica," and mentions Sismondi's concern that by fostering a retrospective resentment of Rome such rhetoric would lead to a devaluation of Italy's classical heritage and an alienation from its most precious moral and mythical resources, Trèves argues that the reaction to Rome was a salutary development, even a necessary condition of the nation's eventual reconciliation with and repossession of Rome: "Only by means of such historical inquiry into its own past could Italy come to understand the dialectical relationship between its classical and universalist heritage and its modern needs as a nation, between the two Romes of yesterday and the third, which it was necessary not to occupy but to create."[9]

Although the nationalistic revival of medieval vocabularies came relatively late to Italian architecture, notably with the work of Camillo Boito in the 1870s and the façade completions of the cathedrals of Florence and Milan,[10] the renewal of interest in the Middle Ages propagated by European romanticism did find expression in the archaeological reconstructions of episodes from Italian history attempted by the *romanzo storico* and history painting of the 1830s and 1840s.[11] Apart from purely sentimental approaches to the theme, such as Diodata Saluzzo's poem "Le rovine," a fantasy inspired by the view of a ruined medieval castle (which nonetheless was celebrated by Di Breme as the prototype of the modern romantic lyric),[12] there did evolve *a contrario*, out of the reactionary cult of the Middle Ages imposed by Restoration pedagogy to erase the memory of Jacobin classicism, that liberal and patriotic revaluation of the medieval communes that I mentioned earlier and whose genesis De Sanctis would recall in his 1866 funeral oration for Massimo D'Azeglio:

> In those days it was fashionable to study the Middle Ages. It was a reaction to the [dangerous example of] Greek and Roman history, to which [the authorities] attributed those revolutionary fantasies which had led us astray. To set us straight they prescribed the study of the medieval period, which represented the grandeur of the papacy and the principle of divine right; they devised a system, half mystical and half feudal, which they intended to be the catechism of the new generation . . .
> But no system . . . can arrest the forces of change. The idea of Italy was already alive in the minds of Italians, and it is the intellect that directs the process of history. D'Azeglio studied the Middle Ages in his own way and joined with other Italian writers. Together they forged a revolutionary image of medieval Italy . . . and it was this that D'Azeglio represented in his paintings and novels.[13]

After a rapid summary of the episodes and protagonists favored by the new historical novel, De Sanctis concludes:

> This was the image of the Middle Ages forged by Massimo D'Azeglio. Recommended and encouraged by the authorities themselves, the study of medieval history turned against the Restoration and became one of the most effective components of our political regeneration. We searched not for . . . parchments, codices, institutions, and the claims to sovereignty of Popes and Emperors, but the traditions and charter of our own nationality . . . the image and proof of our own courage and grandeur as a people.
>
> (285)

Though conscious of the limits of the medieval commune as a political ideal (for it was structurally more sympathetic to the federalist thesis), Mazzini himself applauded every effort to reconstruct "heroic" episodes from any period in Italian history that might serve as *exempla virtutis* to the present generation. In an essay of 1828, "Del romanzo in generale ed anche dei *Promessi sposi* di Alessandro Manzoni" – his first contribution to the ongoing debate on the validity of the historical novel as a genre – he not only defended its political and pedagogical utility but specifically recommended a medieval thematic:

> We exhort Italians to devote themselves ardently to this genre, and to take their subjects from medieval history, for those centuries, which the ruinous indifference of writers condemned so long to obscurity, are rich in edifying examples and sublime memories.[14]

Mazzini's endorsement of medieval themes in the novel concords with the preference for Hayez expressed in a later commentary on the "Pittura moderna in Italia." There Mazzini judges the most valuable contribution of the neoclassical school of Italian painting to have been the search for archaeological accuracy in the reconstruction of a milieu – a goal accordingly politicized by the medievalizing school of history painting headed by Francesco Hayez, who in his great crowded frescoes of historical events first gave concrete representation to the masses:

> By emphasizing the need for historical and architectural exactitude [the neoclassicists] prepared the way for the school which was to follow . . . [But the history painters] are the Precursors of the Nation's Art, just as the political martyrs are the Precursors of the Nation.[15]

Mazzini's aesthetic does not then exclude medieval themes; his approval of archaeological strategies of representation is conditional only on their progressive political function. Mazzini's primary concern is that the accurate reconstruction of a milieu be remembered as the means, and not the end, of the historical mode. He does not share with a Giacomo Durando that fanatical distrust of history that led the latter, in his 1846 manifesto *Della nazionalità italiana,* to reject every prior archaeological effort to forge a national consciousness as mere "idolatry of the antique" – accusing Dante, Machiavelli, Alfieri, Foscolo, et al., of fatally confusing politics and aesthetics:

> We have proposed to regenerate Italy as if it were a question of restoring a statue of Praxiteles, a text of Aristotle or of Cicero, without

taking into consideration that what is "true and beautiful" in an aesthetic sense seldom varies, whereas what is "true and beautiful" in a social and political sense depends on the historical and geographical context. Art has become a tyrant among us . . . Art is destroying us.[16]

Yet Mazzini is fully aware of the dangers of encouraging any inquiry into the past that is not directed by and anchored in an immediate and creative concern for the future. In the spirit of Renaissance humanism as characterized by Thomas M. Greene,[17] Mazzini understands archaeology to be useful only insofar as it implies a "latent pressure on the present and future": the "will to form" that motivates his historical imagination is a dynamic and prospective force, alien to any retrospective or archaizing brand of classicism oriented toward the restoration of a static ideal.

Gioberti's *Primato,* with its promise of the literal restitution of the natural and inalienable title of "primogenito delle nazioni" to the Italian people, was certainly more deserving of Durando's skepticism than Mazzini's abstract and idealistic archaeology. In the following pages I will further question the function of archaeological imagery in the discourse of these two figures, and consider the measure in which it shapes their contrasting modes of representing the "Italian question" in the years leading up to 1848. I do not pretend to provide a more general presentation or critique of the political thought of either figure; as I mentioned earlier, my discussion of Gioberti will be deliberately limited to a single text, the *Primato morale e civile degli italiani* (1843), whereas most of my references to Mazzini will be culled from a series of essays which as part of his ongoing *critica militante* develop the imagery of archaeology in particularly striking ways.[18]

Any discussion of Gioberti's use of archaeology would have to begin by focusing on his "Esortazione ai colti giovani italiani," an explicit appeal to renew the study of classical antiquity in order to refresh the present generation's awareness of the dignity of its origins.

In this chapter of the *Primato* Gioberti deplores in general the neglect of archaeological inquiry in a region like Italy, naturally its privileged terrain:

Italy and Greece are the two parts of Europe which contain the greatest relics of a past civilization, and rest on the ruins of an ancient world which was built and destroyed by the industry and barbarity of men. It is deplorable that there are so few Italians today desirous of studying their country's own ruins, and that this sort of inquiry, regarded as useless, is left to a handful of learned antiquarians.[19]

More specifically Gioberti recommends the revival of such study for its salutary effect on the young. The ritual contemplation of ruins represents in fact the climax of an austere pedagogical program that he proposes in order to remedy the corruption of Italy's present educational system. The "majesty of ruins" is a spectacle reserved for the highest grade of the initiate, who having honed their moral sensibilities through tireless mortification of the flesh ("let them harden their bodies to the hot sun, to the fatigue of running and other gymnastic exercises . . . let them eat frugally, sleep on a hard bed, and subject the body in every respect to the domination of the mind"), and trained their spiritual faculties through solitary communion with nature at its most "sublime" ("let them contemplate . . . divinity . . . in the cool shade, amid the rustling leaves of the forest, or . . . on the high and serene mountain passes"), will finally be prepared, in the contemplation of ruins, to accomplish that spiritual ascent enabling man to "climb against the current of years and centuries to the divine and mysterious source in which all originates."

But archaeology is more than a private spiritual exercise. To each nation as a whole, ruins represent an archive, a repository of information and concrete mode of access to its unwritten history. In a page that Mazzini could only have underscored, Gioberti develops this concept:

> Ruins are like the fossils of extinct nations and civilizations, and perpetuate the ages which have passed, representing their history in vivid and concrete form; indeed, the annals of more than one nation could be deduced from the description of its ruins. To write a history of Greece, Italy, or Spain based on the study of its ruins alone would be a challenging task, worthy of an eloquent philosopher.

From an awareness of history comes the power to shape the future; hence the creative and prospective nature of archaeology as a human science:

> Archaeology, no less than philology, far from being a sterile and moribund science, is a lively and exceedingly fertile discipline; for in addition to renewing the past, it serves to prepare the future of nations. Since the resurrection of a nation's monuments restores the very idea of its identity, it joins a nation's past with its future, and serves . . . to unite resurgent peoples, awakening and keeping their hopes alive . . .

In a passage that inevitably recalls the argument of the *Sepolcri* and the democratic view of ruins as a "common place" in which to mobilize a patriotic opposition, Gioberti declares:

Therefore ruins often serve as the gathering-place of dispersed generations, and ensure the survival of cultures which have been suppressed
and overthrown: scattered or crushed by force or by violence, even if
they have been stripped of their name and language, these nations live
on forever in the monuments of their ancestors.

Just as a single fallen column, in Gioberti's semiology of ruins, signifies
survival rather than decay, the more complex image of a stratified monumental ruin site attests not to the violence of human history but to the overt
presence of a providential plan: a "divine teleology of nations" that guaran-
tees the preservation of one civilization through the temporary superimposition of another. This is the logic to be read in the apparently random
movements of migrating tribes:

> . . . famous ruins serve to determine the patterns of migrating peoples
> and tribes . . . Thus it happens that several distinct civilizations con-
> verge on one site, and that one city rises on the ruins of another . . .
> Therefore I believe that monuments of all kinds are preserved not by
> chance but through a divine teleology of nations; and that a building
> which has survived the ravages of time and the violence of men is
> never a useless heap of bricks and stones.

It is the aura surrounding the monuments of the past that makes their
study so valuable to the young, particularly in a period of moral and political upheaval:

> Ancient monuments are often more important than modern ones;
> especially when they are related to political history, and can renew the
> national consciousness of a people. Therefore educated young Italians
> would be wise not to ignore the ruins of their own country. Like the
> scholars who have patiently reconstructed ancient monuments, either
> lost or legendary, such as Achilles' shield, the tombs of Ozymandias
> and Porsena, the sarcophagi of Ephestius and Alexander, the labyrinth
> of Egypt, etc.; young Italian scholars, examining their own nation's
> history, should renew the most hallowed of its ancient traditions,
> *restoring not its fora, amphitheaters, and baths, but the unity, force, and
> grandeur of the ancient Italian nation.* (Emphasis added)

Mazzini himself could have found little to quarrel with in this generic
invocation of the archaeological metaphor in support of a patriotic discourse. Yet to distinguish his use of the metaphor from that of Gioberti, one
need only consider the nature of those institutions in which Gioberti saw the
"unity, force, and grandeur of the ancient Italian nation" to reside.

Although he implies the exclusion of Austria from a future confederation of Italian states,[20] Gioberti's proposal of a "return to origins" otherwise amounts to little more than an elaborate apology of the existing power structure in Italy. His famous theory of the two components of the Italian national character (elaborated in I, 179 ff.) provides an ingenious "genetic" explanation of the split between lay princes and papacy that revaluates that duality as the sole possible structuring principle of national unity:

> The unique character of Italians in matters of government results from the fusion of two components: one of which is natural, Pelasgic, Doric, Etruscan, Latin, and Roman, and derives from the racial stock and its primitive traditions; and the other supernatural, modern, Christian, Catholic, and Guelph, which results from beliefs and institutions which have taken root in Italy over the past fifteen centuries, and become second nature to the inhabitants of the Peninsula. These two elements, both distinctly Italian – though the first is civic and secular, the second religious and hieratic in nature – harmonize with each other; for inasmuch as they are logically simultaneous and chronologically successive, they complement each other, and correspond to the two great periods in our history before and after Christ, and to the two most powerful and admirable Italian institutions . . . that is, the Latin empire born from the Etruscan and Pelasgic civilization, and the civil dictatorship of the Pope in the Middle Ages . . . Both of these elements, native to Italy and Tuscan and Roman in origin, permeate every part of our political existence, through an elective aristocracy, the natural counselor and auxiliary of the princes . . . and a hieratic authority which presides over and unifies the individual governments, and is the governing principle of ecclesiastical society. Therefore popular governments are not appropriate to the institutions of the Peninsula . . .

Despite the apparent audacity of his proposal that the Pope be appointed head of a league of lay princes, the implications of Gioberti's neoguelph restoration are deeply conservative. The theme of the providential continuity between classical and Christian Rome, a bulwark of the Vatican's own apology of the temporal power, has merely been extended to the entire peninsula and made the basis of a triumphal characterization of a fixed national character, which provides a retrospective, pseudo-scientific sanction to the two forms of authority surviving in Italy but denies the emergence of that third force, the Popolo, which had recently found its spokesman in Mazzini.

The "Popolo" is only an abstraction, a chimera, argues Gioberti in implicit polemic with Mazzini. It can not be considered one of the raw materials of a national Risorgimento because it is an entity nowhere to be found in Italian political precedent. And Gioberti's own greatest strength, according to his pseudo-Machiavellian parenthesis of I, 118 ff. ("Scusa dell'autore se entra a discorrere di cose di Stato"), is his prudence in matters of politics:

> for I venture neither to fabricate new orders, nor to create the slightest new social entity; I have attempted only, with the greatest caution, to suggest the best possible arrangement among those elements which are already in existence.

In more explicit polemic with Mazzini, he warns in the "Esortazione agli esuli italiani" (II, 2) that nothing is more damaging to the cause of national unity than the exhortation to violence. The "intemperate doctrines" learned while in exile will never find widespread support in Italy; they can lead only to abortive revolutions and renewed governmental repression. Such setbacks are the more to be regretted because they derive from the imitation of foreigners (especially the French) and could be avoided by a realistic recognition of the Italian national temper: "because democratic, tumultuous, and licentious doctrines are contrary to our national character."

Elsewhere Gioberti is even more blunt in his rejection of a democratic alternative as both unworkable and undesirable in Italy:

> I believe the maxim to be extremely wise which says that everything possible should be done *for* the people, but nothing or very little *through* their participation; for the worst of all governments, and the one most contrary to the interests of all, is that of the people.

Not by imitating the error of the French – whose many heresies, political and religious, he condemns at length (I, 189 ff. and passim) – but by conforming to the precedents of their *own* history, will the Italians realize their unique and privileged destiny among nations. An impressive vocabulary is enlisted to support the ethnographic end of this argument: "Imitation is all the more repugnant to us, because our Pelasgic lineage is the ruling stock of the great Giapetic family of the Indogermanic branch . . ." (I, 187). But the defense of the *primato* concept returns inevitably to the archaeological metaphor, as he concludes:

> Therefore, since the present is rooted in the past, the Italian statesman must have a broad and profound understanding of history, we might say of the *political archaeology of the nation* . . . (Emphasis added)

If Gioberti reserves his greatest scorn for the imitators of the "cosmopolitans" and "foreigners," seduced by every novelty, he warns too against the possible abuses of archaeology. The peculiar irony of what he calls the "ghibelline heresy" is its anachronistic attempt to return to pagan origins long since superseded and transvalued by the Church. Gioberti cites such figures as Cola di Rienzo, Arnaldo da Brescia, and Machiavelli himself as victims of a single "magnanimous error": a naïve enthusiasm for the study of classical antiquity that divorced them from Christian principles and led them to seek Italy's redemption in a literal restoration of its pagan past.

By ignoring the mediating tradition that had preserved ancient Rome and fulfilled its prefigured destiny, such men invited their own destruction; for they moved to sever the first component of the national character (Etruscan, Pelasgic, Roman, etc.) from the second which had preserved, nurtured, and perfected it. Gioberti's own polemic was not as anachronistic as it might first seem: Arnaldo da Brescia, here so heavily censured, was the hero of Giovanni Battista Niccolini's tragedy of the same year (1843).

Against the parable of such deluded antiquarians Gioberti envisions himself a successful Aesculapius – healing, restoring, re-membering the fragments of Italy's past by mustering every icon and emblem, however decrepit, in the service of a vast rhetorical synthesis. In his attempt to rally the broadest possible range of support among moderates and conservatives, he raises not only the sacred effigy of the Pope ("Doge and standard-bearer of the Italian confederation, paternal arbiter and peacemaker in Europe . . . spiritual father of the human race, heir and guardian of the grandeur of the Latin people," III, 262); but also the standard of the Piedmontese House of Savoy ("Della casa di Savoia e sue lodi," I, 132 ff.) and a host of lesser devices representing each of the surviving indigenous dynasties on Italian soil.

Throughout the *Primato* he is patiently solicitous of these private interests, assuring the princes that the unity of Italy will be accomplished "without wars, without revolutions, without offense to any rights, public or private" (II, 90); for it depends simply on the restoration of an established network of legitimate authorities.

"Certain utopians recommend the overthrow of the social order as a remedy for the current situation in Italy"; yet on the contrary, Gioberti claims, "the concepts of property and the inequality of fortunes are inseparable from all political life and from the laws of our own nature" (II, 215). The emphasis on *diritti* rather than *doveri* is obviously calculated; unlike Mazzini, Gioberti promises to salvage all and sacrifice nothing; and to reassure the new reigning house of Savoy he explains carefully:

> It is not a question of innovation, but simply of reviving an idea which is Italian, Catholic, and ancient in origin; and of implementing it peacefully, in the best interests of all, without offending . . . the rights of any individual.
>
> (I, 140)

Finally Gioberti argues that the reintegration of a fragmented Italy is only a prelude to the reintegration of Europe as a whole, divided against itself since the Protestant schism. In a passage reminiscent of Angelo Mai's oration he orients his public toward the far horizon of heterodoxy, praising the ongoing missionary work of the Church and promising a renewed Catholic crusade to the Orient as the ultimate goal and reward of an Italian *risorgimento*.

In his essentially encomiastic scheme and informing promise to preserve rather than subvert the present power structure of Italy, it is easy to discern the limits of Gioberti's archaeology. But it would be naïve to underestimate the extraordinary appeal of his *Primato* during the years immediately following its publication.[21] If his program for the union of Italy represents little more than a sanguine *description* of her composite features, we must nonetheless recognize the success of this very rhetorical strategy.

His approach to the question of Rome is a case in point. Though repeatedly throughout the *Primato* he returns to the image of Rome as eternal city, a phoenix continually reborn from its own ashes (I, 79), the fulcrum and cornerstone of Italian stability and (in yet another archaeological metaphor) the guardian of its Vestal fire (I, 78), it is only in the context of a panoramic review of Italian geography that he fully develops the crucial panegyric of Rome.

Gioberti's sketch of a "moral geography" of Italy (III, 159–93) is calculated to disarm regional resistance to Rome by framing the monumental image of Saint Peter's within a triumphal rhetorical tour of the entire peninsula that skillfully promotes the illusion of unity through the very description of diversity. Gioberti's stated premise is that "variety does not compromise the principle of unity . . . but on the contrary contributes to produce it." This applies particularly to a region like Italy, where a "genetic" predisposition to order naturally facilitates the harmonious integration of opposites:

> . . . the Pelasgic race . . . is the one which is richest, most capable and best suited to unite all the ethnographic varieties and contradictions in a harmonious fashion, just as the ideal and apparent oppositions in the supreme Being are harmonized.

By virtue of its very diversity, Italy becomes in Gioberti's view not only a microcosm of Europe ("la sintesi e lo specchio di Europa") but an image of the Cosmos ("la più viva immagine del Cosmo"). By elevating Italy's geographic, ethnic, and political heterogeneity to a sign and precondition of

its *primato* Gioberti disarms the opposition and smoothly paves his rhetorical path to Rome.

A practical advantage of his conciliatory mode is that on this rhetorical
journey not even Florence need present an obstacle. Although he concedes
that it is unusual to find two cities so close together, yet with such highly
developed and distinct traditions, he is unwilling to admit any antagonism
between them; even historically he characterizes their relationship as one of
alternating hegemony and mutual regeneration rather than conflict.

In a favorite spatial metaphor that he frequently opposes to the circle
(seen, like the geographical configuration of France, to imply all the dangers
of excessive centralization), he describes Florence and Rome as the "two
foci of the Italian ellipse" (179), logically sharing the function of directing
the destinies of the peninsula. But their peaceful coexistence is ironically
dependent on the surpassing prestige of Rome; if "Roma e Firenze fanno
moralmente una sola metropoli," this is possible only because Rome so
clearly prevails:

> as the sacred and cosmopolitan city, privileged seat of the Idea, guard-
> ian of doctrinal principles, archive of origins, throne of the priest-
> hood, court of religion, and hence the city which inspires and directs
> all thought and action which proceed from the driving force of
> religion.
>
> (173)

Gioberti's formal "Elogio di Firenze" (175–7), complete with its tribute
to the city's distant Etruscan origins, is then an impatient prelude to the
acclamation of Rome (177–82). After a passing reproach to the "fiera e
ingegnosa plebe romanesca," which through its archaic spirit of resistance
to authority retarded the rise of the Church and with it the work of Italian
unification (178), Gioberti admits:

> Yet in the case of Rome, all that is truly needed to excite and occupy
> the admiration of men is the hieratic, cosmopolitan, and monumental
> city. Whoever travels from Tuscany to Rome, passing through Um-
> bria, already in the region of the upper Tiber begins to sense the
> proximity of the sacred city . . .

And in his own version of the "entry into Rome" topos ("Ecco Roma!"),
central to the genre of the travel narrative, he declares:

> If a learned German has compared Venice to an enormous ship an-
> chored to the floor of the Adriatic, we may compare the seven-hilled

city, which rises above the majestic silence of its *campagna,* to an immense pyramid rising in the midst of the desert.

This "desert" is neither the "vuota insalubre region" decried by Alfieri and a generation of Enlightenment intellectuals pressing for reform in the Papal States, nor the melancholy retreat favored by a certain romantic sensibility, but a sparkling visual setting for a monumental city that is the "privileged seat of the sublime." For Gioberti, in fact, Rome with its maze of ruins and monuments is a spectacular image of *order:*

> Rome . . . as a Christian and cosmopolitan city, resembles the monad of Leibniz; and its representative of the universe, whose various components it unites and expresses, not in the disorderly fashion of eclectic philosophy, but as harmoniously distinct, and governed by the principle of *creation.*

Incarnating this principle is of course the Pope,

> who fashioned the new city from the ruins of the ancient metropolis, and built one city on top of the other, just as God shaped our earth from the remains of an earlier globe, whose ruins are buried in the viscera of the mountains.

Noting that Gibbon himself praised the efforts of the popes to restore and preserve pagan monuments (and ignoring the parallel tradition of papal vandalism of ruins), Gioberti concludes:

> Therefore the ruins of pagan culture are scattered amidst the Christian monuments, and form a city of the dead which is intermingled with the city of the living, but subservient to it: for the principle of Christianity triumphs in Rome, and embracing all things in the power of its vast synthesis distributes and orders all things in their appropriate place.
>
> (179)

Gioberti clearly takes his distance from Gibbon, and from every other writer who had read in the Roman landscape the decadence of classical civilization (or indeed, of Italian civilization as a whole) when he envisions, even from the depths of the "città sotterranea e sepolcrale," the indistinct splendors of a "metropoli futura":

> A learned Englishman of the last century who chanced to hear, as he sat on the Capitoline, Christian psalms rising from the temple of

Jupiter, began to reflect on the decline and fall of this long ruined empire, and resolved to reconstruct its history. It gives me greater pleasure to perceive in the solemnity of Christian Rome *a new order which is approaching,* and to announce its advent and greet its arrival. Hail, *oh Rome, city of memories, but even more of our hopes,* for you alone bear the seed of the unity of Italy and of the world . . . Located in the center of Italy, you are the common meeting-ground [*comune ritrovo*] of all her children; arriving from the north and south, from the mountains and the seacoasts, they come together in your womb: and there, speaking your language, they recognize their fellow countrymen, and blessed by the father, embrace as brothers. (Emphasis added)

The edifying parable, prophetic tone, and "comune ritrovo" theme inevitably recall Mazzini; but Mazzini's Third Rome would have risen on the ruins of the papacy. This is in fact the one reproach that qualifies his otherwise favorable review of Didier's *Rome souterraine* that I mentioned at the outset of this chapter.

Although Mazzini is grateful for Didier's solidarity with the Italian cause and congratulates the author for having created, in his character of Anselmo, a protagonist capable of representing that Popolo which he himself regarded as the sole possible source of Italy's redemption, Mazzini argues that the objective limit of Didier's political vision is his attachment to the persistent mirage of the papacy – by which Anselmo, in his maneuvers as double agent for the *carbonari* and *sanfedisti,* is fatally deceived.

Anselmo's continued fascination for the papacy is chiefly explained in the novel by the charismatic presence of the Cardinal de Pétralie – a Julien Sorel figure and "bâtard de la Sicile" grimly, ecstatically determined to rise from his humble origins to the office of pope – and like Julien a skillful *comédien,* secretly patterning his own meteoric career on a text (here, the biography of Sixtus V).[22] Nonetheless, Mazzini insists – a decade before Gioberti's *Primato* and the election of Pius IX – that the Pope will never play a role in the unification of Italy.

The neoguelph illusion from which Anselmo never manages to free himself thus represents for Mazzini the one reactionary tendency in Didier's novel. The ideological limits of Anselmo are those of *carbonarismo* in general. As an ideal "type" of the emerging Popolo Anselmo is flawed, incomplete:

For Anselmo, born of the people (like the *carbonaro* movement itself) has no faith in the people; though he glimpses the republican destiny of Italy, he looks to the papal tiara to provide a sanction for that destiny . . . : between the People and God, the sole terms of the

future, this man of little faith introduces a third term which the century will discard.

(390)

Extending to the *carbonari* in general, for their lack of a coherent political
program and willingness to compromise with the Church for the expulsion
of Austria, a reproach that he repeatedly leveled against a nostalgic "poetry
of ruins,"[23] Mazzini concludes that Anselmo,

> wandering among the sublime ruins of Rome, fell in love with the sun
> which was setting . . . He prostrated himself before that setting sun,
> and allured by the dream of restoring the ruins, was unable to dis-
> tinguish the last ray cast by a dying institution from the first ray which
> shines from a third world still invisible.
>
> (390–1)

If *carbonarismo* was historically unprepared to witness that "primo rag-
gio" ("That first ray will come; but it will rise to illuminate a council, not a
conclave . . ."), it nevertheless began the labyrinthine work of subverting
the present power structure through its obscure maze of mines and counter-
mines – the "catacombes politiques" traced by Didier in an effort to explain
the unlikely collaboration of *carbonari* and *sanfedisti* in a novel pledged to
historical verisimilitude:

> Italy, as we have said, is like ancient Egypt a land of mysteries and
> initiations. Its entire terrain is volcanic; thrones tremble there like the
> earth itself; when its surface is calm and carpeted with flowers that is
> perhaps the very moment when a mine will explode. In this vast
> subterranean network of mines and countermines which intersect in
> the darkness and undermine the foundations of the Italian dynasties, it
> often happens that one man's work aids another; but it is also common
> that, meeting underground as at the seige of Tortona, the miners stain
> the shadows with their blood.
>
> (81)

One can not help recalling the extraordinary elaboration of this theme in
Hugo's chapter, "Les mines et les mineurs," in *Les misérables* (1862). To cite
just a brief portion of it here:

> There are all sorts of excavations beneath the edifice of society . . .
> there is the religious mine, the philosophical mine, the political mine,
> the economic mine, the revolutionary mine. One man uses an idea to

cleave the rock; another is armed with numbers, another with his anger, and they call to and answer each other from the catacombs. Utopias move in these subterranean channels and ramify in all directions; they meet at times and fraternize. Jean Jacques lends his pick to Diogenes, who lends him his lantern in turn; at times, though, they fight, and Calvin clutches Socinus by the hair. But nothing arrests or interrupts the tension of all their energies toward the object . . . Society hardly suspects this excavation, which leaves no traces on its surface and yet changes its entrails. So many subterranean levels, so many different works and varying extractions. What issues from all these profound trenches? – the future.[24]

Mazzini's own rhetoric is equally melodramatic. After congratulating Didier for his discovery of the "true" Italy ("l'Italia invisibile – l'Italia sotterranea"), he further strains the metaphor of a politico-religious "underground" by portraying the Popolo itself as a buried icon, a mystical artifact soon to be excavated and unveiled:

> The youth of Italy glimpsed their nation's own destiny, and drew near to see this destiny revealed. Incautious tyranny had prepared the moment by striking at the veils and symbols which swathed the sacred image of Italy's future, jealously guarded in Italy's subterranean depths. The new generation stripped off the last veil, and the *Word,* the secret of Italy appeared. It was the *People.*
>
> (388)

It was because *carbonarismo* was unready for this revelation that Mazzini considers Didier's text a "historical" novel: a tribute and epitaph to the movement with a useful commemorative function, but itself an inadequate representation of the ongoing political struggle in Italy. This explains his later request to George Sand, in a letter of 1843, to write a novel that would glorify the Giovine Italia as Didier's *Rome souterraine* had the *carbonari,* by portraying "une Italie souterraine qui serait non l'épitaphe de la vieille et réactionnaire Italia . . . mais l'hymne du rajeunissement."[25]

If Mazzini judged Anselmo's attempted rapprochement between the *carbonari* and *sanfedisti* to be a particularly dangerous form of political collaboration, he did believe it necessary for the Giovine Italia to work closely with other sects both in Italy and throughout Europe. One of the unusual features of his program was in fact the requirement that all members of the Giovine Italia belong to other sects as well, in order to direct the older organizations toward its new set of goals. This labyrinth of clandestine activity was complex and not easily penetrated; there were many cul-de-sacs and false leads, and much shifting terrain. But Mazzini's "catacombes politiques" were not the *Carceri* of Piranesi, full of blind staircases and deliberately skewed perspectives. The entire clandestine structure he helped to create was founded on the goal of communication ("On s'appelle et on se répond d'une catacombe à l'autre"); and his monumental city, the "Third Rome," would have shared none of Piranesi's sinister spatial humor.

Given the interest of Didier's *Rome souterraine* not only to Mazzini but to Garibaldi himself as a novelist, it may be helpful to examine the text very briefly here. On the whole the book reads like a revisionary topography of Rome; the table of contents, with its catalogue of monumental sites, would have looked familiar to any dilettante on a classical tour. But Didier's strategy is to exploit each of these settings as a contemporary frame for heroic action, as if by their historical and mythical associations monumental sites could indeed inspire "monumental" deeds (Foscolo's "egregie cose").

Since Didier's characters are constantly on the move, circulating throughout the city and outlying *campagna* in a continuing effort to communicate with and mobilize their fellow conspirators while avoiding detection themselves, the author is able (without abandoning all claim to verisimilitude) to range freely throughout the city of Rome, accompanying his characters like the crow in Pasolini's *Uccellacci e uccellini,* pursuing them tirelessly with edifying commentary on each Roman landmark that crosses their path. If this technique would be less successful today, Mazzini testifies to its popularity at the time ("Reviewers have long noted the many admirable qualities of Didier's novel . . . local color reproduced with marvellous accuracy, lively descriptions, erudition introduced without pedantry into the course of the action," p. 385). A tolerance for such intrusive archaeological narration had certainly been prepared in part by the diffusion of the *roman pédagogique,* at least since Barthélemy's *Anarcharsis.* In any case my point here is not to defend Didier's narrative technique but to suggest that his strategic focus on certain landmarks of the ancient city contributed to an Italian revision of the possibilities of Rome.

To retrace each character's complicated itineraries is not necessary here; but it may be useful to sketch the basic camps into which Didier's Rome is divided.

The locus of power is clearly represented by the Vatican (finally spared from destruction by the invading *carbonari* only through the intervention of Remo, the artist of the group: "Brûler les Loges de Raphael et la Transfiguration! . . . Brûler le Laocoön! Le Jugement dernier de Michel-Ange! Brûler l'Apollo du Belvedere! Sacrilège! Sacrilège! Sommes-nous donc des incendiaires? Que dirait l'Italie? Que dirait le monde?", 346–7); the Quirinal (seat of the Conclave and retreat of the Pope during the insurrection, 190 ff.), the Palazzo Madama (headquarters of the papal police, to whom Antonia, the jealous mistress of one of the insurgents, denounces the conspiracy, 157 ff.); and, ironically, the Piazza del Popolo (where Marius "le Trasteverin" is executed, like Arnaldo da Brescia before him, his scaffold erected at the base of the papal obelisk, 332).

The primary locus of the opposition, instead, is the Forum. Though forced to hide most of their men in the medieval tower of Astura, on the coast at a short distance from Rome, the *carbonari* base their military operations in the Forum itself. One early convocation in the Velabrum is foiled, as we have seen, by the jealous Antonia; but the conspirators escape through an underground passageway unknown to the police (165 ff.).

The Baths of Caracalla are the rendezvous of Anselmo and Marius the intransigent republican; here they debate political strategy while awaiting the decision of the Conclave. The Tomb of Bibulus (a plebeian aedile of the first century B.C.) is the scene of Marius's harangue to the Roman people following the election of the new pope; Didier supplies the entire Latin inscription to help us follow the impassioned epigraphy of this Rienzo reincarnate, who points to the words "Senatus Consulto Populique Iussu" as incontrovertible proof of the natural sovereignty of the Roman people (240).

To each of the principal characters is assigned a separate hill, commanding a distinct perspective of Rome, on which to confess his private life and political ideals. Marius chooses Monte Sacro (site of the popular revolt of 394 B.C. that resulted in the concession of the tribunes) as the site of his sunrise farewell to Anselmo (269 ff.). The Cardinal de Pétralie as a cleric prefers the right bank, and arranges to meet Anselmo on Monte Mario at sunset (118 ff.). Anselmo himself selects the overgrown gardens of the Villa Farnese on the Palatine, with its view of the Forum, as the site of his interview with the Cardinal (289).

But the action naturally climaxes in the Forum itself. Bombarded by papal cannon from the Palatine and surprised from the rear by the entry of enemy troops through their secret escape route, the *carbonari* besieged in the "maison du Forum" are swiftly massacred; but each dies crying "Vive l'Italie!" and the narrator, surveying the wreckage, concludes, "Jamais le Forum, ce vieux champ de bataille des Gracques, des Barbares et des guerres civiles du moyen âge, jamais il n'avait vu une si épouvantable mêlée" (354).

Anselmo alone survives the attack and is left to find a hiding place till nightfall allows him to return safely home. Ironically, it is the Colosseum that affords greatest anonymity; though his meditations there are soon interrupted by the arrival of no less than the mother of Napoleon ("Si cette femme isolée n'était pas la Niobe des nations," the narrator remarks, echoing Byron's phrase, "c'était bien une Niobe comme elle, elle avait à pleurer, elle aussi, bien des enfants, bien des martyrs . . .").

But it is the sight of a procession of penitents in the arena below, praying

for the Christian martyrs, that finally restores Anselmo's faith in the revolution, as he declares to the Capuchin monk who has come to console him on
the death of his comrades: "Ce que les chrétiens étaient pour la Rome de
Néron, nous le sommes, nous, pour la Rome du Vatican." The idyllic
landscape of ruins ("le temps était splendide, les ruines toutes parfumées de
fleurs sauvages . . ."), through the timely superimposition of a Christian
spectacle, has been reclaimed by Didier's hero as a political symbol of an
"avenir reparateur."

A good deal less skillfully Garibaldi, in his novel *Clelia* of 1870,[26] will
exploit the same landscape as the setting for a fictionalized account of the
Roman uprising of 1867, which had ended in disastrous defeat at the Villa
Glori. As if to take up where Didier had left off, he stages the first assembly
of his conspirators in the Colosseum itself – a revolutionary arena which, he
proudly notes, bears no resemblance to the romantic moonlit ramble of
foreign visitors to Rome ("It is customary for foreigners to visit the Colosseum by moonlight – but it should be seen on a black and stormy night – lit
by lightning – rocked by thunder – and resounding with deep and un-
earthly echoes," 11).

That such a public place, in the heart of the papal city, can afford safe
rendezvous for three hundred conspirators, is due (the narrator explains) to
the obscurantism of the clergy itself, which by fostering superstition and
fear has created within its own walls an enclave for the opposition, a desert
within the city abandoned at nightfall not only by the populace but by the
priests themselves (13). Thus the single pair of papal guards who venture
forth to investigate the gathering take flight at first sight of the conspirators,
appropriately mistaking them for ghosts of the ancient Romans.

"It was a dark night – and huge black clouds were gathering over the
holy city – blown by a violent scirocco wind . . ." The scene is set for the
arrival of the Three Hundred, "wrapped in loose robes that looked like
togas in the flickering light." Silently they file into the sole remaining loggia
of the Colosseum: "No thrones, no tapestries adorned the enclosure. –
(What use were ornaments to those who had pledged to die?) – The ruins
were their walls, their rostrum and gallery" (12).

Their leader Attilio has only begun to address the conspirators when the
ceremony is interrupted by a violent storm and the sudden apparition of a
disheveled young woman, stumbling into the middle of the arena. "Povera
Camilla!" exclaims the gallant Silvio, as she shrieks and faints in his arms:
for he knows her to have been seduced and abandoned to a *manicomio* by a
perfidious priest upon the murder of her illegitimate child . . . and it is her
appearance that precipitates the bewildering whirl of events that will make
up Garibaldi's novel.

I will not pursue the plot any further except to note that the political topography of the novel continues remarkably parallel to that of Didier. A second convocation in the catacombs beneath the Baths of Caracalla is, like the *carbonaro* reunion of the Velabrum, betrayed to the papal authorities by a spy, leaving the conspirators to disperse at great peril through the streets and ruins of Rome (100 ff.). Again a ruined medieval tower along the coastline serves as shelter for the fugitives (149), while the *campagna* as a whole is portrayed, along with the great marble wilderness of Rome, as the locus of political resistance, "un deserto . . . seminato di macerie" (95), officially belonging to the priests but effectively the asylum of beggars, bandits, and other victims of papal misgovernment.

That Garibaldi's sense of the political implications of archaeology naturally sought more concrete form of expression than the literary text is clear from his campaign during the 1870s to divert the Tiber from the city of Rome, opening a vast new field for excavation and eventually transforming the ancient river bed into an instructive "passeggiata archaeologica."[27]

This audacious proposal, while the cause of some embarrassment to the governing coalition of the Destra, wholly conformed to the heroic scale of the city envisioned by Mazzini – the Third Rome that he had invoked in a famous passage of 1859.[28]

"Venite meco," he began, leading the "giovani d'Italia" on an imaginary archaeological tour of the *campagna* north of Rome. "Seguitemi dove comincia la vasta campagna che fu, or sono tredici secoli, il convegno delle razze, perch'io vi ricordi dove batte il core d'Italia . . ."

Admonishing them that the ground beneath their feet is the "dust of nations," he invites them now to consider the view:

> The vast *campagna* is still and through its lonely wastes breathes a silence that fills the heart with sadness, as if one were wandering through a cemetery. But whoever, nourished by thoughts which have been steeled through hardship, stops in this solitary place in the evening, feels an indistinct murmur of life beneath his feet, which seems the sound of generations that await the command of a vigorous word to arise and repopulate those sites that seem created for a Council of Peoples . . .

With an increasingly hypnotic momentum he urges his listeners on, to a vantage point on the Via Cassia, "among extinguished volcanoes and Etruscan ruins," and gives this command:

> Stop here and gaze as far as you can toward the south and toward the Mediterranean. In the midst of these vast spaces you will glimpse, like a beacon in the ocean, an isolated point, a sign of distant grandeur.

Kneel then and worship; for there beats the heart of Italy: there lies ROME in its eternal solemnity. And that eminent point is the Campidoglio of the Christian World. And a few steps away is the Campidoglio of the Pagan World. And those two fallen worlds await a third World, even more vast and sublime, which is being fashioned in the midst of its mighty ruins [*potenti rovine*]. And this is the Trinity of History whose Word is in Rome.

Rome's "potenti rovine" never gave birth to the ideal city of Mazzini. It is hard to guess what structures and spaces he might have invented to replace the broken thrones and altars of Europe. In Rome we can imagine a "Pantheon dell'Umanità" inspired by the visionary geometry of Boullée and Ledoux. Instead we have the Victor Emmanuel monument. Yet Mazzini's Third Rome remains, along with the neoguelph capital of Gioberti, one of the most influential nineteenth-century visions of the city, and illustrates the importance of archaeology to the nationalist rhetoric of the Risorgimento.

7

PIUS IX, THE REPUBLIC, AND THE SCENE OF RUIN, 1846–50

N O EVENT seemed more providential to the rising neoguelph nationalist movement than the election of Giovan Maria Mastai-Ferretti in 1846, just three years after the publication of Gioberti's *Primato*. The candidate who had seemed most likely to accede to the papacy upon the death of the octogenarian Gregory XVI was his secretary of state, Lambruschini, a conservative and close collaborator with Metternich; but unexpectedly, the young and relatively liberal cardinal-bishop from Imola was chosen in his place. Not only was the new Pope no friend to Austria (his choice of the name Pius, in homage to the persecuted Pius VII, was taken as a sign of his desire to reassert the papacy's freedom from foreign interference), but he showed immediate interest in certain of the reforms proposed by Gioberti and raised the hopes of liberals and democrats alike by declaring an amnesty to all political prisoners on 16 July 1846, only a month after his election.

Mazzini's republican and unitary goals were, as we have seen, fundamentally incompatible with Gioberti's program of a federalist league of Italian states under the leadership of the Pope. Yet both movements immediately profited from the amnesty, as their members returned from exile to resume their political activity throughout the peninsula. The goal of the moderates was to encourage the Pope to grant a series of limited reforms that would set an example for the other Italian princes and prepare the way for a federalist unification of Italy; but Mazzini's plan was to infiltrate demonstrations of enthusiasm for the Pope, generating a degree of patriotic and national sentiment that would eventually regain the initiative for the democrats and lead to a war of national liberation against Austria.

That the democrats succeeded in their project of discrediting the papacy is clear from the chronicle of events that followed. Pressured into a series of economic and administrative concessions that took on an increasingly political character and culminated in the granting of a constitution on 14 March 1848 (after the example of Ferdinand II of the Two Sicilies, Leopold II of Tuscany, and Charles Albert of Piedmont), Pius IX found himself trapped by his popular image as the "liberal pope" and finally withdrew his support

from the nationalist movement and the war against Austria by the allocution of 29 April. Unable to maintain control in Rome, after the assassination
of his minister Pellegrino Rossi the Pope fled in disguise to Gaeta (24
November 1848), where he remained for seventeen months under the protection of King Ferdinand of Naples. Like Pius VI, exiled a half-century
earlier, from this outpost he watched the second republican experiment in
Rome; but it was Napoleon's own nephew who would restore him to the
Vatican, inaugurating a new period of political reaction throughout Italy
and the last desperate defense of the temporal power.

The events of Pius IX's long and controversial papacy (1846–78) and the
history of the 1849 Roman Republic are well known and do not need to be
reviewed in this chapter.[1] My purpose instead is to examine the role of
archaeological imagery in the rhetoric of both revolution and reaction at this
critical juncture in the Risorgimento movement. If Pius IX was initially
sympathetic to Gioberti's proposal of the archaeological revival of an Italian
primato, like Gioberti he rejected the more subversive implications of the
archaeological metaphor that evolved in the discourse of Italian nationalism.
After calling on the French to overthrow the Republic he retrenched his
papacy amid the fresh ruins of the Janiculum, only to await the decisive
breach of the Aurelian wall at the Porta Pia in 1870 and subsequent redefini-
tion of the entire political landscape of Rome.

Both the traditional genre of encomiastic poetry and the relatively new
popular medium of the lithograph were enlisted to celebrate the reforms
granted by Pio Nono in the first eighteen months of his papacy. By the time
he reluctantly conceded a constitution on 14 March 1848, events were clearly beyond his control. A lithograph produced in Venice to commemorate
the occasion (Fig. 17) shows the extent to which the Pope was now identified with the cause of Italian nationalism, despite his protests that these
reforms were only limited in scope and must never be taken to suggest a
willingness to participate in a war against Austria.

The lithograph, dedicated to Pius IX from "Tutti i popoli riconoscenti,"
shows the Pope, guided by the winged figure of Liberty (dressed in a
Phrygian cap and carrying an olive branch and cross), extending his left
hand to help Italy rise (*risorgere*) from her chains. The figure of Justice holds
the Pope's right hand over Italy's head in a gesture of benediction. Behind
the Pope, two *putti* hold a marble tablet inscribed "Nova carta," representing the new constitution; while a figure of Fame with her trumpet flies
overhead carrying a banner marked "Religion / Libertà / Toleranza" (*sic*).
The view, appropriately, is from the north, as we can tell from the disposition of the two great landmarks of St. Peter's and the Colosseum. Unlike
the later portrait of Garibaldi (1862; Fig. 3), presented just a few months

17. Melchiorre Fontana, "To His Holiness Pius IX, from all the grateful peoples," 1848 (Venice, Litografia al San Marco).

before his march on Rome and defeat at Aspromonte (in which the position of these two monuments is reversed), the political perspective here implied proceeds not from Calabria but from Venice and reflects the hope that the Pope will voluntarily unite the divided provinces of Italy under his leadership.

The figure of Italy, with her crenellated crown and cornucopia of fruit and grains at her feet, is recognizable from many iconographical sources, including Ripa's *Iconologia* (1603); but most recently it recalls Canova's tomb of Alfieri (Fig. 16) and Leopardi's own personification of Italy in his canzone "All'Italia" of 1818 (". . . o qual ti veggio, / formosissima donna! . . . / . . . E questo è peggio, / che di catene ha carche ambe le braccia," lines 9–13), itself inspired by Foscolo's *Sepolcri* as well as by Petrarch's "Italia mia." Like Leopardi's allegorical vision of Italy, this figure is seated; but she is not "negletta e sconsolata," left alone to mourn her state of servitude, but surrounded by "tutti i popoli riconoscenti" who celebrate her imminent *risorgimento* as they gather to praise her liberator, the Pope. All ages, races, and social classes are represented in the group that clusters round Pius, from the bourgeois couple on the extreme right to the bareheaded monk prostrate in the foreground and the workman at his left, leaning to pray on a relief of Romulus and Remus. This image, produced at the height of the neoguelph movement, presents a visual synthesis of its political aspirations and translates the traditional topoi of papal encomium into the language of liberal Catholic nationalism.

Only days after granting the constitution in Rome, Pio Nono was faced with new pressure to join the war against Austria after the flight of Metternich and the victorious insurrections of Venice and Milan. In his *Histoire de la révolution de Rome* of 1851, the highly conservative contemporary historian Alphonse Balleydier describes a demonstration staged in the Colosseum on 23 March 1848 in support of Charles Albert's declaration of war on Austria. Balleydier argues that the Pope never had any intention of sending troops against another Catholic kingdom, but that his authority was subverted by a liberal faction of the clergy who independently roused the people to a "Holy War." On this occasion they exploit the stirring scenography of the Colosseum; and despite his contempt for their motives Balleydier can not disguise his appreciation of the spectacle:

> It was the 23 March! Illuminated by a magnificent spring sun, the Roman sky was cloudless; [the crowd was] radiant with enthusiasm; the soldiers of the civic guard, the members of [patriotic] clubs, the official troops, the nobility, the bourgeoisie, princes, artisans and proletarians were all there, grouped together with the artistic instinct of the Italians; here stood the Dominican draped in his white robe and long black cloak, there the Capuchin with his long beard framed in a brown wool hood, farther on stood the abbé with his short and trim robe; still farther on were the schoolchildren in their blue, red, violet, scarlet and white smocks, forming a human mosaic of color; nearby, the soldier whose brilliant uniform contrasted with the simple and picturesque costume of the laborer from Trastevere, and the women of all classes and social conditions completed the tableau whose arrangement resembled an elaborate stage set. A magnificent theater, indeed, was the Colosseum with its ruins, its great memories, and its immense audience standing beneath the numerous flags which seemed to replace the ancient velarium. This spectacle was magnificent, the moment solemn![2]

But the Colosseum, long consecrated to the Christian martyrs, becomes a tribune for "nationalist demagogues" as the renegade priest Alessandro Gavazzi advances to the sacred pulpit in the center of the arena:

> He is admirably cast in his role, and his costume contributes to the illusion of the scene. A long black cloak, artistically draped, covers his black robe gathered at the waist by a broad belt of the same color. A green, red and white cross shines forth on his chest . . . his long black

hair, loose in the wind, flows to his neck, his gaze is inspired, his
bearing harmonious, his pose dramatic, his voice resounding, as he
begins to preach the crusade of Italian independence: "Brothers," he
cries, "the day of our deliverance is at hand! the hour of the holy
crusade has sounded! To arms! God wills it! To arms!"

Balleydier contemptuously calls Gavazzi a "pale copy of Peter the Hermit" and the resemblance was no doubt deliberately cultivated by the priest,
for the figure of Peter the Hermit had already been revived in the iconography of the Italian revolution by Francesco Hayez's famous painting of 1828
(explicitly commended by Mazzini in his "Pittura moderna in Italia" of
1840).[3] Gavazzi's theatrical manner was widely criticized, even by the democrats (Trevelyan suggests that in his eloquence there was a "certain strain
of vulgarity" and notes that the young poet Mameli "had the strongest
aversion to Father Gavazzi"):[4] but Balleydier himself admits the priest's
ability to rouse the people, against the will of their pope, to a declaration of
war against Austria. In the text of the speech as transcribed by Balleydier we
recognize the exhortatory rhetoric of Foscolo's *Sepolcri,* translated from
Santa Croce to the Colosseum and into the language of the nationalist
crusade of the clergy:

> "Romans! Do you see those stone slabs, these shafts of broken col-
> umns, these ancient ruins, these scattered capitals? Each is a pulpit
> which the fatherland raises before you to receive the names of its
> strong and valiant sons. These names, inscribed in the hearts of Ital-
> ians, will last longer than if they had been engraved in marble or
> bronze. Now, oh Romans, rise up! under the dome of heaven which
> lends us the most beautiful rays of its sun, in the presence of God who
> sees us and reads the truth in our hearts, in the presence of the men
> who hear us, before this symbol of the cross, an emblem of liberty, on
> this ground hallowed by the blood of saints and martyrs, let us all
> pledge never to return to Rome until we have slain the last of the
> barbarians."

> In that moment, as the flags and banners wave overhead, the entire
> audience rises, and with their right hands extended toward the cross
> which stands in the middle of the Colosseum, with a single voice they
> repeat the formula of the oath pronounced by Father Gavazzi.

> It was a sublime spectacle that the Colosseum presented that day.

Unable to resist popular pressure stirred up at the assembly, the Pope
agreed to send troops on the following day. He specified that they were to

be used strictly for the purpose of defending the borders of the Papal States against any possible Austrian incursion; but when General Durando proceeded despite his orders into Lombardy, Pius disclaimed all responsibility for the war in the allocution of 29 April and formally denied any participation or sympathy with the Risorgimento movement.

Unable to recall his troops, who had independently joined forces with Charles Albert against Austria, the Pope found his authority and credibility eroding. His flight to Gaeta finally enabled the democrats to seize control of the government, and the Roman Republic was proclaimed on 9 February 1849.

Throughout the brief history of the Roman Republic its orators used the imagery of ruins and reconstruction to represent the goals of the new regime. Carlo Armellini, soon to be elected triumvir with Mazzini and Saffi, echoed Mazzini's formula of the Third Rome in his address to the Constituent Assembly of 5 February 1849:

> You [fellow deputies] are sitting between the tombs of two great epochs. On the one side are the ruins of imperial Italy, on the other the ruins of papal Italy; it is up to you to build a new edifice upon those ruins . . .[5]

Mazzini himself, in justifying the decision to resist the armies of Oudinot and subject Rome to a potentially disastrous siege, recalled Rome's centrality to the very principle of national unity and argued that the new Italy could only arise on the ruins of Rome:

> To the many other causes which decided us to resist, there was in my mind added one intimately bound up with the aim of my whole life – the foundation of our national unity. Rome was the natural center of that unity, and it was important to attract the eyes and the reverence of my countrymen towards her. The Italian people had almost lost their *Religion* of Rome; they, too, had begun to look upon her as a sepulcher, and such she seemed.
>
> As the seat of a form of faith now extinct, and only outwardly sustained by hypocrisy and persecution . . . Rome was regarded by some with aversion, by others with disdainful indifference. It was therefore essential to redeem Rome; to place her once again at the summit, so that the Italians might again learn to regard her as the temple of their common country. It was necessary that all should learn how potent was the immortality stirring beneath those ruins of two epochs, two worlds . . .[6]

While the revolutionaries stood guard over Rome's *potenti rovine,* preparing to defend the city from the French, the Pope himself was enjoying an unusual excursion to the ruins of Pompeii. Perhaps to console him for the loss of his ancient treasures at the Vatican, the King awarded Pio Nono a Greek marble stele unearthed during their visit to the site. Only later was it discovered that the relief had been planted there deliberately, after lying unattended for many years in the storerooms of the Naples Museum.[7]

But the Pope did not have to settle for such palliatives for long. The French captured the city after a month-long siege on 3 July 1849; and the Pope reclaimed formal possession of the Vatican and the entire Papal States by his triumphant reentry through the Lateran gate on 12 April 1850.

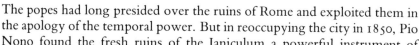

The popes had long presided over the ruins of Rome and exploited them in the apology of the temporal power. But in reoccupying the city in 1850, Pio Nono found the fresh ruins of the Janiculum a powerful instrument of antipapal propaganda. As Mazzini had predicted, the heroic resistance to the French at the Porta San Pancrazio became a national legend and served to mobilize support for the Italian Risorgimento throughout Europe and especially in liberal circles in England. The Villa Corsini, at the height of the Doria-Pamphili gardens (completely destroyed and now marked by a commemorative arch), the Vascello (left in ruins as a national monument), the Porta San Pancrazio (rebuilt in 1854 and now the home of a small Risorgimento museum), Villa Savorelli (Fig. 18; entirely restored and now known as the Villa Aurelia, property of the American Academy in Rome), and the church of San Pietro in Montorio all remained as concrete and eloquent testimony of the violence used against the Republic.

Even after the Unification the Janiculum would remain a sacred ground and strategic focus of patriotic sentiment; the Passeggiata del Gianicolo, lined with the busts of Garibaldini, and the monument to Garibaldi himself in the central piazza, were completed during the reign of Umberto I (1878–1900). In his "Canzone di Garibaldi," D'Annunzio described the hill as a new Marathon:

> Villa Corsina, Casa dei Quattro Venti,
> Fumida prua del Vascello protesa
> Nella tempesta, alti nomi per sempre
> Solenni come Maratona Platea
> Cremera, luoghi già d'ozii di piaceri
> Di melodie e di magnificenze
> Fuggitive, orti custoditi da cieche
> Statue ed arrisi da fontane serene,

18. L. Gallassi, "Palazzo Savorelli, General Headquarters of Garibaldi," lithograph from the series "Ruins of the Roman War of 1849," 1849 (Rome, Museo Centrale del Risorgimento).

Trasfigurati subito in rossi inferni
Vertiginosi.[8]

(Villa Corsini, House of the Four Winds, smoky prow of the Ship thrust forward into the tempest, great names forever solemn as Marathon, Platea, Cremera, once the haunts of idle pleasure and music and frail magnificence, groves guarded by blind statues and watered by peaceful fountains, suddenly transfigured into vertiginous red infernos.)

Like Santa Croce in Foscolo's *Sepolcri,* the Janiculum hill served the Risorgimento movement as a collective tomb and memorial to the cause of national independence; and the Fascists in turn exploited its historic significance by erecting the Monumento ai Caduti per la causa di Roma italiana (1941) on the grassy slope opposite San Pietro in Montorio – its granite altar sheltering a porphyry sarcophagus containing the remains of the poet Goffredo Mameli, killed at twenty-two in the attack on the Villa Corsini and author of the poem "Fratelli d'Italia," which was known as the Italian "Marseillaise" and would become the national anthem of the first Italian republic in 1946.

But the Janiculum was already becoming a legend in early July of 1849 when the American journalist Margaret Fuller, who had been present in Rome throughout the siege, sent this dispatch to the *New York Tribune:*

> Yesterday I went over the scene of conflict. It was fearful even to *see* the Quattro Venti and Vascello, where the French and Romans had been several days so near one another, all shattered to pieces, with fragments of rich stucco and painting still sticking to rafters between the great holes made by the cannonade, and think that men had stayed and fought in them when only a mass of ruins . . . A *contadino* showed me where thirty-seven brave [*sic*] are buried beneath a heap of wall that fell upon them in the shock of one cannonade. A marble nymph, with broken arm, looked sadly that way from her sun-dried fountain; some roses were blooming still, some red oleanders, amid the ruin. The sun was casting its last light on the mountains, on the tranquil, sad Campagna, that sees one more leaf turned in the book of woe . . . O men and women of America, spared these frightful sights – acknowledge as the legitimate leaders and rulers those men who represent the people, who understand their wants, who are ready to die or to live for their good . . .[9]

Contemporary lithographs (Figs. 18 and 19) served to propagate such images – particularly those of Danesi and Gallassi, derived from Lecchi's series of thirty-two calotypes, *Rovine della guerra di Roma del 1849,* executed only days after Garibaldi's retreat. Photographic techniques were still primitive at mid-century, and Lecchi's views were not intended for widespread reproduction except in the standard form of the lithograph; but together with the panoramic view of the Janiculum from Garibaldi's headquarters at the Villa Savorelli – the first full 360-degree panoramic photograph of a battleground – they became a monument not only in Risorgimento iconography but in the history of photography itself.[10]

At the same time more traditional media were inspired by the example of the defense of Rome. The Lombard Federico Faruffini's painting "Cola di Rienzo che dalle alture di Roma ne contempla le rovine" (Fig. 20; presented at Brera in 1856 after the young artist's pilgrimage – on foot – to Rome) was clearly intended as a political allegory to glorify the era of the republican triumvirs and their tribune Ciceruacchio.[11] Nino Costa, who had been present at the siege of Rome, also began but failed to complete a

19. Anonymous lithograph, "Ruins of the Siege of Rome of 1849," 1849 (Rome, GCS).

painting on the same theme; and at Turin in 1850 Carlo Felice Biscarra presented a similar painting of Cola, which was promptly bought by Victor Emmanuel II.

As the Savoy monarchy enlisted the arts in its campaign to discredit the temporal power, the ruins of Rome – both ancient and recent – became an ever more effective instrument of lay propaganda. Yet the papacy had attempted to reclaim control of the ruins in official rhetoric as early as

20. Federico Faruffini, "Cola di Rienzo who from the heights of Rome contemplates its ruins," 1855–6 (Pavia, Musei Civici del Castello Visconteo).

August of 1849, when the temporary government appointed by Pio Nono staged a ceremony in honor of General Oudinot at the Palazzo dei Conservatori on the Capitoline – where a bust of the general was erected in the Sala dei Capitani to commemorate his restoration of order to the city without harm to its most prestigious ancient monuments.[12] Oudinot's effigy,

framed by Tommaso Laureti's sixteenth-century frescoes representing episodes from the history of the original Roman Republic, must have struck
more than one viewer as an incongruous sight; but Pio Nono persisted in
regarding the general as a hero for having liberated Rome from the republican menace.

Yet Rome's marble wilderness was inevitably transfigured by the events of
1848–9. The changing view of the monuments, and of their value in political propaganda, is reflected in the patterns of archaeological patronage of
Pius IX in the years that follow his restoration. The Republic had ordered
new excavations in the Forum during its brief period in power, and Pius
resumed these in 1850. Several important discoveries were made during
these years, including Luigi Canina's successful identification of the temples
of Vespasian (Fig. 11) and Saturn, both excavated under Napoleon but then
believed to be the temples of Jupiter Tonans and Concord.

The Pope's decision to suspend work in the Forum in 1853 reflects a shift
in priorities that had already become evident in the previous year, when he
established the Commissione di Archeologia Sacra to oversee excavation in
the catacombs. Henceforth in his patronage of archaeology Pius would
consistently privilege paleochristian sites. In 1854 he opened the Museo Pio
Cristiano in the Lateran Palace (the first major collection of early Christian
artifacts since Benedict XIV's Museo Sacro in the Vatican), and he ordered
intensive research at the catacombs of Callixtus, where he publicly celebrated mass in 1861.

At the same time Pius IX allowed one of the most important private
collections of pre-Christian artifacts, the Campana collection, to be sold at
auction in 1857 and dispersed in northern Europe, where they still remain
(primarily in the Louvre and the Hermitage in Leningrad). Historians are
still critical of his failure to prevent the export of this rich and broad-ranging
archaeological collection, which his predecessors (Fea, Cardinal Pacca, and
Pius VII) would have protected as part of the legitimate patrimony of
Rome.[13]

Certain impressive classical statues were in fact discovered during Pius's
reign and placed with due prominence in the Vatican museums: most notably the Augustus of Prima Porta (discovered in the Villa of Livia in 1863 and
installed in Pius VII's Braccio Nuovo) and the colossal bronze Hercules
from the Theater of Pompey (which now looms over the Pio-Clementine's
Sala Rotonda). Yet it seems clear that Pio Nono's relative lack of interest in
pre-Christian archaeology, coupled with his emphasis on paleochristian
sites, reflects a growing distrust of the political ambivalence of the ruins and
monuments of pagan Rome, which had been transformed in the century
since David into emblems of revolutionary ideology. Instead the sar-

cophagi, inscriptions, and frescoes retrieved from the catacombs conveyed a clear and unambiguous message to nineteenth-century Europe: the survival of the faith despite all political persecution.

Certainly the notion that classicism was a dangerous tendency in literature was current in conservative circles in Rome; the Jesuit Father Bresciani, director of the *Civiltà cattolica* from 1859 till his death in 1862, was one of the school's most virulent critics. Classical allusions and imagery, in varying contexts, had in fact been widely incorporated into revolutionary discourse; even in Rome the herm of Pericles had given way to the helmet of Scipio.[14]

In his efforts to shore up the power of the Church Pio Nono relied increasingly upon the Jesuits. He called two of the most noted Jesuit theologians, Fathers Perrone and Passaglia, to help draft the Dogma of the Immaculate Conception (1854), which he celebrated in his most dramatic archaeological gesture – the erection of the Column of the Immaculate Conception in the Piazza di Spagna in front of the Palazzo de Propaganda Fide.

Discovered in 1777 in the Campus Martius, the colossal thirty-foot column of veined *cipollino* had been intended by Pius VI for a monument in front of the Curia Innocenziana. But displeased by the designs that were submitted, and more interested in his obelisks, the Braschi pope had abandoned the project, and the column lay forgotten until Paolo Emilio Visconti (as Commissioner of Antiquities) suggested its use in a monument to the Immaculate Conception.[15]

No more eloquent statement of the Church's relationship with antiquity was conceived during the papacy of Pius IX. Like Sixtus V, who had raised the apostolic statues on the columns of Trajan and Marcus Aurelius and inaugurated Tommaso Laureti's "Triumph of Religion" on the ceiling of the Hall of Constantine, Pius IX revived the militant tradition of the Counter-Reformation in this grandiose column in support of his dogma. Like Laureti's dramatic fresco (in which a crucifix replaces the statue of Mercury lying shattered on the ground at the base of its pedestal), this monument proclaimed that Rome would not tolerate the "mercurial" nature of classical images; henceforth they were to be rigorously incorporated into the rhetoric of the Church, just as the ancient spoil column had been resurrected as a pedestal for the effigy of Mary.

━━━ ━━━

But already the papacy relied more on the external support of France than on its own intrinsic strength to uphold the institution of the temporal power. Not even the Dogma of Papal Infallibility (voted by the Vatican Council on 18 July 1870) could prevent the occupation of Rome when Napoleon III's defeat in the Franco-Prussian War caused France to withdraw its protection from the papacy. The taking of Rome inevitably deepened the rift between clerical and secular forces in Italian society; but symbolically it completed the primary task of unifying a nation which – despite the struggles of the Risorgimento – in many ways remains resolutely fragmentary in nature.

SELECTED CHRONOLOGY

1768		When Johann Joachim Winckelmann is murdered in a tavern in Trieste, Giambattista Visconti succeeds him as papal commissioner of antiquities.
1769		Election of Clement XIV Ganganelli (1769–74).
1770		Clement XIV purchases the Fusconi and Mattei collections to form the core of the new Clementine Museum in the Vatican.
1772		Raphael Mengs completes the "Allegory of the Clementine Museum" (Fig. 6) in the Gabinetto dei Papiri in the Vatican library.
1775		Election of Pius VI Braschi (1775–99). Jacques Louis David arrives at the French Academy as recipient of the Prix de Rome.
1779		Vincenzo Monti recites the "Prosopopea di Pericle" in celebration of the *voti quinquennali* of Pius VI.
1784		King Gustav III of Sweden visits the newly opened Pio-Clementine Museum in the Vatican.
1789	20 April	Pius VI erects the obelisk in front of the French church, Trinità dei Monti.
	14 July	Fall of the Bastille.
1793	21 January	Execution of Louis XVI.
1794	28 July	Execution of Robespierre.
1796	March	Bonaparte crosses the Alps into Italy.
	23 June	Article 8 of Bonaparte's armistice with Pius VI at Bologna specifies that one hundred Roman art works must be ceded to France.
1797	February	The Treaty of Tolentino confirms the demands of the Bologna armistice.

	10 April	The first of four convoys of art works leave Rome.
	28 December	Murder of the French general Duphot.
1798	11 February	French troops enter Rome.
	15 February	Proclamation of the Roman Republic.
	20 March	Felice Giani paints the altar erected in the Piazza San Pietro for the Festa della Federazione of the new Republic (Fig. 8).
	28 July	The Laocoön, Torso, and Dying Gladiator (along with the other art works confiscated from Rome) are paraded in their packing cases through the streets of Paris, accompanied by ostriches, camels, and caged lions.
	27 August	Pius VI dies in exile in Valence.
1799	15 February	The Roman Republic celebrates its first (and only) anniversary in the Festa della Rigenerazione at the Roman Forum.
	29 September	Fall of the Roman Republic.
	9 November	Bonaparte's coup of 18 Brumaire.
1800	3 July	Pius VII Chiaramonti (1800–23), newly elected in Venice, makes his triumphal entry into Rome through the Porta del Popolo.
1801	16 July	Concordat is signed between Bonaparte and Pius VII.
1802	30 August	Pius VII appoints Canova for life as inspector general of the fine arts for the Papal States.
	2 October	Carlo Fea, new commissioner of antiquities, drafts an edict prohibiting the export of art works from Rome.
1804	2 December	Pius VII crowns Napoleon as Emperor in Notre Dame.
1806	5 September	Napoleon's Edict of Saint-Cloud is extended to Italy.
1807		Foscolo's *Dei Sepolcri* is printed in Brescia.
1809	17 May	Napoleon abolishes the temporal power and proclaims Rome a free imperial city.
	10 June	Pius VII excommunicates Napoleon.
	6 July	Pius VII is escorted into exile.
1810		Canova completes the tomb of Vittorio Alfieri in Santa Croce (Fig. 16).

1814	6 April	Napoleon abdicates at Fontainebleau and is sent into exile at Elba.
	24 May	Pius VII returns to Rome. Belli composes sonnets for the occasion; the sixteen-year-old Massimo D'Azeglio is also present.
	7 August	Pius VII restores the Jesuit order.
1815	March–June	Napoleon returns from Elba for the Hundred Days. He is defeated at Waterloo and sent into exile on Saint Helena.
	28 August	Canova arrives in Paris to negotiate the return of the art works from the Louvre.
1816	June	Francesco Hayez completes the lunette in the Chiaramonti Museum at the Vatican representing the restoration of the papal collections (Fig. 14).
		The German-Danish historian Niebuhr arrives in Rome, where he will remain until 1823 as Prussian minister to the Holy See.
1818		Childe Harold proclaims Rome a "marble wilderness."
		Leopardi composes the canzone "All'Italia."
		Domenico De Angelis completes the bio-graphical fresco cycles of Pius VI and Pius VII in the library corridor at the Vatican.
1820	January	Leopardi writes the canzone "Ad Angelo Mai" only days after the cardinal announces his discovery of the books of Cicero's *De republica.*
	7 April	The Pacca Edict reinforces the provisions of the Edict of 1802 regarding the export of antiquities.
1820–1		Unsuccessful revolutions in Naples and Piedmont.
1821	23 February	John Keats dies at the age of twenty-six in his rented rooms on the Piazza di Spagna.
1822		Death of Canova.
		Valadier completes the restoration of the Arch of Titus.
		Leopardi makes his first visit to Rome.
1823		Election of Leo XII Sermattei della Genga (1823–9).
1824	19 April	Byron dies at Missolonghi.
1829		Stendhal publishes the *Promenades dans Rome.*

		Election of Pius VIII Castiglioni (1829–30). His reign is uneventful; Pasquino comments, "Nacque, pianse, morì."
1830	27 July–August 9	The July Revolution in France.
1831		Election of Gregory XVI Cappellari (1831–46).
		Giuseppe Mazzini establishes the secret society "Giovine Italia" to bring about the national unification of Italy.
1836	21 April	Angelo Mai addresses the Accademia Pontificia di Archeologia on the anniversary of the founding of Rome.
1842		Pietro Ercole Visconti composes a cantata to celebrate the founding of the Etruscan (1837) and Egyptian (1839) museums in the Vatican.
1843		Vincenzo Gioberti publishes *Il primato morale e civile degli italiani* while in exile in Brussels.
1844		Gregory XVI founds the Museo Profano and Pinacoteca at the Lateran.
1846	16 June	Election of Pius IX Mastai-Ferretti (1846–78).
	16 July	The new pope grants amnesty to all political prisoners.
1847		Camillo Count Benso di Cavour founds the newspaper *Il Risorgimento*.
1848	14 March	Pius IX grants a constitution in Rome.
	29 April	The Pope disclaims any intent to join a war against Austria and denies all sympathy with the Risorgimento movement.
	15 November	Murder of Pellegrino Rossi.
	24 November	Pius IX flees to Gaeta.
1849	9 February	Proclamation of the Roman Republic.
	3 July	Oudinot's army drives Garibaldi from Rome after a month-long siege.
1850	12 April	Pius IX makes his triumphal reentry into Rome.
		Belli welcomes his return in the sonnet "Al signor Giuseppe Mazzini."
1852		Pius IX establishes the Commissione di Archeologia Sacra.
1854	8 November	Official opening of the Museo Pio Cristiano at the Lateran.

	8 December	Pius IX proclaims the Dogma of the Immaculate Conception.
1856		Federico Faruffini completes his painting "Cola di Rienzo who from the heights of Rome contemplates its ruins" (Fig. 20) in expression of his republican sympathies.
1860		Miriam, Kenyon, and Hilda consider Donatello's resemblance to the "Faun of Praxiteles" in the Capitoline museum.
	May	Garibaldi sets sail from Genoa on the Expedition of the Thousand.
1861	17 March	Victor Emmanuel II is proclaimed king of Italy.
	2 November	Pius IX celebrates mass at the catacombs of Callixtus.
1862	29 August	Garibaldi, in his attempt to annex Rome to the kingdom of Italy ("Roma o morte!"), is wounded and arrested at Aspromonte.
1864		The capital of the kingdom of Italy is transferred from Turin to Florence.
1870	18 July	The first Vatican Council proclaims the Dogma of Papal Infallibility.
	20 September	Italian troops, led by General Cadorna, enter Rome through the breach of the Porta Pia.
1871		The capital of Italy is officially transferred to Rome.
		The ashes of Ugo Foscolo are transferred to Santa Croce.

NOTES

INTRODUCTION

1   *Italian Hours;* cited as epigraph by Rose Macaulay, *Pleasure of Ruins* (London: Weidenfeld and Nicolson, 1953).

2   Italian critics were themselves among the first to make this claim; see G. Martegiani, *Il Romanticismo italiano non esiste* (Rome, 1908). For a history of the concept of romanticism in Italian criticism, see Giuseppe Petronio, *Il Romanticismo* (Palermo, 1963). For a thorough historical account of the vicissitudes of the term "romantic" in Italy, see Olga Ragusa, "Italy/Romantico-Romanticismo," in Hans Eichner, ed., *"Romantic" and Its Cognates: The European History of a Word* (Toronto: University of Toronto Press, 1973), pp. 293–340. For a recent attempt to define Italian literary romanticism in terms of a new relationship between conscience and universe, see Gian-Paolo Biasin, *Italian Literary Icons* (Princeton: Princeton University Press, 1985), pp. 18–47. Although unlike Biasin I am not sure that it is necessary to risk a new definition of romanticism that would depend on a sharp distinction between romantic and neoclassical poetics, I find his discussion extremely helpful and his attention to pictorial texts refreshing.

3   On the revival of the epideictic genre in sacred rhetoric during the Renaissance, see John W. O'Malley, *Praise and Blame in Renaissance Rome: Rhetoric, Doctrine, and Reform in the Sacred Orators of the Papal Court, c. 1450–1521* (Durham, N.C.: Duke University Press, 1979).

4   The epigraph is taken from Ariosto's fourth Satire (lines 58–60) and not, as was indicated on the title page of the first edition of Canto IV, from the third.

5   Pietro Romanelli, *The Roman Forum* (Rome: Istituto Poligrafico dello Stato, 1965), p. 20.

6   See especially Jean Starobinski, *1789: Les emblèmes de la raison* (Paris: Flammarion, 1973); Robert Rosenblum, *Transformations in Late Eighteenth-Century Art* (Princeton: Princeton University Press, 1967); and Mario Praz, *Gusto neoclassico* (Florence: Sansoni, 1940).

7   On metonymy and synecdoche in English romanticism (Byron vs. Scott), see Stephen Bann, *The Clothing of Clio: A Study of the Representation of History in Nineteenth-Century Britain and France* (Cambridge: Cambridge University Press, 1984), pp. 93–111.

8   I am quoting from Byron, *The Complete Poetical Works,* ed. Jerome McGann, II

(New York: Oxford University Press, 1980), lines 698–702. All other citations from the poem will be identified by line numbers in the text.

9 Shelley called it "the most consummate personification of loveliness . . . that remains to us of Greek Antiquity" ("Notes on Sculptures in Rome and Florence," in *The Complete Works,* ed. Roger Ingpen and Walter E. Peck, VI [London and New York, 1965], p. 330; cited in Francis Haskell and Nicholas Penny, *Taste and the Antique: The Lure of Classical Sculpture, 1500–1900* [New Haven: Yale University Press, 1981], p. 274). Byron could not have seen the Niobe group now in the Terme Museum in Rome, which was not excavated until the 1870s on the site of the Gardens of Sallust.

10 Alessandro Verri, *Le notti romane,* ed. Renzo Negri (Bari: Laterza, 1967). For a discussion of this text, see my Chapter 2.

11 Keats's "Ode on a Grecian Urn" appeared in 1819, only a year after the publication of Byron's Fourth Canto. On the "anti-archaeological" message of the urn, see Leo Spitzer, "The 'Ode on a Grecian Urn,' or Content vs. Metagrammar," *Comparative Literature,* 7 (1955), 203–25.

12 John Cam Hobhouse, *Historical Illustrations of the Fourth Canto of Childe Harold* (New York: Gilley, 1818), p. 154.

13 E. R. Vincent, *Byron, Hobhouse and Foscolo: New Documents in the History of a Collaboration* (Cambridge: Cambridge University Press, 1949), p. 4.

14 This view is developed by Robert Gleckner, *Byron and the Ruins of Paradise* (Baltimore: Johns Hopkins University Press, 1967).

15 Even today little is known of Cecilia Metella, except that she was the daughter of Quintus Metellus Creticus and the daughter-in-law (not, as Byron says, the wife) of "the wealthiest Roman," M. Lucinius Crassus, a triumvir of the late Republic.

16 Maurice Andrieux, *Rome* (New York: Funk and Wagnalls, 1968), p. 86.

17 Giuseppe Garibaldi, *Clelia: Il governo del monaco (Roma nel secolo XIX)* (Milan: Rechiedei, 1870); see Chapter 6 for a more extensive discussion of this text. On the historical ambivalence of the Colosseum as a religious and political symbol, see Michela di Macco, *Il Colosseo: funzione simbolica, storica, urbana* (Rome: Bulzoni, 1971). For a reading of the Colosseum in a nineteenth-century American context, see William L. Vance, "The Colosseum: American Uses of an Imperial Image," in *Roman Images: Selected Papers from the English Institute, 1982,* ed. Annabel Patterson (Baltimore: Johns Hopkins University Press, 1984).

18 *In lode delle Belle Arti. Orazione e componimenti poetici. Relazione del concorso e de' premi distribuiti in Campidoglio dall'insigne Accademia del Disegno in San Luca nel dì 12 giugno 1786* (Rome: Casaletti, 1786). The Latin version is by D. Severino Erba Bernabita, p. lii. All English versions throughout this book are my own.

19 For a discussion of Mengs's painting, see Chapter 1. On the metamorphoses of Saturn in the visual arts, see Erwin Panofsky, Raymond Klibansky, and Fritz Saxl, *Saturn and Melancholy: Studies in the History of Natural Philosophy, Religion, and Art* (London: Nelson, 1964).

20 In a famous passage Byron describes his cooperation with the *carbonari* in their preparations for an uprising in central Italy:

> My lower apartments are full of their bayonets, fusils, cartridges and what-
> not. I suppose that they consider me as a depot to be sacrificed in case of

accidents. It is no great matter, supposing that Italy could be liberated, who or what is sacrificed. It is a grand object – the very *poetry* of politics. Only think – a free Italy!!! Why, there has been nothing like it since the days of Augustus.

(Byron, *Letters and Journals,* V, p. 205)

21 *Correspondance de Lamartine publiée par Mme Valentine de Lamartine* (Paris: Hachette, 1881), I, p. 172; cited by Franco Venturi, "L'Italia fuori d'Italia," in *Storia d'Italia,* III (Turin: Einaudi, 1973), p. 1201.

22 Lamartine, *Oeuvres complètes,* II (Paris: Furnes, 1834), pp. 238–40.

23 For a detailed account of the querelle arising from Lamartine's poem, see Luigi Foscolo Benedetto, "Come nacque 'La terra dei morti' del Giusti," *Annali della Scuola normale superiore di Pisa,* sec. Lettere, storia e filosofia, 2nd. ser., 9, 227 ff. For the text of Giusti's poem, see his *Opere* (Turin: U.T.E.T., 1976), pp. 297–8.

24 See, among others, Hayden White's groundbreaking study, *Metahistory: The Historical Imagination in Nineteenth-Century Europe* (Baltimore: Johns Hopkins University Press, 1973). More generally, on the need for a rhetorical criticism, see Terry Eagleton, *Literary Theory* (Minneapolis: University of Minnesota Press, 1983), pp. 194–217. See also his *Walter Benjamin, or Towards a Revolutionary Criticism* (London: Schocken, 1981), Part 2, chapter 2, "A Small History of Rhetoric." Especially helpful to me as a practical example of sustained interdisciplinary rhetorical analysis was Stephen Bann's *The Clothing of Clio* (Cambridge: Cambridge University Press, 1984).

25 The phrase is Eagleton's, in *Literary Theory,* p. 205.

26 *The Archaeology of Knowledge,* p. 7.

27 See especially *The Order of Things: An Archaeology of the Human Sciences* (New York: Random House, 1970), pp. 367–73.

CHAPTER I

1 Monti's final version of the poem was transcribed and illuminated with the Braschi insignia by Stefano Piale in 1784 and framed to the left of the Pericles bust, where it can still be viewed today.

2 Ludwig von Pastor, *The History of the Popes,* XXXIX, trans. E. F. Peeler (London: Routledge and Kegan Paul, 1952), p. 83, n. 4. For an inventory of excavations from 1775–80, see Carlo Pietrangeli, *Scavi e scoperte di antichità sotto il pontificato di Pio VI,* 2nd ed. (Rome: Istituto di Studi Romani, 1958). On the growth of the Pio-Clementine Museum, see the two fundamental articles also by Pietrangeli: "Il Museo Clementino Vaticano," *Rendiconti della Pontificia Accademia di Archeologia,* 3rd ser., 27 (1951–2), 87–109; and "I Musei Vaticani al tempo di Pio VI," *Bollettino dei Monumenti Musei e Gallerie Pontificie,* 1 (1959–74), 7–45. For a rapid and readable introduction to the history of the Vatican collections, see the catalogue of the exhibit *The Vatican Collections: The Papacy and Art* (New York: Harry N. Abrams, 1982), and especially the chapter by Georg Daltrop on the Pio-Clementine, pp. 116–29. On the architectural history of the Vatican Palaces, Dioclecio Redig de Campos's *I Palazzi Vaticani* (Bologna: Cappelli, 1967) remains the standard reference.

3 Pastor, p. 37. The Palazzo Braschi, last of the great papal family palaces to be built in Rome, is now the seat of the Museo di Roma.

4 Georg Daltrop cites one such pasquinade in the catalogue entry No. 62, pp. 126–7, *The Vatican Collections*. Boreas may refer to the Swedish origin of the Braschi family.

5 For an account of the dispersal of Italian collections abroad and a brief history of protective legislation, see Francis Haskell, "La dispersione e la conservazione del patrimonio artistico," in *Storia dell'arte italiana*, Pt. 3, III (Turin: Einaudi, 1981), pp. 5–35. On the vicissitudes of individual sculptures, Francis Haskell and Nicholas Penny's *Taste and the Antique: The Lure of Classical Sculpture, 1500–1900* (New Haven: Yale University Press, 1981) is an invaluable reference. On protective legislation in the Papal States from the sixteenth century to the Risorgimento, see Andrea Emiliani, *Leggi, bandi e provvedimenti per la tutela dei beni artistici e culturali negli antichi stati italiani, 1571–1860* (Bologna: Cappelli, 1978), pp. 67–152. For a less technical introduction to the problem, see Giorgio Gualandi, "Neoclassio e antico: Problemi e aspetti dell'archeologia nell'età neo-classica," *Ricerche di storia dell'arte*, 8 (1979), 5–25.

6 L. Hautecoeur, *La renaissance de l'antiquité à la fin du XVIII siècle* (Paris: Fontemoing, 1912), p. 57.

7 Cavaceppi's *Raccolta d'antiche statue restaurate da Bartolomeo Cavaceppi romano* (1768–72), Piranesi's *Scelta delle migliori statue antiche* (1783–91), and Guattani's *Monumenti antichi inediti ovvero notizie sulle antichità e belle arti di Roma* (1784–9) were modeled on the earlier archaeological inventories of Winckelmann and the elder Piranesi. The seven volumes of Ennio Quirino Visconti's catalogue, *Il Museo Pio-Clementino*, were published in Rome between 1782–1807. (The first volume, credited to Giambattista Visconti, was largely the work of his son.) A second edition in reduced format was published in Milan by Bettoni in 1818, with a dedication to Vincenzo Monti. On the history of archaeological publications in eighteenth-century Italy, see the catalogue of the exhibition, *L'immagine dell'antico fra Settecento e Ottocento: Libri di archeologia nella Biblioteca Comunale dell'Archiginnasio* (Bologna: Grafis Edizioni, 1983).

8 Carlo Pietrangeli rejects the attribution of this work to Pompeo Batoni; for a thorough discussion of the painting, see his "Pio VI in visita al Museo Pio-Clementino," *Bollettino dei Monumenti Musei e Gallerie Pontificie*, 5 (1984), 113–20.

9 Hautecoeur, *La renaissance de l'antiquité*, p. 75.

10 Hautecoeur, *La renaissance de l'antiquité*, p. 78.

11 For one reading of the Villa Albani, see Anna Ottani Cavina, "Il Settecento e l'antico," in *Storia dell'arte italiana*, Pt. 2, II (Turin: Einaudi, 1982), pp. 623–33. The most detailed recent work on the Villa Albani is collected in *Forschungen zur Villa Albani: Antike Kunst und die Epoche der Aufklärung*, ed. Herbert Beck (Berlin: Mann, 1982); see especially Elisabeth Schröter, "Die Villa Albani als Imago Mundi," pp. 185–299.

12 On the iconography of Mengs's painting, see Steffi Röttgen, "Das Papyruskabinett von Mengs in der Biblioteca Vaticana, ein Beitrag zur Idee und Geschichte des Museo Pio-Clementino," *Münchner Jahrbuch der bildenden Kunst*, 31 (1980), 189–245.

13   The stone was a gift to Clement XIV from Jacopo Bellotti in 1771 and is today exhibited in the Galleria Lapidaria in the Vatican.

14   Roberto Weiss, *The Renaissance Discovery of Classical Antiquity* (Oxford: Basil Blackwell, 1969), p. 99. The papal bull of April 28, 1462, in which Pius II denounced the vandalism of Roman ruins, like many other such documents, remained a dead letter; it was, however, explicitly recalled as late as 1802 by Pius VII in the influential Chirografo of 2 October (see Chapter 3). Aeneas Sylvius Piccolomini's most famous Latin elegy lamenting the destruction of ancient Rome ("Oblectat me, Roma, tuas spectare ruinas") is included in *Pii Papae II Opera inedita,* ed. G. Cugnoni (Rome, 1883). On the paradox of the humanist pillage of ruins and the "pathology of the double gesture" of emulation and destruction of antiquity in the Renaissance, see Thomas M. Greene, *The Light in Troy: Imitation and Discovery in Renaissance Poetry* (New Haven: Yale University Press, 1982), especially pp. 220–41.

15   See Arabella Riccò Trento, "Le collezioni e i musei archeologici nei libri del XVIII e XIX secolo," in *L'immagine dell'antico,* pp. 123–31. For reproductions of the Caylus and Kircher frontispieces, see pp. 133 and 152.

16   Visconti believed the bust to be the work of Phidias. It is instead catalogued by Helbig as a second-century copy of a Greek original of ca. 429 B.C. (Wolfgang Helbig, *Führer durch die offentlichen Sammlungen klassischer Altertumer in Rom: Die Päpstlichen Sammlungen im Vatikan und Lateran,* I, 4th ed., [Tubingen: Wasmuth, 1963], p. 55).

17   Gennaro Barbarisi, "Vincenzo Monti e la cultura neoclassica," in *Storia della letteratura italiana,* VII (Milan: Garzanti, 1969), p. 21.

18   Vincenzo Monti, "Prosopopea di Pericle: Alla santità di Pio VI," *Opere* (Milan: Ricciardi, 1953), pp. 702–7. All references are to the poem's final version, which is the one framed in the Vatican museum (see note 1). For a review of the golden age *topos* in Italian literature, see Gustavo Costa, *La leggenda dei secoli d'oro nella letteratura italiana* (Bari: Laterza, 1972); on Monti's uses of the *topos,* see pp. 206–12.

19   Cesare D'Onofrio, *Gli obelischi di Roma* (Rome: Cassa di Risparmio, 1965), p. 100.

20   Georg Zoega, *De origine et usu obeliscorum* (Rome: Lazzarini, 1979). The work is dedicated to Pius VI, "qui ut omnia ad veterem gloriam splendoremque revocaret et ad publicam utilitatem referret urbem aeternam aedificiis ingentibus vaticanum libris tabulis bene pictis numis omnis generis studiose comparatis amplificavit locupletavit ornavit. Marmorea aegyptiorum graecorum etruscorum romanorumque monumenta vel e terrae visceribus vel ex abditis locis in apricum prolata in museum publicum comportavit . . ."

21   See Piero Trèves, "La tradizione classica italiana e la romanità napoleonica," in *L'idea di Roma e la cultura italiana del secolo XIX* (Milan: Ricciardi, 1962), pp. 13–18 and passim.

22   James Thomson, *The Complete Poetical Works* (Oxford: Oxford University Press, 1908), pp. 361–3, Pt. 4, lines 134 ff.

23   ". . . Sculpture first, / Deep digging, from the cavern dark and damp, / Their grave for ages, bade her marble race / Spring to new light . . ." (lines 134–7).

24   The cycle is commonly attributed to Demonico De Angelis, although Olivier

Michel, in "*Exempla virtutis* à la gloire de Pio VI," *Bollettino dei Monumenti Musei e Gallerie Pontificie*, 3 (1982), 105–41, argues that it is more probably the work of Domenico Del Frate.

25 For a thorough discussion of this program, see O. Michel, above.

26 On the program of the Hall of Constantine, see André Chastel, *The Sack of Rome, 1527* (Princeton: Princeton University Press, 1983), pp. 50 ff.

CHAPTER 2

1 Alessandro Verri, *Le notti romane*, ed. Renzo Negri (Bari: Laterza, 1967), pp. 253–4. Writing in 1792–1804, Verri situates his fiction in 1780, the year of the discovery of the Scipios's tomb.

2 Verri, *ibid.*, pp. 402–4.

3 "Sonetto pel nuovo Museo Clementino nel Palazzo Vaticano," *I pregi delle Belle Arti celebrati in Campidoglio pel solenne concorso tenuto dall'insigne Accademia di San Luca li 21 aprile 1771* (Rome: Casaletti, 1771), p. 53.

4 For a reproduction of this medal, see Carlo Pietrangeli, "Il Museo Clementino Vaticano," *Rendiconti della Pontificia Accademia Romana di Archeologia*, 27 (1951/52), p. 92.

5 *In lode delle Belle Arti. Orazione e componimenti poetici. Relazione del concorso e de' premi distribuiti in Campidoglio dall'insigne Accademia del Disegno in San Luca il dì 27 aprile 1773* (Rome: Casaletti, 1773), p. 40.

6 "Sonetto," 1773, p. 41.

7 "Ottave sul possesso di Nostro Signore PIO SESTO P.M." (Rome, 1775). The poem was also reviewed and excerpted in the *Effemeridi letterarie di Roma*, 5 (9 March 1776), 73. `

8 (Untitled), *I pregi delle Belle Arti celebrati in Campidoglio pel solenne concorso tenuto dall'insigne Accademia del Disegno in San Luca li 2 giugno 1783* (Rome: Casaletti, 1783), p. xlviii.

9 (Untitled), 1783, p. xlix.

10 "Sul Museo Vaticano," *I pregi delle Belle Arti celebrati in Campidoglio pel solenne concorso tenuto dall'insigne Accademia del Disegno in San Luca li 25 maggio 1789* (Rome: Casaletti, 1789), p. lxvi.

11 Luigi Giuntotardi, "Pel secondo anno secolare della distribuzione de' premi in Campidoglio. Ai prodi Giovani premiati," *Il centesimo secondo dell'anno MDCCXCV co' pregi delle Belle Arti celebrato tanto in San Luca, che nel Campidoglio in occasione del solenne concorso Clementino tenuto dall'insigne Accademia del Disegno di San Luca nel dì 2 giugno di detto anno* (Rome: Casaletti, 1795), p. liv.

12 Marcello Vitelleschi, 1771, p. 58. The most famous literary description of this statue is no doubt that of Byron, in *Childe Harold*, IV, stanzas 140–1. By Byron's time scholars had long dismissed the theory that the statue represented a gladiator, identifying it instead as a Gaul. Again Byron chose to ignore the archaeological evidence, though here he was not alone: "Dying Gladiator" remains the name by which the statue is commonly known today (see Haskell and Penny, pp. 224–7).

13 Angiol Maria della Mirandola, 1779, p. liv.

14 Luca Salvini, 1773, p. 48.

15   "Per la Statuetta di Bronzo rappresentante un nobil Fanciullo Etrusco, ritrovata nella Campagna della Città Tarquinia presso Corneto, e donata alla Santità di Nostro Signore ad ornamento del nuovo Museo Vaticano da Monsignor Francesco Carrara," 1771, p. 69.

16   On the revindication of pre-Roman Italy, see Piero Trèves, *L'idea di Roma e la cultura italiana del secolo XIX* (Milan: Ricciardi, 1962), pp. 19–35.

17   "L'obelisco del Sole eretto da Pio VI," 1795, p. lvii.

18   The reference is to the draining of the Pontine marshes; this was a recurrent theme in Braschi propaganda (see my discussion later in this chapter).

19   On the transvaluation of the imagery of light and darkness in eighteenth-century France, see Ronald Paulson, *Representations of Revolution (1789–1820)* (New Haven: Yale University Press, 1983), pp. 45–7, 102 ff., and passim.

20   Antonio Scarpelli, "Sonetto sull'Ara antica donata dall'Eᵐᵒ e Rᵐᵒ Sig. Card. Casali a Sua Santità, collocata nel Museo Clementino, e rappresentante diversi fatti della guerra di Troja, e dell'origine di Roma," 1773, p. 45.

21   For a detailed contemporary history of the Academy, see Melchior Missirini, *Memorie per servire alla storia della romana Accademia di S. Luca fino alla morte di Antonio Canova* (Rome: De Romanis, 1823).

22   *In lode delle Belle Arti. Orazione e componimenti poetici detti in Campidoglio in occasione della festa del concorso celebrata dall'insigne Accademia del Disegno di San Luca* (Rome: Casaletti, 1775), pp. 8 ff.

23   *La distribuzione de' premi solennizzata sul Campidoglio il 16 agosto 1810 dall'insigne Accademia delle Belle Arti Pittura, Scultura, ed Architettura in San Luca* (Rome: Salvioni, 1810), pp. xiii–xxxii.

24   *Effemeridi letterarie di Roma*, 11 July 1778.

25   *I voti quinquennali celebrati dagli Arcadi nel Bosco Parrasio ad onore della Santità di Nostro Signore Papa Pio VI.* (Rome: Salomoni, 1779), p. 5. This volume of verse was reviewed in the *Effemeridi*, 9 (8 Jan. 1780).

26   *Adunanza tenuta dagli Arcadi per la morte di Anton Raphael Mengs* (Rome: Salomoni, 1780), p. cvii.

27   Giuseppe Gioacchino Belli, *Roma del Belli*, ed. Roberto Vighi (Rome: Palombi, 1963), p. 129.

28   Georg Daltrop cites this passage in *The Vatican Collections: The Papacy and Art* (New York: Harry N. Abrams, 1982), p. 202. The Lateran collections were transferred to the Vatican in 1963 by Pope John XXIII. They are now housed in a new wing north of the Pinacoteca, completed in 1970.

29   On the Etruscanizing style of Pelagio Pelagi and Fortunato Pio Castellani, see Sandra Pinto, "La promozione delle arti negli Stati italiani dall'eta delle riforme all'Unità," in *Storia dell'arte italiana*, Pt. 2, II (Turin: Einaudi, 1982), p. 970.

30   Peter Brooks, *The Melodramatic Imagination: Balzac, Henry James, Melodrama, and the Mode of Excess* (New Haven: Yale University Press, 1976).

31   Pietro Ercole Visconti, "Le Corone del Tempio della Gloria," *Distribuzione de' premi del concorso di Carlo Pio Balestra celebrata sul Campidoglio il dì 4 di febbraio 1842 dall'insigne e pontificia Accademia romana di San Luca* (Rome: Tipografia delle Belle Arti, 1842), p. 30.

32   Brooks, pp. 38–9.

CHAPTER 3

1   Abbé Grégoire, "Rapport sur le vandalisme, 14 Fructidor, An II," in *Oeuvres,* 16 vols, Liechtenstein, II, p. 277; cited in Haskell and Penny, *Taste and the Antique,* p. 108. For a detailed account of the confiscations in Italy and growth of the Musée Napoléon, see Cecil Gould, *Trophy of Conquest* (London: Faber and Faber, 1965).

2   Since its discovery in the Baths of Caracalla in the sixteenth century the Hercules had enjoyed enormous prestige. It was bought by the Farnese and displayed in the courtyard of their palace in Rome until 1787, when it was shipped to Naples. In 1799 it was confiscated and prepared for shipment to Paris, but reprieved by the collapse of the Parthenopean Republic. Napoleon was later to tell Canova that its absence from the Musée was the most serious gap in his collection (see Haskell and Penny, p. 229).

3   Despite reservations voiced both by Winckelmann and E. Q. Visconti as to its identity, the bronze head had long been considered a portrait of Lucius Junius Brutus, perhaps a fragment of the very statue that in antiquity had been placed on the Capitol and, according to Plutarch, inspired Marcus Brutus's assassination of Caesar. The fame of the bust grew with the French Revolution; long before Napoleon requisitioned the original, the painter David had brought a copy of the bust with him from Rome, which he lent to a production of Voltaire's *Brutus* in Paris in 1790. For a history of the vicissitudes and shifting political associations of the sculpture, see Haskell and Penny, pp. 163–4.

4   Quatremère de Quincy, *Lettres sur le préjudice qu'occasionneraient aux arts et à la science, le déplacement des monuments de l'art de l'Italie* (Paris, 1796).

5   For a lively and detailed chronicle of the Roman Republic, including the festivals that I describe in this chapter, see Antonio Cretoni, *Roma giacobina: Storia della Repubblica romana del 1798–9* (Rome: Istituto di Studi Romani, 1971). For a review of the earlier literature, see Vittorio E. Giuntella, ed., *Bibliografia della Repubblica romana del 1798–9* (Rome: Istituto di Studi Romani, 1957). On the festivals themselves, see also Antonio Pinelli, "La rivoluzione imposta o della natura dell'entusiasmo: Fenomenologia della festa nella Roma giacobina," in *Quaderni sul neoclassico,* IV, *Miscellanea* (Rome: Bulzoni, 1978), pp. 97–146.

6   On Cola di Rienzo, see Roberto Weiss, *The Renaissance Discovery of Classical Antiquity* (Oxford: Basil Blackwell, 1969), pp. 38–42. The *Lex de imperio* tablet is now displayed in the Capitoline museum, overlooking the spot where Cola was proclaimed tribune (1341) and executed (1354). The site is marked by a monument commissioned after the unification of Italy (Girolamo Masini, 1887).

7   Cited in Cretoni, p. 181.

8   *Monitore di Roma,* 1 (21 February 1798); cited in Cretoni, p. 53, n. 1.

9   See Mona Ozouf, *La fête révolutionnaire, 1798–9* (Paris: Gallimard, 1976). Related studies of the imagery and iconography of the French Revolution include Maurice Agulhon, *Marianne au combat: L'imagerie et la symbolique républicaines de 1789 à 1880* (Paris, 1979; English version, Cambridge, 1981); and most recently Lynn Hunt, *Politics, Culture, and Class in the French Revolution* (Berkeley, 1984).

10 On the genealogy of the liberty tree as a symbol of revolution, see Hunt, p. 59.

11 Cited in Cretoni, p. 134. Variations on this epigram appear in journals and diaries of the period (see Cretoni, p. 161, n. 18).

12 Cited in Cesare D'Onofrio, *Gli obelischi di Roma* (Rome: Cassa di Risparmio, 1965), p. 9.

13 Cited in Cretoni, p. 49.

14 Giuseppe Antonio Sala, *Diario romano degli anni 1775 ad 1800*, ed. G. Cugnoni (Rome, 1882–6), I, p. 106 (cited in Cretoni, p. 144).

15 See John A. Pinto, "Nicola Michetti and Ephemeral Design in Eighteenth-Century Rome," *Memoirs of the American Academy in Rome*, XXV, ed. Henry A. Millon (Cambridge and London: M.I.T. Press, 1980), pp. 289–322.

16 For a more detailed description of this monument (as well as Barberi's Arch of Triumph), see Italo Faldi, "La festa patriottica della Federazione in due dipinti di Felice Giani," *Bollettino dei musei comunali di Roma*, 2 (1955), 14–18.

17 Contemporary illustrations of these arches include Pinelli's engravings in the Museo Napoleonico (catalogue nos. 686 and 737).

18 Cited in Cretoni, p. 355.

19 This in the account of one of the participants, Nicola Lasagni, Commander of the Guardia Nazionale Sedentaria (quoted in Cretoni, p. 357).

20 *L'iconographie grecque* was published in Paris by Didot in 1818. Before his death in 1818 Visconti managed to complete only the first volume of *L'iconografie romaine* (Paris: Didot, 1818); successive volumes, published by Antoine Mongez, were only partially based on Visconti's work. For additional information on Visconti, see Piero Trèves, ed., *Lo studio dell'antichità classica nell'Ottocento* (Milan: Ricciardi, 1962), pp. 3–73.

21 The cycle is composed of a series of lunettes, each representing various aspects of Pius VII's patronage of archaeology and the arts. The central lunette, painted by Vincenzo Ferreri, portrays the signing of the Chirografo of 1802. For a more detailed description of this program, see my discussion later in this chapter.

22 The entire text of the edict is reprinted in Andrea Emiliani, *Leggi, bandi e provvedimenti per la tutela dei beni artistici e culturali negli antichi stati italiani, 1571–1860* (Bologna, 1978), pp. 110–24. This passage is cited from pp. 111–12. All other references will appear in parentheses in the text. For the text of the Pacca Edict of 1820, renewing the terms of the 1802 law, see Emiliani, pp. 130–45.

23 To cite Raphael's famous letter of protest to Leo X of 1517:

> Ma perché ci dorremo noi de' Gotti, de' Vandali et d'altri perfidi inimici del nome latino, se quelli che, come padri et tutori dovevano difendere queste povere reliquie di Roma, essi medesimi hanno atteso con ogni studio lungamente a distruggerle et a spegnerle? Quanti pontefici . . . hanno permesso le ruine et disfacimento delli templi antichi, delle statue, delli archi et altri edifici, gloria delli lor fondatori? . . . Quanta calcina si è fatta di statue et d'altri ornamenti antichi? che ardirei dire che tutta questa nova Roma che hor si vede, quanto grande ch'ella vi sia, quanto bella, quanto ornata di palazzi, di chiese et di altri edifici, sia fabbricata di calcina fatta di marmi antichi . . .

24 On the history of the ownership of the Barberini Faun, see Haskell and Penny, pp. 202–5. On Carlo Fea's stormy career as Commissioner of Antiquities, see Orietta Rossi Pinelli, "Carlo Fea e il chirografo del 1802: cronaca, giudiziaria e non, delle prime battaglie per la tutela delle Belle Arti," *Ricerche di Storia dell'Arte*, 8 (1979), 27–41.

25 Work began almost immediately on the Museo Chiaramonti, which was opened in 1807. This museum, devoted to marble statues, busts, and reliefs, occupied the north end of the eastern corridor connecting the papal palace to the Palazzetto del Belvedere, parallel to the library wing. The south end of this corridor was reserved for the Galleria Lapidaria, where Gaetano Marini arranged the over three thousand stone inscriptions now belonging to the papal collection. The Braccio Nuovo, Pius VII's only construction *ex novo* in the Vatican museum complex, was not built until after the fall of Napoleon and restoration of the art works from Paris (R. Stern, 1817–21).

26 On the Perseus figure, see Fred Licht, *Canova* (New York: Abbeville Press, 1983), pp. 181–7. On the pugilists Creugas and Damoxenas, see pp. 187–8.

27 Two major restorations of the Colosseum date to Pius VII's era: Raffaele Stern's 1807 buttress on the Lateran side (made necessary by the earthquake of 1806 and illustrated in a Vatican fresco, Fig. 2) and Valadier's restoration on the side toward the Forum (1822).

28 Felice Giani's painting of the arch of triumph built in 1798 for the Festa della Rigenerazione depicts the elaborate marble trompe-l'oeil of the arch. Its eight Doric columns were painted to resemble red granite, while the capitals, bases, architrave, and cornice were of *giallo antico,* the plinths of mottled red and black *africano,* and the attic story of veined purple *pavonazzetto.* The friezes representing Napoleon's campaigns were, like Appiani's later group in the Royal Palace in Milan, grisaille imitations of low-relief sculpture; and the white "marble" group surmounting the arch was almost certainly of stucco (see Faldi, p. 17).

29 Stendhal (Henri Beyle), *Promenades dans Rome* (Florence: Parenti, 1958), pp. 15–16. On this controversial restoration, see S. Casiello, "Aspetti della tutela dei beni culturali nell'Ottocento e il restauro di Valadier per l'arco di Tito," *Quaderni di restauro,* 5 (1973), 77 ff; and P. Marconi, "Roma 1806–26: un momento critico per la formazione della metodologia del restauro," *Ricerche di storia dell'arte,* 8 (1979), 63–71.

30 A layman's reduction of the official Vatican report on these excavations is Toynbee and Perkins's *The Shrine of St. Peter* (London: Longmans, Green & Co., 1956).

31 *La distribuzione dei premi solennizzata sul Campidoglio li 27 novembre 1801 dall'insigne Accademia delle Belle Arti, Pittura, Scultura, ed Architettura in San Luca* (Rome: Salomoni, 1801).

32 Carlo Fea, who had defended the Barberini's right to the statue, regarded this decision as a victory for Rome; but the ultimate irony came when the Barberini themselves applied to sell the Faun to an even richer client, the Crown Prince Ludwig of Bavaria. Fea disputed the case for nearly a decade but was finally powerless to prevent the sale, and the Faun left Rome for the Glyptothek of Munich in 1819; see Orietta Rossi Pinelli, "Artisti, falsari o filologhi? Da Cavaceppi a Canova, il restauro della scultura tra arte e scienza," *Ricerche di storia dell'arte,* 13–14 (1981), 43–54.

33 Giuseppe Alborghetti, "Elegia," 1801, pp. xxii–xxv. This text is accompanied by a Latin translation by Giuseppe Capogrossi.

34 Giuseppe Antinori, "Al Signor Antonio Canova," 1801, p. xliii.

35 *La distribuzione dei premi solennizzata sul Campidoglio li 4 luglio 1805 dall'insigne*

Accademia delle Belle Arti Pittura, Scultura ed Architettura in San Luca (Rome: Salomoni, 1805), p. lxi.

36 Although Canova received the commission in 1803, once completed the tomb was inevitably read in the light of Foscolo's influential text, which renders its political message explicit. The figure of Italy, mourning at the poet's tomb, is the first representation of the Italian nation in nineteenth-century monumental sculpture; and the theme of pan-Italian unity is underscored by the fact that Alfieri was the first non-Tuscan to be permitted burial in Santa Croce and Canova the first non-Tuscan to be invited to work there (see Licht, pp. 75–80).

37 Ercole Dandini, "Orazione," pp. xvii–xxx. The passage here cited is from pp. xxix–xxx.

38 On the programs of the Napoleonic administration in Rome, see Attilio La Padula, *Roma 1809–14: Contributo alla storia dell'urbanistica* (Rome: Palombi, 1958).

39 Melchior Missirini cites Canova's own record of his conversations with Napoleon in *Della vita di Antonio Canova,* 2 vols. (Milan: Bettoni, 1825), II, pp. 10–27.

40 "I want to see Rome," Canova quotes Napoleon as saying; to which he replied, "that city deserves to be seen by Your Majesty, and you will find much there to arouse your imagination, as you view the Capitoline, Trajan's Forum, the Sacred Way, the columns, the arches . . . ." (cited by Missirini, p. 13).

41 Maurice Andrieux, *Rome,* trans. Charles Lam Markham (New York: Funk and Wagnalls, 1968), p. 399.

42 For a detailed account of Napoleonic excavations and urban planning in Rome between 1809–14, see Camille de Tournon, *Études statistiques sur Rome et la partie occidentale des États romains,* III, (Paris: Wurtz, 1831) pp. 237–88. On de Tournon's Pantheon project, see p. 286. On Fascist archaeology and urban planning, see Italo Insolera, *Roma moderna: Un secolo di storia urbanistica, 1870–1970* (Turin: Einaudi, 1976), pp. 115–43, and Antonio Cederna, *Mussolini urbanista: Lo sventramento di Roma negli anni del consenso* (Bari: Laterza, 1979).

43 Louis Madelin, *La Rome de Napoléon: La domination française à Rome de 1809 à 1814* (Paris: Plon, 1906), p. 411.

44 For a map and elevations of the imperial palace designed by Perosini, see Attilio La Padula, *Roma e la regione nell'epoca napoleonica* (Rome: Istituto Editoriale Pubblicazioni Internazionali, 1969), pp. 190–1. On Napoleon's refurbishment of the Quirinal, see Daniel Ternois, "Napoléon et la décoration du Palais Impérial de Monte Cavallo en 1811–13," *Revue de l'art,* 7 (1970), 68–89.

45 The obelisk erected by Pius VII in 1822 on the Pincio had been dedicated by Hadrian to Antinous, rediscovered near the Porta Maggiore in the sixteenth century, and finally given by Cornelia Barberini to Pius VI, who intended it for the Vatican Cortile della Pigna (D'Onofrio, pp. 295 ff.). It was by Mazzini's initiative that the busts of Italian patriots were commissioned to line the avenues of the Pincio.

46 One of the first acts of Pius VII's papacy upon his return from exile in France was the restoration of the Jesuit order on 7 August 1814. Valadier's restoration of the Arch of Titus was completed in 1822.

47 For a detailed description of the program and account of the individual commis-

sions, see Ulrich Heisinger, "Canova and the Frescoes of the Galleria Chiara-monti," *The Burlington Magazine,* 120 (1978), 655–65.

48 Heisinger, p. 661.

49 Tambroni's preface is cited by Heisinger, p. 662.

50 On pictorial restoration under Pius VII, see Alessandro Conti, "Vicende e cultura del restauro," in *Storia dell'arte italiana,* Pt. 3, III (Turin: Einaudi, 1981), "Restaurazione pontificia," pp. 74–6.

51 On the question of its attribution to De Angelis, see my note 24, Chapter 1. Legrelle lists the subjects of each of the scenes in his guidebook *Musei e gallerie pontificie,* V: *Guida delle gallerie di pittura* (Rome, 1925); but to my knowledge the program has never received any extended critical attention.

52 Antonio Canova, "Prolusione alla nuova apertura dell'Accademia Romana di Archeologia," *Atti dell'Accademia Romana di Archaeologia* (1810), pp. 31–5.

53 Massimo D'Azeglio, *I miei ricordi* (Florence: Barbera, 1920), p. 111.

54 Leopardi wrote the canzone "Ad Angelo Mai" in 1820, only days after the cardinal had announced his discovery of the books of Cicero's *De republica* in a Vatican palimpsest. But on his arrival in Rome in 1822, he was disappointed to find it even more stultifyingly provincial than his own Recanati. In a letter written to his father Monaldo on 9 December 1823, Leopardi reported:

> As for the men of letters, of whom you inquire, I have met very few of them, and those few have rid me of the desire to meet any others . . . In their opinion, the height of human wisdom, indeed the sole true science of man is Antiquarianism. I have not yet managed to meet a single Roman scholar who understands literature as anything other than Archaeology. Philosophy, morals, politics, the science of the human heart, eloquence, poetry, philology, all of this is foreign to Rome, and seems child's play when compared to the problem of determining if a piece of copper belonged to Marcus Antonius or Marcus Agrippa. (Leopardi, *Tutte le opere,* ed. Walter Binni [Florence: Sansoni, 1969] I, pp. 1133–4)

55 D'Azeglio, *I miei ricordi,* p. 116.

56 Cited in Piero Trèves, *Lo studio dell'antichità classica nell'Ottocento* (Milan: Ricciardi, 1962), p. 388.

57 Leopardi, I, p. 251 (Canto I, stanzas 16–17).

58 On the relationship between Leopardi and Mai, see Trèves, pp. 347–60, and Leopardi's letters to Mai in his *Opere,* I, 1091, pp. 1118–19, and *passim.*

59 *Ragionamento letto alla Pontificia Accademia Romana di Archeologia nel Dì Solenne 21 di aprile Anniversario della Fondazione di Roma;* the entire text of the oration is reprinted in Trèves, pp. 388–97.

60 The 120-meter gallery was painted in 1580–3 by the Dominican friar Ignazio Danti of Perugia.

CHAPTER 4

1 See "Il sole," "La restituzione delle provincie alla S. Sede," and "Musa mia, ferma in campo," all composed for the return of Pius VII, in *Belli italiano,* ed. Roberto Vighi, I (Rome: Colombo, 1975), pp. 247–51.

2 On Belli's life, see the helpful chronology assembled by Pietro Gibellini in the volume of selected *Sonetti* edited by Giorgio Vigolo (Milan: Mondadori, 1978), pp. xci–cxx; or the breezy biography by Massimo Grillandi, *Belli* (Milan: Rizzoli, 1979).

3 Many of these poems are anthologized by Robert Vighi under the rubric "Le antichità," in *Roma del Belli* (Rome: Palombi, 1967), pp. 106–58. All citations in this chapter are from Belli, *Tutti i sonetti romaneschi,* ed. Bruno Cagli, 5 vols. (Rome: Compton, 1980).

4 Stephen A. Larrabee, *English Bards and Grecian Marbles* (New York: Columbia University Press, 1943), p. 45.

5 For examples, see in *Belli italiano:* "Alla tomba di Scipione Affricano Secondo" (I, pp. 285–8); "Agli etimologisti" (I, p. 554); and "Il nuovo istrione" (II, p. 372).

6 *Tutti i sonetti,* I, p. 97.

7 Belli (1791–1863) and Rossini (1790–1857) were exact contemporaries. For a review of Rossini's work, see the Palazzo Braschi exhibition catalogue, *Luigi Rossini Incisore: Vedute di Roma 1817–50* (Rome: Multigrafica, 1982).

8 Belli's verses are scattered with garbled spellings, puns, obscenities, and mispronunciations. My English versions do not attempt to reproduce these; they are intended as only the barest prose crib.

9 On the excavations at Tusculum, see Sandra Pinto, "La promozione delle arti negli Stati italiani," in *La storia dell'arte italiana,* Pt. 2, II (Turin: Einaudi, 1982), p. 970. For another satire of Biondi, see "Il nuovo istrione" in *Belli italiano,* II, p. 372.

10 The arch marks the entryway to the Forum of Augustus, beside the temple of Mars Ultor. In Belli's time it was still buried up to three quarters of its height.

11 On the history of the animated statue theme, see Theodore Zioldkowski, *Disenchanted Images: A Literary Iconology* (Princeton: Princeton University Press, 1977), pp. 18–77. On humanist ambivalence toward the archaeological gesture and atavistic fears and superstitions regarding the underworld, see Thomas M. Greene, *The Light in Troy: Imitation and Discovery in Renaissance Poetry* (New Haven: Yale University Press, 1982), pp. 235–41.

12 For an account of the episode see Carlo Cecchini, *S. Agnese fuori le mura e S. Costanza* (Rome, 1924), pp. 18–19.

13 On the excavation of Raphael's remains and the dispute regarding their authenticity, see Sandra Pinto, "La promozione . . . ," p. 969.

14 The arch was actually built by Titus's successor, Domitian. In *Rome, Naples et Florence* (1817), Stendhal notes the refusal of Jews to pass under the Arch of Titus, and adds somewhat maliciously that they have cleared a path alongside it to gain access to the Forum "when their business requires it" (cited in Cagli, *Tutti i sonetti,* I, p. 27, note 8).

15 *Belli italiano,* III, p. 9. On the restoration of Pius IX, see also "Il giugno 1849," p. 7, and Belli's parody of the Petrarch sonnet "Padre del ciel," celebrating Rome's reconversion to Catholicism after republican tyranny ("Deh fa che s'ella mai, padre, ti spiacque, / riduca i pensier vani a miglior luogo / oggi che, resa al Pastor suo, rinacque," p. 8).

CHAPTER 5

1 The Edict of St.-Cloud of 1804, extended to the Cisalpine state on 5 September 1806, prohibited burial within cities and required that all tombstones and inscriptions be similar in format.

2 Schliemann began his excavations at Hissarlik, a village in Asia Minor a few
miles from the mouth of the Dardanelles, in 1870. Three years later he discovered the remains of the city he believed to be Homeric Troy.

3 *Ultime lettere di Jacopo Ortis,* in Foscolo, *Opere,* IV, Edizione Nazionale (Florence: Le Monnier, 1970), p. 90.

4 See my article "Petrarch and Leopardi: The Two Canzoni All'Italia," *Canadian
Journal of Italian Studies,* 10 (1987).

5 On the polemics following the publication of the *Sepolcri,* see the excerpts
reprinted in Foscolo's *Opere,* VI (Florence: Le Monnier, 1972), pp. 519–83.

6 Fernando Mazzocca, "Il ritratto tra storia, propaganda e consumo," in *Storia
dell'arte italiana,* Pt. 3, II (Turin: Einaudi, 1981), pp. 376–81. On Bettoni's
career, see L. Pecorella Vergnano and O. Valetti, *Nicolò Bettoni e il suo tempo:
Mostra iconografica* (Brescia, 1979). Among the analogous series published after
Bettoni's example were Stella's *Vite e Ritratti* (1815), Silvestri's *Dizionario degli
Uomini illustri* (1823), and Locatelli's *Iconografia Italiana* (1837). Catalogues of
sepulchral monuments throughout Italy include *Monumenti sepolcrali della
Toscana* (1819), *Monumenti sepolcrali del Cimitero di Bologna* (1826–7), and *I più
pregevoli Monumenti sepolcrali della città di Venezia e sue isole* (1827). For details,
see Mazzocca, pp. 377–8.

7 Lionello Sozzi, "I *Sepolcri* e le discussioni francesi sulle tombe negli anni del
Direttorio e del Consolato," *Giornale storico della letteratura italiana,* 144 (1967),
567–88. I am indebted to Franco Fido for bringing this article to my attention.

8 Volney's *Les Ruines, ou méditations sur les révolutions des Empires* first appeared in
1791 and was among the books owned by Foscolo (Sozzi, p. 586). On the
imagery of ruins in French literature, see Roland Mortier, *La poétique des ruines
en France: Ses origines, ses variations de la Renaissance à Victor Hugo* (Geneva: Droz,
1974). For his remarks on Volney, see pp. 136–41.

9 *Dei Sepolcri,* lines 151–52. All citations are from the National Edition of Foscolo's *Opere,* I. (Florence: Le Monnier, 1972) and will be identified by line
numbers in the text.

10 "Elegy written in a Country Churchyard," lines 41–2. All citations are from
Thomas Gray, *The Complete English Poems* (London: Heinemann, 1973). Along
with Gray's lines, editors of Foscolo frequently cite Cesarotti's 1772 translation
of the "Elegy": "Ah l'animato busto / O l'urna effigiata al primo albergo / Può
richiamar lo spirito fugace?" This reference (unless provided for the conve-
nience of Italian readers) is not strictly necessary; though the existence of such a
prestigious translation testifies to Gray's reputation in Italy, there is no need to
prove its availability to Foscolo, who at the time of writing the *Sepolcri* was
himself an accomplished translator of Sterne.

11 "The breezy call of incense-breathing morn, / The swallow twittering from the
straw-built shed, / The cock's shrill clarion or the echoing horn / No more
shall rouse them from their lowly bed."

12 "For them no more the blazing hearth shall burn, / Or busy housewife ply her
evening care: / No children run to lisp their sire's return, / Or climb his knees
the envied kiss to share."

13 "Oft did the harvest to their sickle yield, / Their furrow oft the stubborn glebe

has broke; / How jocund did they drive their team afield! / How bowed the woods beneath their sturdy stroke!"

14 "Perhaps in this neglected spot is laid / Some heart once pregnant with celestial fire; / Hands that the rod of empire might have swayed, / Or waked to ecstasy the living lyre."

15 "Full many a gem of purest ray serene / The dark unfathomed caves of ocean bear: / Full many a flower is born to blush unseen / And waste its sweetness on the desert air."

16 "Their lot . . . nor circumscribed alone / Their growing virtues, but their crimes confined; / Forbade to walk through slaughter to a throne, / And shut the gates of mercy on mankind."

17 On the theme of exile in Foscolo, see Glauco Cambon, *Ugo Foscolo: Poet of Exile* (Princeton: Princeton University Press, 1980). For his reading of the *Sepolcri,* see pp. 155–81.

18 Foscolo, *Opere,* IV, p. 206.

19 "Lettera a Monsieur Guill . . . su la sua incompetenza a giudicare i poeti italiani," *Opere,* VI, pp. 501–18.

20 Eugenio Donato also stresses this point in his perceptive reading of the poem, "The Mnemonics of History: Notes for a Contextual Reading of *Dei Sepolcri,*" *Yale Italian Studies* I, No. I (1977), 4.

21 For a discussion of this phenomenon see Paolo Valesio, *Novantiqua: Rhetorics as a Contemporary Theory* (Bloomington: Indiana University Press, 1980), p. 4.

22 J. B. Lechevalier, *Voyage dans la Troade, fait dans les années 1785 et 1786,* 2 vols. (Paris: Dentu, 1802).

23 Note Foscolo's inclusion of Galeazzo di Tarsia's sixteenth-century sonnet "Già corsi l'Alpi gelide e canute" in his own *Vestigi della storia del sonetto italiano, Opere,* VIII, pp. 135–6.

24 On the politicization of the genre of landscape painting in Napoleonic Italy and its impact on later Risorgimento iconography, see the exhibition catalogue *Garibaldi: Arte e storia,* II, pp. 28–35. For four views of the Roja pass described by Jacopo Ortis, see the watercolors by Giovanni Battista DeGubernatis of 1833–5 (pp. 33–5). On the Alps as a topos in Romantic literature and painting, see Biasin, *Italian Literary Icons,* pp. 26–32.

25 I am indebted to Paolo Valesio for bringing this to my attention.

26 Victor Hugo, *Notre-Dame de Paris,* I (Paris: Hetzel, 1831), p. 129.

27 Parini was buried in 1799 in a common plot in the cemetery of Porta Comasina; for Foscolo's protest, see lines 53–90 of the *Sepolcri.* On Canova's tomb of Alfieri (1806–10), see my note 36, Chapter 3.

28 "I have dedicated the poem to Cavalier [Pindemonte], mindful of his complaints and of your own, and to atone for my offenses, which are perhaps too clearly political" (Milan, 6 September 1806; *Opere,* XV, pp. 142–3).

29 Ippolito Pindemonte, "I Sepolcri; A Ugo Foscolo," in *Lirici del Settecento,* ed. Bruno Maier (Milan: Ricciardi, 1959), pp. 1023–49.

30 Mazzini, *Scritti editi ed inediti,* XCIV (Imola: Galeati), pp. 211–36. For an overview of Foscolo's influence on Mazzini, see Giovanni Cattani, *Mazzini nella letteratura* (Rome: Bulzoni, 1975), pp. 19–32.

31 The statue that now marks Foscolo's tomb was completed in 1938 by Antonio
Berti. Among the visitors to Foscolo's tomb at Chiswick was Garibaldi himself, exiled from Italy after his arrest at Aspromonte. His follower Giuseppe
Cesare Abba recalls a visit to Garibaldi at Caprera in which the general recited
the verses of Foscolo:

> "Credo che gli ultimi quattro versi dei *Sepolcri* abbiano svegliato negli
> italiani l'amor della patria più di qualunque altro grido di poeta," [disse il
> Generale.] "Io non ho mai sentito la grandezza della patria e della morte
> come leggendoli. Per questo e per gratitudine, l'anno scorso, volli visitare
> la tomba di Ugo, nel cimitero di Chiswick; una povera pietra, quasi ai piedi
> d'una gran torre antica, e pietra e torre pare che parlino tra loro." Così
> aveva detto il Generale, e poi si era messo a recitare dei brani dei *Sepolcri*
> . . . Mai forse, mai altri diede meglio di lui a quei . . . versi il tono che
> dovettero avere . . . quando eruppero dall'anima di Foscolo . . . (G. C.
> Abba, *Cose garibaldine. A Caprera* [1865], cited in Lamberto Vitali, *Il
> Risorgimento nella fotografia* [Turin: Einaudi, 1979], p. 161).

CHAPTER 6

1 In referring to "democratic" and "liberal" schools of Risorgimento thought, I
am adopting the distinction first proposed by De Sanctis in his lectures of 1872–
4, published as *La letteratura italiana nel secolo XIX,* II (Bari: Laterza, 1953).

2 Charles Didier, *Rome souterraine* (Paris: Gosselin, 1841).

3 "*Rome souterraine* par Charles Didier," originally published in vol. VI of *Giovine
Italia,* reprinted in Mazzini's *Scritti editi ed inediti,* I (Imola: Galeati, 1906), pp.
385–92. This edition will be abbreviated henceforth as *S.E.I.*

4 On Lamartine's "La terre des morts" and Giusti's rebuttal, see my Introduction.

5 I should note here that this chapter's discussion of Gioberti will be limited to his
Primato morale e civile degli italiani (1843), rather than to his later political writings. For as Chabod argues in his *Storia della politica estera italiana dal 1870 al
1896,* I (Bari: Laterza, 1951), "quel che pesò sulla storia d'Italia fu, appunto, il
Primato" (p. 199, note 2).

6 Chabod, pp. 190–200.

7 Vincenzo Cuoco, *Platone in Italia,* 2 vols. (Bari: Laterza, 1924), and Giuseppe
Micali, *L'Italia avanti il dominio dei Romani* (Florence: Piatti, 1810).

8 "The Greek manuscript whose translation I now present to you, oh reader, was
discovered by my grandfather in the year 1774, as he dug the foundations for a
country house he wished to build on the very site of ancient Eraclea," "Al
lettore," I, p. 3.

9 Piero Trèves, *L'idea di Roma e la cultura italiana del secolo XIX* (Milan: Ricciardi,
1962), pp. 30–1.

10 See Carroll Meeks, "History of the Façades of the Cathedrals of Florence and
Milan," in his *Italian Architecture 1750–1914* (New Haven: Yale University
Press, 1966), pp. 220–37.

11 On romantic history painting, see Fortunato Bellonzi, *La pittura di storia dell'Ottocento italiano* (Milan: Fabbri, 1967), and the exhibition catalogue *Romanticismo
storico* (Florence: Centro Di, 1974).

12 Both the poem and Di Breme's defense, "Intorno all'ingiustizia di alcuni giudizi

letterari italiani," are reprinted in Carlo Calcaterra, ed., *I manifesti romantici del 1816* (Turin: U.T.E.T., 1968), pp. 81–124.

13 De Sanctis, *Nuovi saggi critici* (Naples: Morano, 1888), p. 283.

14 Mazzini, *S.E.I.*, I, pp. 34–5.

15 *S.E.I.*, XXI, pp. 272 and 292.

16 Giacomo Durando, *Della nazionalità italiana* (Lausanne: Bonamici, 1846), pp. 10–11.

17 Thomas M. Greene, *The Light in Troy* (New Haven: Yale University Press, 1982), especially pp. 220–41.

18 The bibliography on the Risorgimento is vast; for a general introduction, see Stuart Woolf, *A History of Italy 1700–1860: The Social Constraints of Political Change* (London: Methuen, 1979), which also appeared in an earlier Italian version in *Storia d'Italia*, III (Turin: Einaudi, 1973). Useful anthologies include Franco della Peruta, ed., *Scrittori politici dell'Ottocento* (Milan: Ricciardi, 1969) and the twin volumes edited by Vito Lo Curto, *Gli scrittori cattolici dalla Restaurazione all'Unità* (Bari: Laterza, 1976), and Giovanni Pirodda, *Mazzini e gli scrittori democratici* (Bari: Laterza, 1976). See also Ettore Passerin d'Entrèves, "Ideologie del Risorgimento," in *Storia della letteratura italiana*, ed. E. Cecchi and N. Sapegno VII, (Milan: Garzanti, 1969), pp. 201–413, which provides a particularly helpful bibliographical essay. The most recent major study of the Risorgimento in English is Clara M. Lovett's *The Democratic Movement in Italy, 1830–1976* (Cambridge: Harvard University Press, 1982).

19 Vincenzo Gioberti, *Del primato morale e civile degli italiani*, 3 vols., ed. Gustavo Balsamo-Crivelli (Turin: U.T.E.T., 1932), I, pp. 205–6. All additional references will be identified as necessary in the text by page number.

20 Gioberti avoids any explicit criticism of the Austrian presence in Italy in the *Primato*, but he dedicated the work to Silvio Pellico, the martyr of Austrian repression.

21 The first 1500 copies of the *Primato* were rapidly followed by reprints and Vieusseux proposed a popular edition of 5000 copies. As Balbo wrote to Gioberti: "You are now a leader of a school." (Woolf, p. 343).

22 The parallels between the two figures are probably not fortuitous; *Le rouge et le noir* was first published in 1830. On Stendhal's novel, see Peter Brooks, *Reading for the Plot: Design and Intention in Narrative* (New York: Alfred A. Knopf, 1984), pp. 62–89.

23 See especially "Pensieri. Ai poeti del secolo XIX" (1832), *S.E.I.*, I, pp. 349–74; "Dell'arte in Italia, a proposito del *Marco Visconti*, romanzo di Tommaso Grossi" (1835), VIII, pp. 3–65; and "Byron e Goethe" (1840), XXI, pp. 187–241.

24 Victor Hugo, *Les misérables* (Paris: Gallimard, 1951), pp. 757–8.

25 George Sand, *Correspondance*, VI, ed. Georges Lubin (Paris: Garnier, 1969), p. 34: cited by Franco Venturi in "L'Italia fuori d'Italia," *Storia d'Italia*, III (Turin: Einaudi, 1973), p. 1362.

26 Giuseppe Garibaldi, *Clelia: Il governo del monaco (Roma nel secolo XIX)* (Milan: Rechiedei, 1870).

27 See Gabriele Morolli, "I progetti di Garibaldi per il Tevere," in the exhibition catalogue *Garibaldi: Arte e Storia*, I, pp. 94–112, and Alberto Caracciolo, *Roma*

capitale: Dal Risorgimento alla crisi dello Stato liberale (Rome: Editori Riuniti, 1974), pp. 110–18.

28 "Ai giovani d'Italia," *S.E.I.*, LXIV, pp. 155–215. Part of this passage is cited by Chabod, p. 196.

CHAPTER 7

1 For a highly apologetic biography of Pius IX, see E. E. Y. Hales, *Pio Nono: A Study in European Politics and Religion in the Nineteenth Century* (London: Eyre and Spottiswoode, 1956). The tradition of liberal Risorgimento scholarship is best represented by George Macaulay Trevelyan's classic study, *Garibaldi's Defense of the Roman Republic* (London: Longmans, Greene, and Co., 1912), which thoroughly maps out the diplomatic and military maneuvers involved in the defense of the Janiculum. For a basic bibliography on the Italian revolutions of 1848–9, see Stuart Woolf, pp. 497–8.

2 *Histoire de la Révolution de Rome: Tableau réligieux, politique et militaire des années 1846, 1847, 1848, 1849 et 1850 en Italie*, 2 vols. (Paris: Comon, 1851), I, p. 90.

3 On Mazzini's view of Hayez, see my Chapter 6. For a reproduction and brief discussion of Hayez's painting, "Pietro l'Eremita predica la Iª Crociata," see the exhibition catalogue *Garibaldi: Arte e Storia*, II, pp. 108 and 120. For Mazzini's review, see his *S.E.I.*, XXI, pp. 272 ff.

4 Trevelyan, pp. 76–7.

5 *Le assemblee del Risorgimento*, 15 vols. (Rome: Camera dei Deputati, 1911), IX, p. 21; cited in Clara Lovett, *The Democratic Movement in Italy*, p. 138.

6 I cite Trevelyan's translation of this passage from the *Note autobiografiche*, p. 112.

7 Filippo Magi gives a brief account of the episode in "La stele greca della Biblioteca Vaticana," in *Mélanges Eugène Tisseraut*, VII (Vatican City: Biblioteca Apostolica Vaticana, 1964), pp. 1–9. With the Pope's restoration in 1850 the relief passed into the Vatican collections and is now located in the Sala Clementina of the Library, No. 4092. For a reproduction see the exhibition catalogue *The Vatican Collections*, p. 205.

8 Trevelyan cites these lines as the epigraph to his chapter on the French occupation of the Villa Corsini, p. 161.

9 Cited in Joseph Jay Deiss, *The Roman Years of Margaret Fuller* (New York: Crowell, 1969), pp. 271–2.

10 For a history of the rise of photography in Italy, see Piero Becchetti, *Fotografi e fotografia in Italia 1839–80* (Rome: Quasar, 1978). On the role of photography in the Risorgimento, see Lamberto Vitali, *Il Risorgimento nella fotografia* (Turin: Einaudi, 1979) and "I luoghi dell'epopea garibaldina: reportage bellico e 'veduta' nella fotografia dell'Ottocento," in the exhibition catalogue *Garibaldi: Arte e Storia*, II, pp. 273–334. On the Lecchi calotype series and lithographs by Danesi and Gallassi, see pp. 298–302.

11 For a discussion of Faruffini's painting, see Sandra Pinto, "La promozione delle arti negli Stati italiani," p. 979.

12 For an enthusiastic account of the ceremony, see Balleydier, II, pp. 355–61.

13 On the sale of the Campana collection see Pinto, pp. 974–6, and Haskell, "La dispersione e la conservazione del patrimonio artistico," pp. 28–9.

14 In the words of Mameli's "Fratelli d'Italia," "L'Italia s'è desta, / Dell'elmo di Scipio / S'è cinta la testa . . ."

15 For a history of the vicissitudes of the column and a description of its nineteenth-century sculptural ornament, see Cesare D'Onofrio, *Gli obelischi di Roma,* pp. 295–302.

INDEX OF NAMES